CONTENTS

1

The Nature of the Soviet Challenge

2

An Assessment of the Balance

PREFACE

While we hope to move beyond containment, we are only at the beginning of our new path. Many dangers and uncertainties are ahead. We must not forget that the Soviet Union has acquired awesome military capabilities. That was a fact of life for my predecessors, and that's always been a fact of life for our allies. And that is a fact of life for me today as President of the United States.

George Bush
12 May 1989

This edition of *Soviet Military Power* marks the eighth in the series that began in 1981. Although much has changed in the Soviet Union and in the United States since the beginning of this decade, the purpose of this publication remains fixed: to provide an authoritative report on the Soviet Union's military forces and the threat they represent to the United States, and our allies and friends.

This year we have continued with an approach that is similar in organization to that adopted by my predecessor. Part 1 of this document focuses exclusively on the elements of Soviet military power. Chapter I provides an overview of Soviet military strategy, policy, organization, and doctrine. Chapter II discusses Soviet foreign policy under General Secretary Gorbachev. Chapter III describes the resource base — both manpower and materiel — that constitutes the foundation upon which Soviet military strength rests. Chapter IV analyzes Soviet strategic offensive, strategic defensive, and space forces, while Chapter V examines Soviet conventional military power.

Part 2 places Soviet military capabilities in perspective through a discussion of the significant military power balances. To understand fully the potential implications of Soviet military strength, it is necessary to examine the Soviet Union's military capabilities in relation to those of the United States and our allies. Thus Chapter VI contains our assessment of the military balances in Europe, Southwest Asia, the Far East, and Central America, as well as the maritime, strategic nuclear, and space balances. Because both the United States and the Soviet Union rely heavily on technology to improve their respective military capabilities, Chapter VII provides a comparative assessment of the US-Soviet technological competition, to include world-wide technology developments and their implications for our security. Chapter VIII reviews the changes occurring in the Soviet Union, as well as what has *not* changed, and concludes with some thoughts on how we in the West might best respond to preserve our security against the Soviet threat while seeking opportunities to enhance international stability.

This year we also have initiated the use of sidebar commentary to address particularly topical issues in greater depth than otherwise possible. Discussion on issues such as estimating Soviet defense spending (Chapter III), the impact of the Warsaw Pact's announced force reductions (Chapter V), and the Soviets' publishing of their force data (Chapter VI), among others, are given the extended treatment they merit.

Thus *Soviet Military Power 1989* examines the context within which change is occurring in the Soviet Union and the implications of such change in terms of Soviet military capabilities and the military balance between East and West. General Secretary Gorbachev has taken far-reaching initiatives in domestic, foreign, and military policy that mark a significant change in the Soviet Union's strategy and tactics for achieving its national goals.

While the United States encourages the evolution of the Soviet Union toward a more open society, a Soviet Union demonstrably dedicated to democratic principles, we cannot react unilaterally to Soviet initiatives that are not yet implemented or to proposals which, if implemented, can easily be reversed.

For example, despite Gorbachev's stated commitment to a defensive military doctrine, the Soviet Union continues upgrading its forces and improving their capabilities. Indeed, while some Soviet military units and equipment have been withdrawn from Eastern Europe, the Soviet Union will remain the world's largest military power, even if the General Secretary's promised unilateral reductions take place.

The General Secretary also has announced that the Soviets will reduce their defense budget by 14.2 percent over the next two years. Yet, since 1985 Soviet defense expenditures have *increased* by an average of 3 percent per year in real terms, while US defense spending has *declined* in real terms by over 11 percent during the same time period. Consequently, the Soviet Union still confronts the United States and its allies with very large, modern, conventional ground, sea and air forces, and with formidable strategic and theater nuclear forces as well.

The most striking feature of Soviet military power today is the extraordinary momentum of its offensive strategic nuclear force modernization. The Soviets are deploying the new silo-based SS-18 Mod 5 heavy ICBM. These SS-18s have at least ten nuclear warheads each, and possess greater accuracy and throw-weight than earlier versions, increasing the Strategic Rocket Forces' capability to destroy hard targets such as US ICBM silos.

While the United States grapples with the selection of a mobile missile force and its funding, the Soviets are continuing to field fifth-generation mobile ICBMs — roughly 170 SS-25 road-mobile missiles and some 18 rail-mobile SS-24s, the latter with ten nuclear warheads. Deploying these systems in large numbers has significantly increased the survivability of the USSR's Strategic Rocket Forces.

In the last year the Soviets also have augmented their strategic ballistic missile submarine force by launching the sixth units of the Typhoon- and Delta IV-class submarines. The Soviet manned strategic bomber force continues deploying new operational units of the Bear H and supersonic Blackjack bombers as launch platforms for their 3,000-kilometer-range, air-launched nuclear cruise missiles.

While the Soviets are unilaterally withdrawing some ground forces opposite NATO, they also are continuing to reorganize and modernize their general purpose forces, upgrade the command, control and communications for those forces, and research and develop future generations of weapon systems.

The modernization of Soviet ground forces proceeds apace, with continued emphasis on tank production. Modern Soviet tanks, like the T-64, T-72, and T-80, are entering the force in quantities so great that in less than two years they will more than offset the Soviets' announced tank reductions from Eastern Europe. As for the Soviet air forces, modernization continues, although replacement of older systems by newer, more capable aircraft, like the Su-27 Flanker and MiG-31 Foxhound, generally is being accomplished on a less than one-for-one basis.

Despite the scrapping of some obsolete submarines, the USSR opened a second production line for the Akula-class cruise missile submarine. Furthermore, while the tempo of Soviet out-of-area deployments decreased, new major surface combatants — such as the Udaloy and Sovremennyy-class guided-missile destroyers, a Kirov-class nuclear-powered cruiser, and a Kiev-class aircraft carrier — joined the Soviet fleet. Indeed Soviet naval force reduction initiatives make no mention of the two new 65,000-ton Tbilisi-class carriers now fitting out, or that the keel has already been laid at Nikolayev for still another new carrier.

It is, therefore, clear that despite the dramatic changes occurring in the Soviet Union and the Soviet leadership's declaration of benign *intentions* toward the Western democracies, Soviet military *capabilities* continue to constitute a major threat to our security. We should encourage Moscow to continue pursuing those policies that promote pluralism at home and international stability abroad. Even more important, however, is our continuing support of our successful alliance strategy and collective security efforts, which are based on a strong military deterrent, until the Soviets reduce their armed forces to significantly lower levels. As the NATO heads of state and government declared at the May 1989 summit in Brussels, "Peace must be worked for; it can never be taken for granted. The greatly improved East-West political climate offers prospects for a stable and lasting peace, but experience teaches us that we must remain prepared."

Richard B. Cheney
Secretary of Defense

September 1989

PART

1

The Nature of the Soviet Challenge

1

CHAPTER I

Soviet Defense Policy, Strategy, and Structure

CHAPTER II

Soviet Foreign Policy

CHAPTER III

Military Resource Allocation

CHAPTER IV

Nuclear, Strategic Defense, and Space Programs

CHAPTER V

General Purpose Forces

CHAPTER I

Soviet Defense Policy, Strategy, and Structure

UNITED NATIONS

In his December 1988 United Nations speech, General Secretary Mikhail Gorbachev announced large-scale unilateral force reductions along with other dramatic proposals affecting Soviet economic, political, and military policies. Although in the ensuing months some change has occurred as the result of such policy initiatives, it must be viewed within the context of continuing Soviet strategic and conventional force modernization.

INTRODUCTION

To assess how Soviet military power may be used, and how that power is likely to develop in the future, we need to understand the objectives and strategy of the Soviet rulers. While we can try to interpret and predict Soviet objectives and strategy, there are severe limits on how precisely and confidently this can be done. Accordingly, *Soviet Military Power* focuses primarily on Soviet military capabilities — what Soviet forces could do, not what they will do. It assesses current Soviet mil-

itary capabilities and how promised or possible changes in Soviet practices would affect those capabilities, not whether or when those changes will come to pass.

Even in the past, when Soviet pronouncements spoke in unison and Soviet policies seemed unchanging, there was room for disagreement on the objectives and meaning of those policies. Did the enormous and costly peacetime military build-up of the 1960s and 1970s have as its aim to conquer and coerce other countries, or only to increase Soviet confidence that their existing empire was secure? Did the invasion of Afghanistan manifest a desire to expand the Soviet empire further by direct employment of military force, an intention to menace oil supplies vital to the West, or only an attempt to forestall instability in Soviet Central Asia?

Now that Soviet policies are undergoing significant changes, there is even more room for uncertainty about Soviet objectives. Are promised Soviet military cutbacks intended only to divide and relax Western defense efforts, gain time for Soviet economic modernization, and permit a later acceleration of military competition under conditions more favorable to the Soviet Union? Or, whether motivated by economic necessity or political choice, do these policy changes manifest a fundamental change in the goals of the Soviet regime? Whoever is wrong in this debate may become right in the future, since Soviet objectives and intentions are not only debatable but changeable.

This chapter will not offer an interpretation or prediction of Soviet objectives and strategy. Rather, following a brief description of long-standing Soviet national security policies and the problems that appear to have contributed to recent changes, the various elements of Gorbachev's policy initiatives will be discussed in turn: economic reform, political reform, new formulations of military doctrine, announced reductions in military forces and spending, and "new thinking" on Soviet foreign policy. In each case, the key questions are how far changes have proceeded, the degree to which they may be reversible, and their possible implications for the future of Soviet military power.

THE CONTEXT OF CHANGE

A useful starting point for considering changes in Soviet policy is to note three principal features of Soviet defense policy under former General Secretary Leonid Brezhnev. First, the Soviet Union undertook to build military forces capable of defeating the combined strength of all potential adversaries. This included nuclear forces to checkmate US long-range nuclear guarantees and the modernization of large conventional forces so as to attain recognized military superiority in the Eurasian theater. Second, consistent with long-standing policies, the Soviet Union retained political domination over its neighbors in Eastern Europe, by stationing its own troops there as well as by the implicit threat and actual practice of armed intervention. Third, the Soviet Union supported revolution (so-called "wars of national liberation") in the Third World, either as a means of expanding communism, gaining useful military outposts, or weakening the global influence and presence of the industrial democracies.

According to Soviet statements, these policies are being reconsidered or modified to some degree under Gorbachev. Two sets of circumstances help explain why some policy change appeared advisable.

First, Soviet economic difficulties, and associated social problems and technological limitations, suggested the need for change in the Soviet economic system and/or resource allocation. The priority allocation of resources to build large standing military forces created an additional burden on a Soviet economy already suffering from the effects of central economic planning on incentives and efficiency. The result has been a faltering industrial base, uneven technological development, an agricultural system incapable of adequately feeding its people, citizen disillusionment, growing health and environmental problems, and the waning of socialism's appeal to the Third World.

In addition to the general effect of these problems, the economy's status became a military concern as well. Starting about 1980, some Soviet military writings began to reflect the idea that advanced technologies held more promise for enhancing military strength than did ever-increasing force levels. These writings also suggested that the Soviet industrial base could not adequately support a new revolution in weapon technologies in competition with the West.

Second, the impressive Soviet military capabilities built and maintained at great cost were unsuccessful in demoralizing Soviet adversaries (witness the acceleration of US military spending Soviet efforts provoked), in coercing the NATO Alliance (witness the failure of the Soviet campaign against INF), or in defeating the Afghan resistance.

ECONOMIC REFORM: *PERESTROIKA*

Gorbachev's program of economic *perestroika* (restructuring) is a potentially far-reaching attempt to overcome the gross inefficiencies and stultifying effects of the Soviet economic system. He has said that the USSR stands at a "crossroads," and the "historic fate of the country and the position of socialism in the modern world" depend on economic revitalization. Gorbachev's ambitious goal is a "fundamental breakthrough" in productivity, efficiency, and the quality of economic output to reverse the long-term slide in economic growth rates.

Gorbachev's economic policies have evolved from an initial emphasis on organizational change and tighter labor discipline to a long-term program for restructuring the economy and modernizing the technological base of industry. Soviet economic plan data indicate Gorbachev was counting, during his first years in power, on significant gains in the efficiency and productivity of civilian and military industries to fuel rapid growth in both sectors without a major reallocation of resources. These improvements, however, have not materialized. The lack of progress in economic reform and industrial modernization, the rise in consumer dissatisfaction, and the leadership's new emphasis on raising living standards to promote labor productivity have increased pressures on resources. Gorbachev has recently looked to the defense sector, which has long produced civilian goods in addition to military weapons and equipment, as a logical source of additional assistance to the economy.

Key elements of the economic reform apparently envisioned have not yet been instituted, in particular a rational pricing system and wide substitution of wholesale trade for centrally planned allocation of intermediate products. The scope of "individual labor activity," i.e., a limited private sector, has increased, but remains small. *Perestroika* is hampered both by political obstacles to the institution of reform, and by the fact that reforms to date appear not to have improved the Soviet economic situation.

TASS/SOVFOTO

The military leadership is generally supportive of Gorbachev's programs, including arms control strategies, force reductions, and technological modernization. It may, however, resist any attempt at substantial budget cuts, excessive downplaying of the Western threat, and significant reduction of the armed forces' influence in national security matters.

In the near term, the success or failure of *perestroika* may have a major effect on the longevity of Gorbachev's rule and the fate of his other policies. In the long term, the military implications of Soviet economic rejuvenation are uncertain. For example, economic reinvigoration without a corresponding growth of democratic institutions and practices could provide the economic and technological foundation for a more formidable Soviet military threat than exists today. Whether the intended or unintended social and political effects of successful reform would inhibit such a threat cannot be known today.

POLITICAL REFORM: *GLASNOST*

The policy of *glasnost* (openness) has permitted a much more wide-ranging political debate in the Soviet Union than has been allowed in the past. The principle of "democratization" has been carried so far as to allow contested elections for the Congress of People's Deputies, although members of the Communist Party still dominate this legislature. One apparent impulse behind these policies is Gorbachev's attempt to build a political power base in support of economic reform. While he advocates decentralized decisionmaking in day-to-day economic matters, Gorbachev seems to believe that the first step to decentralizing the economy is centralizing his political power. With the June 1988 All-Union Party Conference, the first of its kind since 1941, and with plenums of the Central Committee and elections to a newly reformed Supreme Soviet structure, Gorbachev achieved two critical objectives: he assumed the post of head of state, and he engineered changes that produced a more loyal, though still questioning, leadership.

The Soviets are demonstrating greater tolerance for political diversity. Expanded public participation in the political process signifies a hesitant recognition of political interests outside the Party, but the leadership is attempting to contain and manage this process in a way that will minimize public unrest.

In December 1988, the Supreme Soviet approved Gorbachev's plan to amend the Soviet Constitution. The amendments set up a new legislative body, the USSR Congress of People's Deputies, comprising 2,250 deputies who meet once a year. A much smaller 542-member Supreme Soviet, elected by this congress, will meet for up to eight months per year (in contrast to the current Supreme Soviet that meets for only a few days). Gorbachev also intends to enhance the role of Supreme Soviet commissions. Foreign Minister Eduard Shevardnadze has advocated changes that, if implemented, would expand significantly these commissions'

participation in strategic and foreign policy decisions. The most likely outcome in the short term, however, is a modest increase in the legislature's real power in the decisionmaking process.

The other part of Gorbachev's plan to change the relationship between the Party and state includes a series of measures that, while leaving the Party leadership in ultimate control, will limit meddling by lower-level party *apparatchiks* in day-to-day government business. Six specialized Central Committee commissions on Party organization and personnel, ideology, socioeconomic policy, agriculture, foreign policy, and legal issues have been created. The commissions will report directly to the Politburo and rely on a smaller Central Committee bureaucracy for staff support. The staff cutbacks may marginally reduce Party influence and result in a corresponding increase in the autonomy of state bodies.

Gorbachev also is attempting to advance measures designed to provide voters with a choice of candidates in elections. The new election law encourages multicandidate elections and involves a broader spectrum of individuals and organizations in the nomination and campaign processes. Moreover, many previously appointed jobs, like enterprise director, now have become elective positions, requiring a majority vote by workers. Both of these measures are facing tough resistance from local party bosses and enterprise officials who may now lose their jobs to other Communist Party candidates in competitive election. The new system still remains weighted in favor of party members and no opposition political parties are tolerated.

A related trend is greater official tolerance for "informal groups" — grassroots organizations that have sprung up outside officially created and sanctioned institutions. While some of these groups focus on cultural or social issues, many are explicitly political, each pressing its own agenda for change and indirectly challenging the Party's monopoly on power. While leadership policy toward these groups and their activities has not been consistent, the general lessening of political controls has generated an upsurge of political ferment throughout the country.

One important consequence has been efforts by Soviet ethnic groups to publicize previously suppressed grievances and to demand rectification of Stalin's policies. The three Baltic republics — Lithuania, Latvia, and Estonia — have transformed demonstrations for national independence into "Popular Front" movements that invoked Gorbachev's reform program. Ukrainian nationalism also has begun to reemerge after many years

At the June 1988 All-Union Party Conference, General Secretary Gorbachev succeeded in garnering additional support for his programs of sweeping reform.

of suppression. Although Ukrainian nationalists have stressed preservation and renewal of Ukrainian culture and language — but not political independence — Soviet authorities nonetheless fear a growth of Baltic-style nationalism there.

The Armenian-Azerbaijani dispute over control of the Nagorno-Karabakh Autonomous Oblast is an example of the serious ethnic problems facing the Soviet leadership. Nagorno-Karabakh is located within Azerbaijan, and Armenians comprise the majority of its residents. At the core of the dispute is historical hatred between the Christian Armenians and Moslem Azeris, combined with Azeri economic, cultural, and religious discrimination against Armenians. Limited Central Committee concessions to Armenians in the disputed region failed to end mass strikes and demonstrations, and the Soviets employed emergency measures and large-scale security forces to restore order. Ultimately, the Supreme Soviet determined that the region would be placed under the administrative control of Moscow, at

least temporarily avoiding a no-win decision on whether to transfer control of the region to the Armenians, or retain the status quo. Senior leaders based their decision, at least in part, on concerns that transfer of the disputed territory would lead to demands from other ethnic groups seeking to resolve territorial grievances. Strikes have recurred periodically in the region, and troop presence remains at higher-than-normal levels.

One of the greatest dangers that ethnic unrest poses to internal Soviet stability is the possibility of a Great Russian backlash and the rise of ultranationalist Russian groups. Another possible effect of ethnic grievances and conflicts would be to provoke restrictions on political openness and discourage further democratization of the political system.

It is uncertain how far Gorbachev wants democratization to go, and to what extent his intentions will be realized. The turmoil generated by reform could lead to reactions against it, or to unpredictable

The three Baltic Republics — Lithuania, Latvia, and Estonia — have transformed demonstrations for national independence into "Popular Front" movements that invoked Gorbachev's reform program and pushed *glasnost* to the limit.

instabilities. A truly democratic Soviet Union would greatly increase the confidence other countries could have regarding its military policies, but that outcome is, to say the least, not an immediate prospect. It appears that Gorbachev wants political changes that will provide a greater variety of policy options for the leadership at all levels, as well as greater legitimacy for their policies. Such changes are also intended to introduce a sense of accountability to Soviet leaders and to encourage them to carry out their duties energetically and conscientiously by making them, to some degree, responsible to an electorate. But it does not appear that the current Soviet leadership intends to concede the primacy of the Communist Party. It is, therefore, unlikely to sanction a rival political party in the Western sense.

MILITARY POLICY

Military doctrine has been another area of discussion and revision in recent years. Officials have suggested a new standard of "reasonable sufficiency" or "defense sufficiency" for sizing Soviet military forces, and a new doctrine of "defensive defense" for military operations. But the interpretation of these principles remains subject to debate, leaving a wide range of uncertainty as to the future composition of Soviet military forces.

Many on the General Staff use the term "defense sufficiency" to imply retaining a capability to execute an offensive-oriented defense that would defeat an enemy by conducting counteroffensive operations deep in his territory. In contrast, civilian advisers to Gorbachev advocate the principle of "reasonable sufficiency," which they believe would involve structuring forces for a defensive-oriented defense on a strategic and operational scale. This would permit repelling an aggressor but would preclude offensive operations in an enemy's territory.

The debate is evident in Gorbachev's incorporation of the "concept of war prevention" into Soviet military

Soviet Military Power

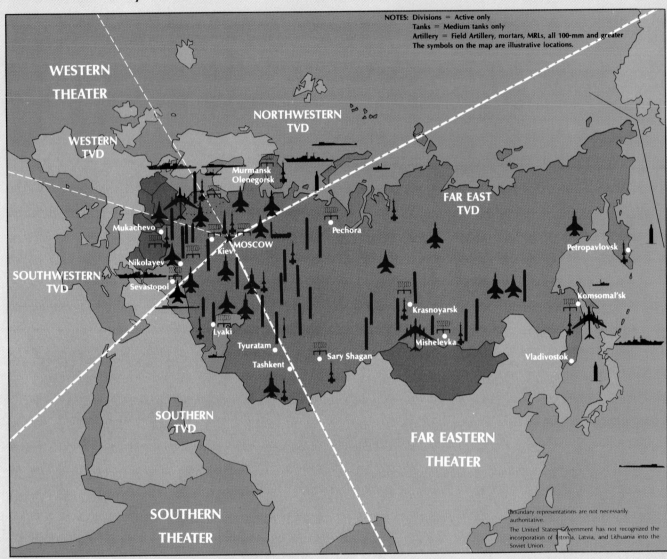

NOTES: Divisions = Active only
Tanks = Medium tanks only
Artillery = Field Artillery, mortars, MRLs, all 100-mm and greater
The symbols on the map are illustrative locations.

Boundary representations are not necessarily authoritative.
The United States Government has not recognized the incorporation of Estonia, Latvia, and Lithuania into the Soviet Union.

WESTERN THEATER

WESTERN TVD			NORTHWESTERN TVD		SOUTHWESTERN TVD			BALTIC FLEET	
DIVISIONS	64 (USSR);	29 (NSWP)	DIVISIONS	12	DIVISIONS	29 (USSR);	19 (NSWP)*	VSTOL AIRCRAFT CARRIERS	0
TANKS	19,800 (USSR);	10,800 (NSWP)	TANKS	1,300	TANKS	7,750 (USSR);	5,450 (NSWP)	LARGER PRINCIPAL SURFACE COMBATANTS	22
APC/IFVs	23,500 (USSR);	12,550 (NSWP)	APC/IFVs	3,600	APC/IFVs	6,100 (USSR);	5,700 (NSWP)	SMALLER FRIGATES AND CORVETTES	25
ARTILLERY	17,550 (USSR);	7,200 (NSWP)	ARTILLERY	2,050	ARTILLERY	6,400 (USSR);	3,900 (NSWP)	MCM SHIPS	21
TACTICAL SSMs	480 (USSR);	220 (NSWP)	TACTICAL SSMs	90	TACTICAL SSMs	220 (USSR);	160 (NSWP)	ASW/ASUW PATROL COMBATANTS	40
			TACTICAL AIRCRAFT	160	TACTICAL AIRCRAFT	600 (USSR);	750 (NSWP)	AMPHIBIOUS WARFARE SHIPS	22
TACTICAL AIRCRAFT	2,300 (USSR);	1,510 (NSWP)						BALLISTIC MISSILE SUBMARINES	4
					*DOES NOT INCLUDE 6 HUNGARIAN DIVISION EQUIVALENTS			ATTACK SUBMARINES	32
								OTHER SUBMARINES	1
								NAVAL AVIATION	220

SOUTHERN THEATER

FAR EASTERN THEATER

SOUTHERN TVD

DIVISIONS	30
TANKS	5,100
APC/IFVs	6,200
ARTILLERY	4,900
TACTICAL SSMs	190
TACTICAL AIRCRAFT	700

CASPIAN FLOTILLA

VSTOL AIRCRAFT CARRIERS	0
LARGER PRINCIPAL SURFACE COMBATANTS	0
SMALLER FRIGATES AND CORVETTES	5
MCM SHIPS	11
ASW/ASUW PATROL COMBATANTS	2
AMPHIBIOUS WARFARE SHIPS	15
BALLISTIC MISSILE SUBMARINES	0
ATTACK SUBMARINES	0
OTHER SUBMARINES	0
NAVAL AVIATION	0

FAR EAST TVD

DIVISIONS	59*
TANKS	14,950
APC/IFVs	17,050
ARTILLERY	13,800
TACTICAL SSMs	360
TACTICAL AIRCRAFT	1,200

*4 IN MONGOLIA, ONE OF WHICH IS IN THE PROCESS OF RETURNING TO THE USSR

PACIFIC OCEAN FLEET

VSTOL AIRCRAFT CARRIERS	2
LARGER PRINCIPAL SURFACE COMBATANTS	33
SMALLER FRIGATES AND CORVETTES	34
MCM SHIPS	26
ASW/ASUW PATROL COMBATANTS	30
AMPHIBIOUS WARFARE SHIPS	19
BALLISTIC MISSILE SUBMARINES	26
ATTACK SUBMARINES	83
OTHER SUBMARINES	9
NAVAL AVIATION	480

FIXED AND MOBILE ICBMs

SS-11	380
SS-13	60
SS-17	110
SS-18	308
SS-19	320
SS-25	About 170
SS-24 (MOD 1)	About 18
SS-24 (MOD 2)	About 40

LRINF[1]

SS-4	30
SS-20	262

SLBMs

SS-N-5	36
SS-N-6	256
SS-N-8	286
SS-N-17	12
SS-N-18	224
SS-N-20	120
SS-N-23	96

BOMBERS[2][3]

BLACKJACK	10
BACKFIRE	350
BEAR	160
BADGER	265
BLINDER	75

TACTICAL AIRCRAFT[3]

TACTICAL AIRCRAFT	5,170

GROUND FORCES[4]

MOTORIZED RIFLE DIVISIONS	152
TANK DIVISIONS	53
AIRBORNE DIVISIONS	7
STATIC DEFENSE DIVISIONS	2

NAVAL FORCES

VSTOL AIRCRAFT CARRIERS	4
LARGER PRINCIPAL SURFACE COMBATANTS	116
SMALLER FRIGATES AND CORVETTES	131
MCM SHIPS	114
ASW/ASUW PATROL COMBATANTS	119
AMPHIBIOUS WARFARE SHIPS	81
BALLISTIC MISSILE SUBMARINES	69
ATTACK SUBMARINES	256
OTHER SUBMARINES	34
NAVAL AVIATION[5]	1,300

STRATEGIC DEFENSE FORCES

ABM/BMEW RADAR	
INTERCEPTORS[3]	2,200
ASAT	
SAM LAUNCHERS[6]	8,000
ABM LAUNCHERS	100

[1] Deployed missiles as of 16 June 1989.
[2] Includes 160 Backfire in Soviet Naval Aviation (SNA). Excludes some 175 SNA Badgers.
[3] There are over 5,000 additional Soviet combat capable trainers and over 1,000 non-Soviet Warsaw Pact combat capable trainers in the non-Soviet Warsaw Pact countries.
[4] Ground forces maneuver division totals exclude three Soviet mobilization divisions and one Soviet independent army corps. Totals include 13GTD from SGF and 32GTD and 25GTD from WGF. Two MRDs from Afghanistan may not be active.
[5] As of 1 June 1989. Excludes SNA-subordinated fixed- and rotary-wing aircraft to include SNA Headquarters- and fleet air force-subordinated transport and other support types, aircraft which are subordinated to SNA school and test and development units, and aircraft which are assessed to be maintained in storage.
[6] In USSR only — does not include Soviet strategic SAMs (SA-2/3/5) in Mongolia or with Groups of Forces.

NORTHERN FLEET

VSTOL AIRCRAFT CARRIERS	2
LARGER PRINCIPAL SURFACE COMBATANTS	29
SMALLER FRIGATES AND CORVETTES	34
MCM SHIPS	30
ASW/ASUW PATROL COMBATANTS	20
AMPHIBIOUS WARFARE SHIPS	11
BALLISTIC MISSILE SUBMARINES	39
ATTACK SUBMARINES	118
OTHER SUBMARINES	18
NAVAL AVIATION	355

BLACK SEA FLEET

VSTOL AIRCRAFT CARRIERS	0
LARGER PRINCIPAL SURFACE COMBATANTS	32
SMALLER FRIGATES AND CORVETTES	33
MCM SHIPS	26
ASW/ASUW PATROL COMBATANTS	27
AMPHIBIOUS WARFARE SHIPS	14
BALLISTIC MISSILE SUBMARINES	0
ATTACK SUBMARINES	23
OTHER SUBMARINES	6
NAVAL AVIATION	245

MEDITERRANEAN FLOTILLA*

SHIPS, AVERAGE	31-42**
LARGER PRINCIPAL SURFACE COMBATANTS	6-10
ATTACK SUBMARINES	5-7

*UNITS ARE DRAWN FROM BLACK SEA AND NORTHERN FLEETS
**INCLUDES 20-25 AUXILIARIES

NOTES: Divisions = Active only
Tanks = Medium tanks only
Artillery = Field Artillery, mortars, MRLs, all 100-mm and greater
The symbols on the map are illustrative locations.

STRATEGIC RESERVES

DIVISIONS	20
TANKS	4,850
APC/IFVs	3,900
ARTILLERY	5,050
TACTICAL SSMs	100
TACTICAL AIRCRAFT	150

Stavka of the Soviet Supreme High Command - 1989

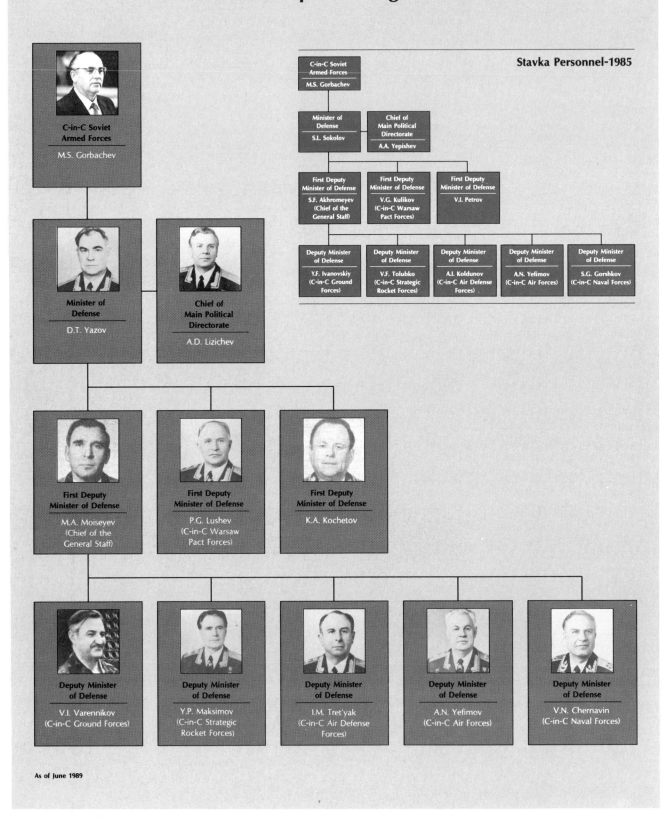

C-in-C Soviet Armed Forces

M.S. Gorbachev

Minister of Defense

D.T. Yazov

Chief of Main Political Directorate

A.D. Lizichev

First Deputy Minister of Defense

M.A. Moiseyev (Chief of the General Staff)

First Deputy Minister of Defense

P.G. Lushev (C-in-C Warsaw Pact Forces)

First Deputy Minister of Defense

K.A. Kochetov

Deputy Minister of Defense

V.I. Varennikov (C-in-C Ground Forces)

Deputy Minister of Defense

Y.P. Maksimov (C-in-C Strategic Rocket Forces)

Deputy Minister of Defense

I.M. Tret'yak (C-in-C Air Defense Forces)

Deputy Minister of Defense

A.N. Yefimov (C-in-C Air Forces)

Deputy Minister of Defense

V.N. Chernavin (C-in-C Naval Forces)

Stavka Personnel-1985

C-in-C Soviet Armed Forces

M.S. Gorbachev

Minister of Defense

S.L. Sokolov

Chief of Main Political Directorate

A.A. Yepishev

First Deputy Minister of Defense

S.F. Akhromeyev (Chief of the General Staff)

First Deputy Minister of Defense

V.G. Kulikov (C-in-C Warsaw Pact Forces)

First Deputy Minister of Defense

V.I. Petrov

Deputy Minister of Defense

Y.F. Ivanovskiy (C-in-C Ground Forces)

Deputy Minister of Defense

V.F. Tolubko (C-in-C Strategic Rocket Forces)

Deputy Minister of Defense

A.I. Koldunov (C-in-C Air Defense Forces)

Deputy Minister of Defense

A.N. Yefimov (C-in-C Air Forces)

Deputy Minister of Defense

S.G. Gorshkov (C-in-C Naval Forces)

As of June 1989

doctrine. Although the Soviets have stated that they regard the prevention of war as a cardinal principle, the concept has yet to be defined in terms of strategy and force structure. The General Staff may hope to influence this process, with the goal of retaining capabilities for an offensive-oriented defense.

Another point of contention is the proposal to introduce legislative oversight on military and foreign policy decisions. Until now, the formulation of national security policy has been highly centralized, with military professionals dominating the process of staffing proposals and developing options. Soviet Foreign Minister Shevardnadze has publicly advocated a procedure that would make key security decisions (including use of Soviet combat forces abroad, defense plans, and the defense budget) subject to approval by Supreme Soviet commissions.

While the outcome of debates about military doctrine and policy procedures could eventually have major effects on Soviet military power, those effects will become clear only if and when they change the size and character of deployed Soviet military forces.

MILITARY CUTBACKS AND NEGOTIATIONS

In the past year, reductions in Soviet military spending and deployed Soviet military forces have been announced by the Soviet rulers. Thus the effect of Gorbachev's initiatives on Soviet military power is no longer a matter of speculation, it is a matter of announced policy. But it is not yet a matter of accomplished fact, and many uncertainties remain concerning the character of the promised reductions.

In his United Nations speech of December 1988 Gorbachev announced that there will be reductions over the next two years in several categories of Soviet military equipment and in total Soviet armed forces, including the withdrawal of six tank divisions and 5,000 tanks from Eastern Europe. The effect of these planned changes on Soviet military power will be considered in Chapter V. In early 1989, Gorbachev announced that Soviet defense spending will be reduced by 14.2 percent by 1991 (see Chapter III). And the Soviets have proposed negotiated reductions in conventional forces in Europe, accepting in principle the idea of parity between NATO and Warsaw Pact forces (see Chapter V).

NEW THINKING ON FOREIGN POLICY

Finally, Soviet discussions of the overall goals and

approach of its foreign policy have been another area of innovation in recent years. The statements that inspire the greatest hope in the West have gone so far as to renounce "any threat or use of force and interference in the internal affairs of other states under any pretext whatsoever." In his United Nations speech, Gorbachev spoke of the "multi-optional nature of social development in different countries" and said that "the use or threat of force can no longer and must no longer be an instrument of foreign policy."

If these principles are followed, they would require a radical departure from past Soviet policies toward Eastern Europe and elsewhere. The Soviet withdrawal from Afghanistan, signing of the INF Treaty, and willingness to negotiate conventional parity in Europe offer grounds for hope that the Soviet Union has indeed

The 1989 Sino-Soviet summit, the first such summit in 30 years, is one of Gorbachev's most significant foreign policy achievements. Since his 1986 Vladivostok speech, Asia has become a high-priority foreign policy target.

recalibrated its security policies. But these events also lend themselves to other explanations. Chapter II considers the character of current Soviet policy toward various regions.

A shift in thinking, by itself, cannot be confidently verified, and it can be reversed by even newer thinking. Furthermore, it will take time for the tangible effects of "new thinking" on Soviet military forces to become manifest. Should the Soviets adopt a policy that truly renounces the use of force except for self defense, we should see much larger reductions in Soviet military power than those promised so far.

CHAPTER II

Soviet Foreign Policy

The Soviet leadership's "new thinking" in world affairs has begun to have a major impact on Soviet military power, as reflected by the withdrawal of Soviet forces from Afghanistan. Under Gorbachev, the Soviet leadership has begun to reassess the utility of military force as the most effective means of achieving the Kremlin's foreign policy objectives.

INTRODUCTION

Soviet foreign policy initiatives in the late 1980s confirm in some measure the frequently proclaimed Soviet intention to pursue more businesslike and less ideological relations with other nations, including those of the Western alliance. Among the more promising developments are the Soviets' military withdrawal from Afghanistan, their participation in negotiation of the INF accords, their announced plan to withdraw troops and tanks from Eastern Europe, and their constructive approach to mutual conventional armed force reductions in Europe. According to Soviet public statements, the foreign policy of the USSR is, in accordance with its domestic program, entering a new era of international cooperation, in which its chief aim will be "to show (through domestic economic success) that socialism can provide man with more than any other sociopolitical system."

The USSR under Gorbachev has pursued foreign policies evidently aimed at expanding Soviet contacts and influence in a variety of countries, while discouraging confrontational behavior by its existing regional clients. In 1989, for example, China and the USSR announced the normalization of Sino-Soviet relations and the future withdrawal of most Soviet troops from Mongolia. At the same summit, officials of the two countries discussed the accelerated resolution of Sino-Soviet border disputes and the Vietnamese occupation of Cambodia. In Africa, the Soviets played a helpful role in the successful US-mediated settlement leading to the withdrawal of foreign troops from Angola and the establishment of Namibian independence. To the extent that these initiatives reflect a redirection of Soviet foreign policy toward quiet diplomacy, improved political relations, and a reduction of regional tensions, they are consistent with the "new thinking" in foreign affairs recently proclaimed by Soviet officials.

While recent Soviet behavior gives some evidence of a more benign foreign policy, promises of a radical transformation of East-West relations must be viewed cautiously. First, the new Soviet initiatives do not amount to an abandonment of the long-term Soviet objective of shifting "the correlation of forces" in its favor. The USSR is likely to continue striving to increase its power and influence at the expense of the West through diplomacy, economic and military aid, and support of movements and regimes hostile to Western interests. For example, the USSR has not renounced its support for indigenous "national liberation movements," although its support for leftist insurgencies throughout the world may become more indirect and low-profile, with most of the aid channeled through Soviet clients. Nor has "new thinking" stopped Gorbachev from increasing military aid to Nicaragua from $280 million in 1985 to well over $500 million in 1988. Furthermore, military assistance and sales will continue to dominate Soviet relations with many developing countries, with a view to obtaining hard currency as well as regional political influence.

Second, Soviet arms control initiatives are at least partly intended to weaken the NATO Alliance, increase US-European tensions, and undermine Western military programs while protecting planned Soviet force modernization and development.

Third, the Soviets' desire for reduced trade barriers and greater economic cooperation with the West is partly aimed at securing access to Western technology and financial credits that have hitherto been denied them.

Fourth, the foreign policy changes announced by General Secretary Gorbachev are part of a more sweeping program of political and economic reform whose success is by no means assured. Virtually all of the policy changes could be reversed, especially if the failure of Gorbachev's economic policies leads to a domestic political crisis for the current regime.

Finally, friendly Soviet pronouncements notwithstanding, it is simply impossible to know with any certainty what Soviet intentions are in the long term. Nor can it be ascertained whether and to what extent recent Soviet foreign policy initiatives undertaken by Gorbachev will be preserved by his eventual successors.

SOVIET ALLIES AND CLIENTS

Soviet policies of "new thinking" and *perestroika* have been unsettling for some East European leaders and Soviet leftist client states, who see them as obstacles to the accomplishment of their own domestic and regional objectives. Some East European leaders see Gorbachev's policies as promoting a dangerous unleashing of latent nationalistic sentiments and demands for greater freedom and consumer comforts, while Soviet Third World allies and clients view these policies as a threat to indigenous revolutions, to nationalistic interpretations of Marxism-Leninism, and to continuing Soviet political and military support.

Eastern Europe

While some formulations of Soviet "new thinking" about international relations would seem to call into question past Soviet policy toward Eastern Europe, the Soviets appear determined to maintain their political dominance of the Warsaw Pact nations.

Moscow has several goals with respect to Eastern Europe:

- greater bloc cohesion and viability;
- increased economic integration;
- acceptable levels of defense spending, as well as a

Soviet Global Power Projection

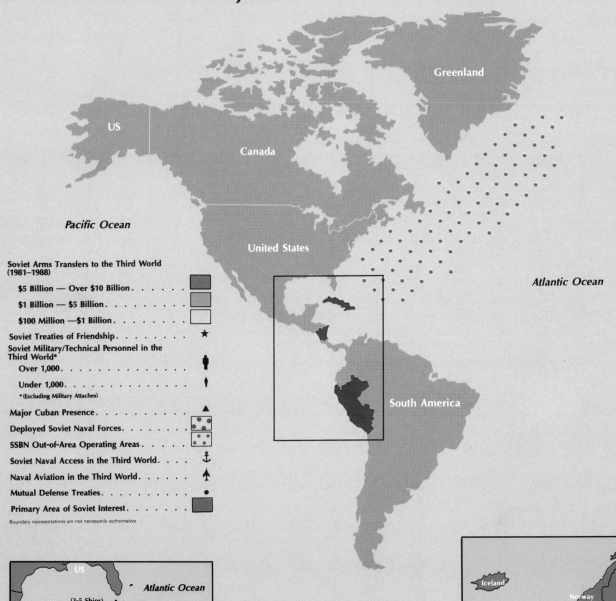

Greenland

US

Canada

Pacific Ocean

United States

Atlantic Ocean

South America

Soviet Arms Transfers to the Third World (1981–1988)

$5 Billion — Over $10 Billion . . . . . .

$1 Billion — $5 Billion . . . .

$100 Million —$1 Billion . . . .

Soviet Treaties of Friendship . . . . ★

Soviet Military/Technical Personnel in the Third World*

  Over 1,000 . . . .

  Under 1,000 . . . .

  *(Excluding Military Attaches)

Major Cuban Presence . . . . ▲

Deployed Soviet Naval Forces . . . .

SSBN Out-of-Area Operating Areas . . . .

Soviet Naval Access in the Third World . . . ⚓

Naval Aviation in the Third World . . . . . . ✈

Mutual Defense Treaties . . . . ●

Primary Area of Soviet Interest . . . . . .

Boundary representations are not necessarily authoritative.

US

Atlantic Ocean

(3-5 Ships)

Cuba

Dominican Republic

Haiti

Mexico

Belize

Jamaica

Guatemala

Honduras

El Salvador

Nicaragua

Costa Rica

Panama

Venezuela

Colombia

Ecuador

Brazil

Peru

Bol

Pacific Ocean

SOVIET MILITARY PERSONNEL IN THE THIRD WORLD[1]	
	(Est)
Latin America (Including Cuba) . .	7,500+
Sub-Saharan Africa	4,000+
Mideast and North Africa . .	6,000-7,000
Asia (Including Vietnam) . . .	4,000-4,500
Afghanistan	less than 200
India	400+

CUBAN MILITARY PERSONNEL IN THE THIRD WORLD[1]	
Latin America	1,000-1,500
Sub-Saharan Africa[2]	43,000-45,000
Mideast and North Africa	400

[1] As of June 1989
[2] Reduced by November 1989 to 25,000

Iceland

Sweden

Norway

Finland

Est
Lat
Lith

Denmark

United Kingdom

Neth
GDR
Poland

Ire

Bel
FRG
Czech

France
Switz
Aus
Hung
Rom

Yugo
Bul

Portugal
Spain

Italy
Alb

Med
Sea
Greece

Tur

(31-42 Ships)

Mor

Algeria

Egy

Libya

Western Sahara

Mauritania

Mali

Niger

Chad

Senegal

Guinea
Bissau

Guinea
Ghana

Benin

Nigeria

Sudan

Ivory Coast

(2-3 Ships)

Atlantic Ocean

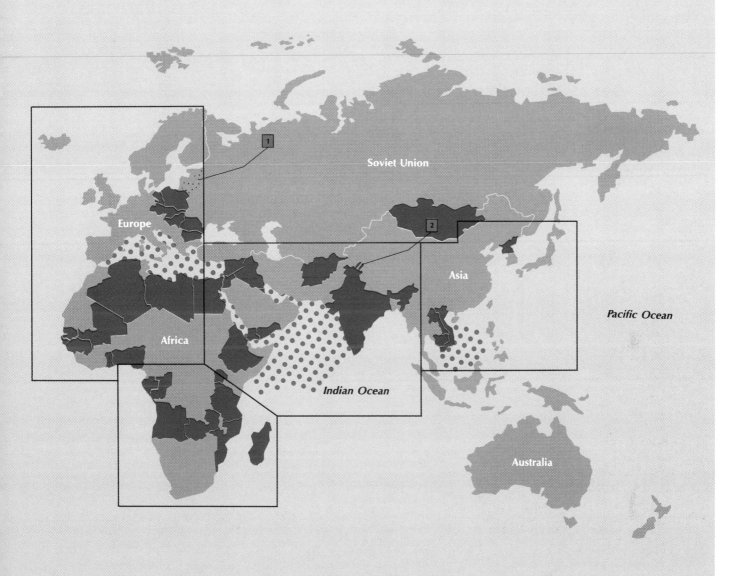

Soviet Union

Europe

Asia

Pacific Ocean

Africa

Indian Ocean

Australia

1 The United States Government has not recognized the incorporation of Estonia, Latvia, and Lithuania into the Soviet Union.

2 Area controlled by China, claimed by India.

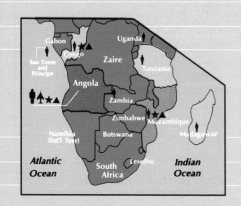

Gabon
Uganda
Congo
Zaire
Tanzania
Sao Tome and Principe
Angola
Zambia
Zimbabwe
Mozambique
Madagascar
Namibia (Int'l Terr)
Botswana
Lesotho
South Africa
Atlantic Ocean
Indian Ocean

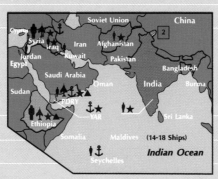

Cyprus
Syria
Iraq
Iran
Afghanistan
Soviet Union
China
2
Jordan
Kuwait
Egypt
Pakistan
Saudi Arabia
Oman
Bangladesh
Sudan
India
Burma
PDRY
YAR
Sri Lanka
Ethiopia
Somalia
Maldives
(14-18 Ships)
Seychelles
Indian Ocean

Mongolia
N. Korea
S. Korea
Japan
China
Pacific Ocean
(18-22 Ships)
Laos
Thailand
Vietnam
Cambodia
Philippines
Malaysia

THE AFGHANISTAN EXPERIENCE

In February 1989, the Soviets ended more than nine years of direct military intervention in Afghanistan. The immediate objective of the 1979 invasion was to prevent the imminent collapse of the communist government in Kabul resulting from popular reaction to the heavy-handed implementation of the regime's radical economic, social, religious, and educational programs. Soviet military action, however, was part of a larger political strategy that included placing a more compliant faction in charge of the government. After seizing Kabul, units of the Soviet 40th Army then occupied major cities and patrolled lines of communication to defend them against insurgent attacks.

The Soviets are now publicly examining the origins of their involvement in Afghanistan. The Gorbachev regime is distancing itself from the decision to invade Afghanistan. Recent statements by the military leadership have portrayed the invasion as a decision made by a small number of civilian leaders without full consultation and against the recommendations of the Soviet General Staff. Others contend that this action had the full support of the military and the Politburo. It is alleged that the decision was based upon mistaken estimates of the existing political situation within Afghanistan at that time.

In 1980 Moscow's primary long-term goal was to develop an Afghan communist government capable of dominating the country politically and militarily by itself, ultimately making the presence of Soviet troops unnecessary. The 40th Army's combat role was subordinated to this overall political strategy. It was not required to win a victory by purely military means or to suppress the Mujahedin resistance fighters completely. The Soviet occupation force remained limited in size in accordance with its constrained mission: to protect the government from resistance forces and keep the insurgency at a tolerable level; to enable the Afghan armed forces to take over the combat burden gradually; to forego significant attacks against the Mujahedin across the borders of Pakistan or Iran; and to keep Soviet personnel casualties and equipment losses low.

Soviet operations in Afghanistan generally employed mechanized tactics designed for modern warfare in Europe rather than adopting an aggressive counterinsurgency approach. Relying on massive artillery firepower and close air support to minimize casualties, Soviet forces seldom pressed their attacks to a final infantry assault, thereby frequently enabling insurgent groups to escape. Many operations were competently executed but had no lasting effect; the Soviets and their Afghan allies abandoned areas after the fighting, and the Mujahedin simply returned. However, the Soviets also occasionally conducted severe reprisal operations which were designed to exact a heavy penalty from civilian populations suspected of supporting the Mujahedin.

Mujahedin groups conducted an effective guerrilla campaign of harassing operations intended to disrupt government control, wear down enemy forces, and maintain popular support for the resistance. The Mujahedin understood that they were not able to overrun major Soviet bases, and they sensibly avoided large enemy field forces when tactical conditions were unfavorable. While the overall strength of anti-Soviet sentiment was always evident, the organization of the insurgency was never politically or militarily efficient because of the large number of Mujahedin parties and guerrilla groups, reflecting the tribal, ethnic and religious diversity of Afghanistan. Military cooperation among many groups did improve greatly in the latter years of the Soviet occupation, but lack of experience in controlling large-scale operations remained a problem.

By the mid-1980s increasing foreign material assistance to the Mujahedin consisted of a broad range of weapons, equipment, and supplies such as ammunition, transport vehicles, food, and clothing. Some advanced weapons had a notable impact on the battlefield. The Stinger shoulder-fired antiaircraft missile, for example, reduced the effectiveness of Soviet air superiority, boosted resistance morale, and enabled the Mujahedin to operate more freely. However, the sheer volume of less sophisticated lethal and nonlethal military equipment was equally important to the improvement of the resistance's combat capabilities by 1987.

By 1986 it was clear to the Soviets that the Kabul government remained incapable of consolidating its power. Moscow was unable to resolve or suppress chronic factionalism in the regime, even with a change in Afghan communist leadership from Karmal to Najibullah, and there seemed little chance that the performance of the government or the Afghan Army would improve significantly.

In addition, the Soviet leadership under Gorbachev recognized that the continued presence of Soviet troops in Afghanistan was an obstacle to progress on higher-priority diplomatic and strategic initiatives in East-West relations. At the same time, the resistance was growing stronger, further dimming the prospect of bringing the insurgency under control for many years. These factors resulted in Moscow's decision to pull out its troops.

Major Soviet Equipment Delivered to the Third World 1980–1988[1]

	Near East and South Asia	Sub-Saharan Africa	Latin America	East Asia and Pacific	Total
Tanks/Self-Propelled Guns	5,750	985	840	350	7,925
Light Armor	11,075	1,625	750	650	14,100
Artillery	13,050	4,685	1,875	860	20,470
Major Surface Combatants	37	4	5	4	50
Minor Surface Combatants	36	29	66	63	194
Submarines	15	0	2	0	17
Missile Attack Boats	16	9	6	6	37
Supersonic Aircraft	1,740	405	145	330	2,620
Subsonic Aircraft	170	15	0	25	210
Helicopters	1,150	310	155	90	1,705
Other Combat Aircraft	405	110	80	95	690
Surface-to-Air Missiles	22,000	6,110	2,600	1,500	32,210

[1] Revised from previous editions to reflect current information.

strengthening of the Pact's political apparatus;
- retention of Communist Party authority in each country; and
- continued support for Soviet foreign policy.

The USSR seeks improved economic performance out of Eastern Europe as a means of improving long-term security. Appeals by Moscow for Western joint ventures and the pressing need to acquire Western technology notwithstanding, Eastern Europe will remain the USSR's primary external source for industrial components and consumer goods. In fact, the Soviets are attempting to promote greater integration among Council for Mutual Economic Assistance (CEMA) members. However, the same signs of economic failure seen in the USSR now abound in most of Eastern Europe: long lines of consumers queuing up to buy shoddy, sub-standard products; rampant pollution of the environment; obsolete factories and industrial processes; and shortages of basic goods, all compounded by massive Polish and Hungarian foreign debts, and lesser debts elsewhere. Some East Europeans have been periodically trying to enact economic reforms for 40 years — e.g., Poland's Gomulka in 1956, Gierek in 1970, and Kania in 1980 — with scant success, mainly because economic change has usually implied or led to attempts at political change unacceptable to either Moscow or the indigenous communist leaders. Nevertheless, leaders in Poland, Hungary, and Czechoslovakia are once again loosening economic controls and allowing greater political free-

dom, though watching for Moscow's reaction at each step. However, the Soviets have not given the East Europeans definitive guidance on how far they may go.

The largely conservative leadership in other East European nations, especially East Germany and Romania, want little or no change, fearing it would lead to their downfall. Here the Soviet challenge will be to encourage economic and political reforms without jeopardizing communist rule.

Despite some significant changes in Soviet relations with its East European allies, the 1968 invasion of Czechoslovakia, prompted by the Prague Spring, is one Brezhnev action that Gorbachev has not condemned. Although the Soviets have promised to address the "blank spots" in Soviet-East European history — and even obliquely admitted the responsibility of Soviet secret police for the 1940 Katyn Forest massacre of 10,000 Polish officers — no reappraisal of the Prague Spring and its aftermath has appeared yet. Soviet and Czechoslovak police broke up August 1988 commemorative demonstrations in Moscow and Prague, and the official position in both countries is still that the Prague Spring was an out-of-control situation abetted by Western provocations that justified the Pact invasion. At his Council of Europe speech in July 1989, Gorbachev said "Any interference in internal affairs ... , any attempts to limit the sovereignty of states, ... is impermissible." However, he also said that "overcoming the division

Soviet-Cuban differences over economic reform were muted during Gorbachev's April 1989 visit to Cuba. Bilateral cordiality was outwardly maintained most notably by the signing of a 25-year treaty of friendship and cooperation.

of Europe" should not be understood to mean "the overcoming of socialism" which would be "a course for confrontation, if not something worse."

Cuba

Cuba remains the Soviet Union's principal client in the Western hemisphere and a huge recipient of Soviet military aid ($1.5 billion in 1988) and economic support ($4 billion in 1988). Soviet assistance pays for the presence of tens of thousands of Cuban military personnel in Angola, Ethiopia, and Nicaragua. Cuba also provides the USSR with military and intelligence collection support, and Soviet naval task forces use Cuban bases in joint exercises in the Caribbean.

Soviet-Cuban relations, while still close, have begun to experience more tension during Gorbachev's tenure. The chief source of friction appears to be the Soviet insistence that the Cuban economy be put on a sounder footing. Recent Soviet economic aid has increasingly been tied to specific development projects, and the USSR no longer subsidizes Cuban sugar sales to CEMA members. In addition, the Castro regime has resisted pressure to imitate the domestic political and economic reforms under way in the Soviet Union, as was evident during Gorbachev's April 1989 trip to Havana.

Vietnam

Vietnam's ailing economy and enormous military forces continue to be underwritten by substantial Soviet aid. Soviet financial and military support sustains the Vietnamese occupation of Cambodia. In return, the Soviets have been permitted to develop Cam Ranh Bay into the largest Soviet naval base outside of the USSR.

Under Gorbachev, the USSR has exerted some pressure on Vietnam to bring an end to the occupation of Cambodia, which Moscow sees as an "intolerable" burden on Vietnam's economy (and therefore on the Soviet treasury). Although the Soviets continue to view the Cambodian situation as an obstacle to improved relations with China, recent progress toward a settlement indicates that this issue will diminish as a source of tension between Moscow and Hanoi.

Angola

While the USSR will strive for the cessation of foreign — especially US — assistance to the Angolan insurgents, it will continue to supply significant quantities of weapons to the Popular Movement for the Liberation of Angola (MPLA), the Marxist regime currently in power, claiming that this materiel is being supplied to fulfill a legal agreement between two sovereign governments. While future arms agreements may be less generous, Moscow will attempt to find a reasonable balance between the regime's needs for combatting UNITA and Angola's ability to pay over the long term. Angola, however, does have natural resources, which provide some reimbursement options unlike other Soviet client states in Africa. Under the rubric of noninterference in the domestic affairs of Angola, Moscow will argue publicly that the composition of a postwar government in Luanda is a matter for the government and UNITA to work out between themselves. The Soviets may encourage the MPLA to pursue a "talk-fight" strategy of the type conducted so skillfully by Hanoi during the Vietnam War, but they appear to now accept the need for some form of powersharing as a means of peacefully resolving the conflict. The Soviets, in any event, will

Moscow's behind-the-scenes contribution to the negotiation of the December 1988 accord on Cuban troop withdrawal from Angola reflects the USSR's new focus on resolving regional conflicts. This policy has not included a significant diminution of political and military support to traditional Third World allies.

try to reinforce their influence in a postwar Angola by supplying most of the regime's military equipment.

Ethiopia

Relations between Addis Ababa and Moscow are in a period of transition, and tension has developed over conflicting objectives and personal leadership styles. Ethiopia's President Mengistu is highly resistant to the changing priorities and more pragmatic policies of General Secretary Gorbachev. The Soviets have urged Mengistu to seek a political settlement with the northern insurgents, to temper his radical pursuit of socialist economic policies, and to improve relations with the West to secure more economic aid.

The domestic deprivations caused by Mengistu's economic policies and relentless pursuit of a military resolution to the northern insurgencies led to an unsuccessful coup attempt in May 1989. Although Mengistu remains in power, he purged a large number of the most senior and experienced military leaders who were involved in plotting and executing the coup. The resultant degrading of the armed forces has led Mengistu to make some peace proposals to the insurgents. Moscow probably will take this occasion to further prod Mengistu to pursue serious negotiations in order to create the stable environment necessary to ensure that Soviet access arrangements in Asmara and the Dahlak Archipelago, regions claimed by the insurgents, are not threatened.

Nicaragua

Moscow wants to preserve the Marxist Sandinista regime, and will likely counsel Nicaragua's President

Moscow will continue to support the Sandinista regime of Daniel Ortega in Nicaragua. Although Soviet aid amounted to well over $500 million in 1988, future support may become more indirect and low-profile. It is possible that new aid may be channeled through client states, such as Cuba or those in Eastern Europe.

Following Chancellor Helmut Kohl's 1988 visit to Moscow, General Secretary Gorbachev geared his mid-June 1989 visit to West Germany to cultivate further a more benign Soviet image in Western Europe.

Daniel Ortega to use the respite from the anti-Sandinista insurgency to consolidate his regime and improve Nicaragua's economy. In May 1989, Gorbachev informed the United States that the USSR had stopped sending arms to Nicaragua in response to a favorable turn in US Central American policy. Nevertheless, Soviet military supplies continue to arrive in Nicaragua. Furthermore, Soviet weapons could be provided indirectly, through Cuba for example, or from Eastern Europe. Evidence also available shows that some arms of Soviet origin are being provided by Nicaragua to leftist insurgents in El Salvador and other Central American nations. The Soviet Union has ample time before it must decide whether or not to support the next phase of Nicaragua's planned military build-up, scheduled to begin in 1991. This build-up would further the expansion of the armed forces, militia, and other paramilitary organizations toward a Nicaraguan target of 500,000 personnel.

Panama

In Panama, the Soviets will continue efforts to establish relations with the Noriega regime or a successor government. They will castigate the United States for interference in Panama's internal affairs and otherwise try to fuel anti-US sentiment, while working with Panamanian communists to build a leftist infrastructure.

SOVIET REGIONAL POLICIES

The Atlantic Community

For Moscow, a long-standing, fundamental strategic goal has been to decouple the United States from

Both the US and USSR continue to implement the INF Treaty since its entry into force. Here Soviet SS-12 shorter-range missiles arrive at the Saryozek station in Kazakhstan for destruction in accordance with provisions of the treaty.

its West European allies. Despite the high priority that Gorbachev has placed on US-Soviet relations, Western Europe remains a pre-eminent concern of Soviet foreign policy. One of the Kremlin's favorite themes is the need to construct a "common European home" which includes the Soviet Union. References to this theme — a maneuver designed, among other things, to weaken NATO ties — are aimed at mitigating Western fears of Soviet aggression and dampening West European support for NATO and for defense spending. Economically, Gorbachev has used the commonality theme through appeals for widening cooperation, and has emphasized the USSR's desire for more East-West trade, unrestricted Western loans, and an easing of restrictions on technology transfer to the Soviet bloc.

The Soviets are exploiting the momentum generated by the INF Treaty to press for further arms control measures in Western Europe. During West German Chancellor Helmut Kohl's October 1988 visit to Moscow, Gorbachev expressed opposition to NATO's plan for modernizing its short-range nuclear systems which are deployed in West Germany. The Soviet announcement that 500 tactical nuclear warheads will be withdrawn was clearly intended to exploit differences in NATO. The Soviets also are advocating establishing a 300-kilometer-wide corridor in Central Europe, embracing both East and West Germany, that would be free of nuclear or chemical weapons.

During a September 1988 visit to Denmark, Foreign Minister Shevardnadze expanded on Gorbachev's October 1987 Murmansk speech which set forth a series of proposals on Nordic security and economic cooperation. He proposed exchange visits by warships, praised the research under way in Denmark and elsewhere in Europe on "nonoffensive defense," and promoted Gorbachev's concept of a "common European home." Shevardnadze called for broad economic cooperation between the USSR and the Nordic states, with all that such cooperation implies for Soviet access to modern technology. During a press conference in Copenhagen, Shevardnadze stated that the Coordinating Committee for Multilateral Export Controls (COCOM) list of items prohibited from export to the Soviet bloc should be shortened to foster the spirit of East-West cooperation.

The ongoing Soviet withdrawal from Mongolia has greatly facilitated Gorbachev's efforts to improve relations with China. Moscow timed the beginning of the pullout's second phase to coincide with Gorbachev's arrival in Beijing in May 1989.

East Asia and the Pacific

The Soviet Union seeks to expand its role in Asia and the Pacific. The Soviets have stepped up their diplomatic activity, advanced arms control initiatives, and sought to establish stronger economic links with nations in the region. Moreover, Moscow has shown greater flexibility on issues of concern to the region, such as Afghanistan, the Cambodian conflict, and deployment of intermediate-range missiles east of the Urals. The Soviets also have accelerated efforts to improve relations with China by normalizing ties at a historic leadership summit in May 1989. They also have devoted greater attention to nonsocialist states, particularly Japan, as well as growing economic powers like the Republic of Korea and the ASEAN nations. These moves appear designed to overcome perceptions that the USSR seeks to dominate the region, and to promote economic ties beneficial to the Soviet Union. While the Soviets have announced significant force reductions, they continue to modernize their military forces in the region.

Despite the skill and vigor with which the Soviets are pushing their new agenda, they face substantial impediments. Moscow has few products that it can successfully market in the region, and many leaders remain deeply suspicious of Soviet intentions. For example, because of the extensive military and economic support provided to Vietnam and military aid provided to North Korea, many regional states view the Kremlin as ultimately responsible for Vietnam's occupation of Cambodia and past North Korean acts of terrorism.

The Soviets are particularly covetous of Japanese economic expertise and investment but remain unwilling to modify their position on Japan's Northern Territories, which the USSR has occupied since the end of World War II.

The Middle East/North Africa

A February 1989 visit to the Middle East by Soviet Foreign Minister Shevardnadze was aimed at placing the Soviet Union in the forefront of Middle East affairs and at strengthening bilateral relations with Israel, the PLO, and Iran. Shevardnadze did not present a new "peace plan" for the Middle East; rather, he sought

Moscow has become more supportive of Yassir Arafat as he has moderated the PLO's approach to a Middle East peace settlement. Arafat's new position is more in keeping with new, more flexible Soviet Middle East policies designed to expand the Soviet role in the peace process.

to portray the USSR as a superpower deeply involved in Middle East issues and negotiating actively with all parties to the various conflicts. He also stressed the need for US-Soviet cooperation in resolving these conflicts.

The Soviets are striving to broaden their base of influence in the Middle East by establishing ties with moderate Arab states and Israel. By demonstrating that it has interests in the region that go beyond its traditional arms clients — with which it is often at odds politically — Moscow calculated that it will be assured a place in any Middle East negotiations.

Moscow will strive to enhance its political influence through the use of economic and arms agreements. By its supply of additional and sophisticated arms, Moscow also will attempt to reassure Syria, Libya, and Iraq — its traditional Middle East arms clients — that its support has not diminished. Most disturbing to the West has been the sale of Su-24 Fencer long-range aircraft to Libya and the conclusion of a major Soviet arms sale agreement with Iran.

Southwest Asia

India will remain the focal point of Soviet regional policy, and the special relationship between Moscow and New Delhi will continue. Moscow will, however, attempt to strike a better balance in its regional relations now that its forces have withdrawn from Afghanistan.

Moscow has taken steps to forestall the collapse of the Afghan communist government, as well as to ensure that the Kremlin can retain relations with the follow-on government. Last fall, an Afghan-Soviet economic agreement was signed to prepare a framework for continued Soviet influence in post-withdrawal Afghanistan. The agreement provided for Soviet assistance in extracting Afghan mineral deposits, in increasing oil and gas production, in expanding Soviet electrical distribution in northern Afghanistan, and in improving the transportation system, to include highway and railroad construction. These national-level protocols followed an unprecedented web of province-to-province economic agreements designed to increase Afghan border trade and cooperation with the USSR. Moscow is calculating that these agreements would be honored by a successor regime. As of mid-1989, massive military assistance was also flowing to the regime in Kabul in an effort to sustain it against the non-communist resistance.

The Soviet withdrawal also removes a major impediment to improving the USSR's relations with Pakistan. Moscow will likely expand governmental contacts and initiate limited economic development projects there. The Soviet commitment to India, however, will limit any Moscow rapprochement with Islamabad.

Latin America

Soviet leaders believe regional trends favor the expansion of their influence in Latin America through overt as well as covert means, and under Gorbachev they have placed increased emphasis on state-to-state ties. The growth of democratic governments provides opportunities for leftist organizations to expand their activities and influence legally, thus reducing the likelihood of clashes with the United States over such activities. Moscow will probably encourage communist parties to consolidate factions and build their infrastructure while exploiting political processes to gain influence. Soviet support to leftist insurgencies will be selective and covert, and provided primarily via Cuba and Nicaragua, and to a lesser degree through Latin American communist parties.

Sub-Saharan Africa

Although Sub-Saharan Africa is peripheral to the Soviet Union's major strategic interests, which lie predominantly in Europe, East Asia, and along the USSR's southern border, the Soviets seek to broaden their influence in the region. The Kremlin is particularly eager to buttress its ties with Africa's "Frontline States," (Tanzania, Mozambique, Zambia, Zimbabwe, Botswana, and Angola) with a view toward ensuring that Soviet interests are served during the transition period in Namibia and, later, Moscow believes, in South Africa. At the same time, in line with Moscow's traditional dual foreign policy of seeking links both with established governments and their opponents, the Soviets intend to cultivate improved relations with Pretoria while maintaining their relationship with the African National Congress. In short, the Soviet Union wants to keep its options open, both in terms of dealing with a multiplicity of African governments and political movements, and of utilizing a broad variety of tools — including military assistance, economic cooperation, propaganda, disinformation, and other overt and covert means.

CONCLUSION

Soviet foreign policy's new public emphasis on cooperation and negotiation serves a variety of objectives. The Soviets probably hope to broaden their interests and influence, and gain support for initiatives such as arms control and regional denuclearization, increased access to advanced technologies, and expanded economic opportunities. Shevardnadze has acknowledged that Soviet Third World activities affect East-West relations (previously Moscow rejected this concept of "linkage"). The economic cost of some Soviet Third World involvements may also militate in favor of negotiations or retrenchments. Moreover, less provocative Soviet policies may create an atmosphere in which US allies question the utility of supporting a US military presence in their respective regions.

Despite Soviet concern to be seen as nonthreatening and cooperative, specific Soviet policy choices will depend heavily on circumstances, opportunities, and the policies of other countries.

CHAPTER III

Military Resource Allocation

Under the terms of the INF Treaty the Soviets are dismantling and destroying some weapon systems; others are being converted for use in the civilian sector. One of the first such conversions is this former transporter-erector-launcher for an SS-20 missile, now fitted with a crane for industrial use.

INTRODUCTION

In their pursuit of long-term economic strength, and in recognition of the critical problems facing their economy, the Soviets have given some indications of shifting emphasis away from the military to the civilian sector. General Secretary Gorbachev has stated his intention to "maintain the country's defense capability at a level of reasonable and dependable sufficiency," to seek to "demilitarize international relations," and to address the problem of "converting the armaments economy into a disarmament economy."

In January 1989 Gorbachev elaborated upon his plans for the defense sector, declaring that the defense budget would be cut by 14.2 percent and the production of military weapons and equipment by 19.5 percent during 1989-90.

The poor performance of the Soviet economy makes such defense cuts advisable. Almost four years into Gorbachev's economic revitalization program, the economy has averaged about the same growth rate as in the last years of the Brezhnev regime, a time Gorbachev calls the "period of stagnation." The Soviets were faced at the end of 1988 with another year of lackluster industrial performance, a disappointing harvest, and continuing frustration in their efforts to modernize industry and reform the economic system. They also saw rising popular dissatisfaction over the lack of improvement, and in some respects deterioration, in living conditions over the last few years. Gorbachev acknowledged that consumer welfare must be substantially improved soon if the regime hopes to develop broad-based support for *perestroika.*

In addition to these problems, state revenues have stagnated, primarily because world market prices for Soviet oil exports slumped in the mid-1980s and state liquor tax earnings, a major source of government income, fell with Gorbachev's campaign to curb alcohol abuse. At the same time, state spending under Gorbachev increased for investment, defense, and subsidizing unprofitable factories and farms. The combined effect of declining revenue and increased spending substantially boosted the Soviet budget deficit and, in turn, fueled inflationary pressures in the economy. In a 6 January 1989 speech, Gorbachev said that the question of reducing the budget deficit and restoring financial order "is so acute that we will have to look at our expenditures on defense too."

The poor progress in economic reform and modernization, coupled with a growing budget deficit and new concern for raising living standards, has prompted the Soviets to reassess and revise their economic policies. They have launched major policy changes designed to boost substantially the production of consumer goods and services, postpone reforms that would require consumer sacrifices, and reduce the budget deficit. New budget deficit reduction plans include trimming state investments, reducing state subsidies to unprofitable enterprises, and cutting defense expenditures. More important than the budgetary effect of a defense spending cut is the potential transfer of resources from the military to the civilian sectors of the economy. The Soviets apparently concluded that the civilian sector was unable to provide all of the resources required to modernize industry and expand food and consumer goods supplies, and they decided to draw more upon the resources of the defense sector to assist in revitalizing the economy. The conversion of defense industries to civilian production, however, remains in a preliminary state.

The issues of defense spending and military-civilian resource allocation have also come to the fore because of the time requirements of the Soviet economic planning process. Political leaders are currently weighing their estimates of future military requirements against resource availability and economic potential in preparing the 13th Five-Year Plan (FYP), which will cover the period 1991–95. Based on the guidelines these leaders must provide on the amount of resources that will be allocated to defense, the military will draft its five-year defense plan. Thus the timing of Gorbachev's statements on reducing military spending and converting defense plants was consistent not only with the pressing needs of the economy, but also with the need to keep the preparation of the 13th Five-Year Plan on track by reaching basic decisions on future resource allocations.

While Gorbachev's announcements on defense are in response to strong economic incentives and represent his intention to reduce the economy's defense burden, they also contain a strong political element. They are most certainly intended to further Soviet efforts to constrain Western military modernization, give added impetus to the arms control process, and enlist Western support for the USSR's economic program. In light of these political implications, it is essential for the West to consider closely the Soviet military-economic reforms. The potential for significant changes in traditional Soviet military resource allocation priorities must be analyzed carefully in an attempt to separate rhetoric from reality and ascertain the factors that will help shape future Soviet military power.

SOVIET MILITARY SPENDING

In their new show of candor on military spending issues, the Soviets have acknowledged the persistence of traditional resource allocation priorities favoring the military during Gorbachev's first three years in power, despite the high priority placed on economic modernization. In an address to the new Congress of People's Deputies on 7 June 1989, Soviet Prime Minister Nikolay Ryzhkov said, "When forming the plans for 1986–90, because of the international situation prevailing at the time and our military doctrine, we were compelled to envision a traditional growth of defense expenses at a pace exceeding the growth of the national income." Ryzhkov's statement indicates that the Soviets had planned for an increase in the defense burden on the economy during the 12th Five-Year Plan (1986–90), even while they began a crash industrial investment program which they hoped would achieve substantial gains in productivity and economic growth. Their subsequent failure to achieve a breakthrough on the economic front is not surprising.

This continuation of traditional military resource allocation patterns is reflected in Western estimates of military spending under Gorbachev, which show that total military outlays have grown at a rate of about 3 percent a year in real terms since 1985. Expenditures on research and development (R&D) and weapon procurement have been the primary contributors to growth. This growth rate is somewhat higher than existed in the early 1980s, although it does not appear to represent a change in defense spending policy under Gorbachev. Rather, the growth has been driven largely by the startup or acceleration of several new weapon systems that were under development before Gorbachev took office.

All major categories of weapon systems continued to receive high levels of funding. Historically, the Soviets have allocated the largest percentage of their procurement budget to land armaments. Spending for this category has remained at a relatively stable, but high, level under Gorbachev, enabling the military to proceed with its broad-based modernization of ground forces. Meanwhile, naval procurement costs have grown dramatically, especially in general purpose submarines and major surface combatants. The rising costs of new fighter aircraft reflect their increased sophistication and capabilities, which have permitted lower levels of production. Both tactical and strategic missile procurement has grown, primarily due to increases in the output of surface-to-air missiles and a rebound in ICBM production after a dip in 1984–86.

The Soviets have attempted to trim some military expenditures over the past few years. The Soviet Navy, for example, has reduced distant operations, probably in response to both economic and operational requirements, and is accelerating the scrapping of obsolescent submarines and surface ships. Articles in the Soviet military press indicate some ground force units have been given specific goals to reduce the use of fuel and other resources. Apparently, the Soviets also reemphasized their efforts to extend the service life of various weapons. Nevertheless, the rising costs of Soviet weapon programs more than offset these attempts at military economizing. As a result, total military spending continued to grow faster than the overall economy, signifying an increasing defense burden.

For the future, the key issue for the West is the extent to which the recent Soviet statements on military spending cuts will be translated into real changes in traditional military resource allocation priorities. On their surface, the Soviet statements indicate a new willingness to release military expenditure data formerly considered secret, and they suggest the prospect of dramatic changes in military spending. Despite this new show of openness, however, the Soviet statements remain far from a clear guide to their intentions.

The inaugural meeting of the USSR Congress of People's Deputies in late May and early June 1989 proved another occasion for revelations on military spending. General Secretary Gorbachev provided for the first time a total figure for military expenditures, which he said will amount to 77.3 billion rubles in 1989. He claimed that military spending was "frozen" in the 1987-88 period, saving 10 billion rubles, and he proposed to reduce military expenditures "as early as 1990–91" by 14 percent, or another 10 billion rubles. Prime Minister Ryzhkov provided the first breakdown of the defense budget into such categories as weapon procurement; research and development; personnel, operations and maintenance; and military construction. Ryzhkov said the USSR intends to "strive for reducing by one-third to one-half the relative share of defense expenses in the national income by 1995."

Although the Soviets emphasized that they had calculated the defense budget "in full and precisely," their statements contain significant inconsistencies and discrepancies. While considerably higher than any previously announced Soviet defense budget, Gorbachev's figure of 77.3 billion rubles is unrealistically low in comparison to the resources required to equip, maintain, and operate a military force the size of the USSR's. This figure is approximately half of Western estimates of Soviet military spending in current terms. It represents about 9 percent of Soviet gross national product (GNP), in contrast to the 15–17 percent of GNP that the West estimates for the Soviet defense burden.

Several reasons could account for the large difference between Gorbachev's defense budget total and Western estimates. Western estimates could simply be too high. However, all of the several estimates derived independently by Western government agencies, as well as academics and private researchers, are significantly higher than 77.3 billion rubles. Moreover, a February 1989 press article by a Soviet economist admitted it is "obvious" that defense spending "is far in excess of 100

ESTIMATING SOVIET MILITARY SPENDING

Monetary measures provide a common yardstick for representing a diversity of military activities, from weapon procurement, to operations and maintenance, to the training of military personnel. Traditionally, the Soviets have released very little information on their military expenditures. Consequently, the West must derive independent monetary estimates.

Due to the complexity of the assessment problem, several different measures exist. Each serves different purposes and has its own particular limitations. No monetary estimate, however sophisticated, can provide a summary measure of the capabilities or effectiveness of Soviet weapons and forces, which depend upon a number of nonmonetary factors. When applied appropriately however, these estimates can provide insights on the magnitude, trends, and economic impact of Soviet defense efforts that cannot be obtained from official Soviet data. Three of the most commonly used Western estimates are described below.

Dollar Cost Estimates

Dollar cost estimates provide the best means of comparing the relative size of Soviet and US defense activities in terms readily understood by US audiences. They are made in constant US dollars to portray trends in real terms without the effects of inflation.

Dollar cost estimates are derived by calculating what it would cost in the United States, using prevailing US prices and wages, to duplicate Soviet military programs. They are not obtained by converting Soviet defense figures expressed in rubles into dollars at the official exchange rate. This would be misleading because the USSR's official exchange rate is administratively set and does not accurately relate the costs and values of goods and services in the USSR to those in the United States. The dollar

costing method requires detailed information on Soviet weapon procurement, force structures, operating procedures, and the numerous other activities encompassed by Soviet defense programs. Dollar cost estimates can be made for detailed categories of Soviet defense activities — such as procurement, research and development, construction, personnel, and operations and maintenance — as well as for the total Soviet defense effort.

Dollar cost estimates show that the Soviet military effort greatly exceeded that of the United States over the last decade. Even with the rapid growth of US outlays during the 1980s, primarily for procurement, the total dollar cost of Soviet military programs in 1988 — roughly $300 billion — still exceeded total US outlays.

While dollar cost estimates are a valid means to compare Soviet and US defense activities, they do not represent what the USSR actually spends on its military. Actual Soviet military spending can only be understood in terms of rubles and in the context of the Soviet economy.

Constant Ruble Estimates

Constant ruble estimates measure the real growth over time in Soviet military spending, excluding the effects of inflation. They identify trends in the levels of resources going into the Soviet defense sector as a whole and into its various categories of activities. Constant ruble estimates also are based on detailed information about the physical components and activities of Soviet military programs. For some activities — the pay of military forces, for example — the costing is done directly in rubles on the basis of known pay factors and prices. Other programs — the procurement of a given ICBM, for example — are costed in US dollars and then converted to rubles on the basis of information on the relationship of dollar

prices to known ruble prices for comparable programs. Constant ruble estimates indicate that total military spending under Gorbachev has increased at a rate of about 3 percent annually in real terms.

Current Ruble Estimates

Although current ruble estimates reflect both increasing real costs and inflationary price changes for military goods and services, they probably represent the perspective of Soviet leaders on the levels and trends in their defense spending. Most references in Soviet literature to defense spending are in terms of current rubles, which the leadership presumably uses, along with various physical indicators such as fuel allotments, to measure trends in resource allocations to the military. Current ruble estimates also are appropriate for measuring the defense burden — that is, the share of Soviet economic output devoted to military programs in any year.

Estimates in current rubles are calculated in two ways. The first is based on detailed analysis of Soviet economic and financial data. Results are usually expressed in aggregate terms and cannot be broken down easily into detailed expenditure categories. The second is similar to the constant ruble method of identifying activities and then costing them. In this case, however, instead of using prices of a fixed base year, the prices are allowed to change to reflect inflationary pressures.

Western current ruble estimates show that the Soviet defense burden increased from 12-14 percent of GNP in 1970 to 15-17 percent of GNP by the mid-1980s, and that it has continued to rise under Gorbachev. In contrast to the recent Soviet announcement that total defense spending in 1989 will be 77.3 billion rubles, Western estimates in current rubles would put Soviet defense spending at roughly 150 billion rubles.

billion rubles a year." Prime Minister Ryzhkov pointed to a possible source of discrepancy when, after detailing the activities he said constituted the total defense budget, he separately listed additional expenditures of 3.9 billion rubles for military-related space programs. This is perhaps representative of several categories of expenditures the Soviets could have excluded from a narrowly defined defense budget.

Probably the greatest uncertainty lies in the realm of Soviet prices. The Soviets had pledged since 1987 to release a total defense budget after they carry out a price reform that makes their defense spending figures comparable to data on Western defense spending. Although the leadership has postponed the controversial price reform because of their concern for public discontent over higher consumer prices, Gorbachev went ahead with the release of a defense budget. This was probably in response to both Western pressures and the urging of domestic advocates of reform. Therefore,

Soviet Production 1982–84 and 1986–88[1]

Equipment Type	Pre-Gorbachev Yearly Average (1982–84)	Gorbachev Yearly Average (1986–88)
Tanks	2,800	3,400
Other Armored Vehicles	5,400	4,600
Towed Field Artillery	1,300	1,000
Self-Propelled Field Artillery	900	900
MRLs	600	480
Self-Propelled Antiaircraft Artillery	200	100
Submarines	9	9
Surface Warships	9	9
Minor Surface Combatants	57	55
Bombers	40	47
Fighters	950	680
Military Helicopters	580	450
ICBMs	116	116
LRINFs	125	50
SRBMs	480	520
Long-Range SLCMs	50	200
Short-Range SLCMs	950	900
SAMs[2]	15,000	16,000

[1] Totals include exports
[2] Excludes man-portable SAMs

it is unknown to what degree the 77.3-billion-ruble figure reflects subsidies on military goods and services or other price adjusting factors, which could account for a considerable part of the difference with Western estimates.

Unless the Soviets provide more detailed information and more convincing explanations for the discrepancies in their announced defense budget, it will be difficult for Western observers to assess the significance of their intentions to reduce military spending. For example, a 14 percent cut in a defense budget that is half the size of Western estimates could mean a much smaller impact on Soviet military programs. Similarly, a reduction by one-third in the share of national income going to defense could be achieved, based upon recent Soviet national income growth, simply by holding military spending levels steady during the 13th Five-Year Plan, after the 14 percent cut Gorbachev proposed for 1990-91. A reduction by more than one-third in the share of national income devoted to defense, however, would require additional spending cuts. With such budgeting and defense accounting uncertainties, Soviet intentions will remain ambiguous until they provide substantial evidence of actual reductions in Soviet forces and the flow of weapons and equipment to them.

THE DEFENSE INDUSTRIAL BASE

The defense industry has remained the fastest-growing sector of the Soviet economy under Gorbachev, turning out a wide range and high volume of military materiel. The overall quantities of weapons and equipment produced for general purpose forces in the last three years declined only slightly from the three-year period before Gorbachev came to power. Since the start of 1986, production of the premier ground-force weapon, the tank, rose about 5 percent as output of new models, such as the T-80, increased. While the numbers of lighter armored vehicles have dropped, production of the newest APC, the BTR-80, is rising, and a new version of the Soviet BMP infantry fighting vehicle is expected to enter serial, i.e. mass, production in 1989. While the average number of older, less-advanced towed field and antitank artillery pieces turned out each year has declined under Gorbachev, a new 152mm towed howitzer may now be in production. The Soviets continued producing modern self-propelled artillery pieces at the rate of about 900 per year in 1989. Similar trends have occurred in the production of antiaircraft artillery. The number of new models with improved capabilities has increased as older items have been phased out.

The quantities of aircraft being produced are well below the levels of a decade ago, but the quality and capabilities of individual systems have greatly improved. Soviet fighter aircraft production, which had been declining since the early 1980s, leveled off in 1987 and 1988 as plants were expanded and reequipped to produce modern, more capable aircraft. Although transport aircraft production drifted lower, output of the types used by the military, such as the massive An-124 Condor, continued to rise.

Naval shipbuilding has shown no change under Gorbachev in terms of numbers produced or tonnage. Although over the past two decades production numbers have been decreasing, output in tonnage has not. Naval ship output has averaged about 150,000 standard tons annually, split nearly equally between submarines and surface combatants. Moreover, costs have risen with the increasing complexity of weapons and electronics. Additional Delta IV-, Victor III-, Akula-, Oscar-, and Kilo-class submarines were produced in 1988. Surface warships completed during 1988 included the third Kirov guided-missile cruiser, three destroyers of the Udaloy and Sovremennyy classes, a Krivak III-class frigate, and four Grisha-class corvettes. Hulls 1 and 2 of the Tbilisi-class aircraft carrier are fitting out at Nikolayev shipyard, while a follow-on is in an early stage of construction. Ongoing construction activity will deliver new ships into the early 1990s. The fourth Kirov-class guided-missile cruiser, *Yuriy Andropov,* was launched during mid-1989 and a keel for what may be another similar ship laid down. The first of a new frigate class, with a helicopter hanger, is in an advanced state of fitting out at Kaliningrad. Additional Udaloy- and Krivak III-class ships also are being constructed.

Strategic weapons output increased, largely as new designs were accepted for serial output. The first series manufacture of the intercontinental Blackjack bomber began in the mid- to late-1980s. Since Gorbachev came to power, production of long-range (3,000 kilometer) cruise missiles, designed to be launched from bombers and submarines, rose by a factor of three. Active ballistic missile production included SS-18, SS-24, and SS-25 ICBMs, and SS-N-20 and SS-N-23 SLBMs. Total ICBM output was very low in 1984-86, but production now has returned to the levels of the early 1980s. At the same time, the Soviets have continued to augment their strategic defensive systems, increasing production of airborne warning and control systems (AWACS), strategic SAMs, and ABMs.

The Soviets also have made substantial improvements in their defense industrial facilities through a comprehensive modernization program begun in the early 1970s and accelerated in the latter part of the decade. A large portion of the best domestically produced machinery

was allocated to defense industry, which also benefitted from a surge in clandestine and open acquisition of Western manufacturing equipment.

One result of these Soviet budget priorities has been success in producing the current generation of military materiel. This skewed emphasis, however, has also resulted in an increasingly out-of-date manufacturing base for consumer durables and capital equipment. The relative neglect of manufacturing technologies has led not only to a shortage of new machinery needed for civilian production lines, but also to a widening gap with the West in industrial equipment design and production capabilities that threaten the military industrial sector's ability to produce future, high-technology weapon systems. While the legal and illegal acquisition of Western technology has helped bridge the gap in several significant areas, as evident in the Toshiba technology transfer case, imported technology cannot compensate for the general lack of innovative ability in the Soviet industrial sector. This gap in manufacturing technologies is even more worrisome to the military because the defense industry is becoming more dependent on materials, components, and subassemblies produced by civil industry. Soviet military leaders have expressed concern at least since the early 1980s about the economy's ability to support the development of future state-of-the-art weapon systems.

Gorbachev's economic modernization program offers the prospect of long-term benefits for the defense industrial sector. Areas targeted for priority investment and development — computers, electronics, machine tools, and robots — are keys to boosting economic productivity, manufacturing advanced weaponry, and improving the quality of less sophisticated military sys-

In addition to increased production of new tanks like the T-80, older tanks like the T-55, shown here, continue to be retrofitted with add-on armor and laser rangefinders.

tems. In return for these long-term benefits, the defense industry is being pressured to contribute more to economic modernization. A series of governmental decrees over the last two years has established higher targets for defense-industry production of consumer goods, machinery, and equipment for civilian industry.

Soviet leaders clearly have been dissatisfied with the response, however, as indicated by their unusual public criticism of defense industrial ministers. In March 1988, the civilian ministry responsible for producing machinery and equipment employed in light industry and the food-processing sector was disbanded and the bulk of its 260 plants placed under the control of defense industrial ministries. This move probably was an effort to force the defense industry to become more directly responsible for modernizing these civilian industrial sectors, which play a central role in efforts to improve the lot of consumers.

Gorbachev's January 1989 announcement that weapon production will be cut by 19.5 percent indicates

Soviet leaders may be moving to modify long-standing priorities in resource allocation, and channel more defense industrial resources into modernization of the overall economic base. Although the process of reducing weapon production is likely to extend well into the 1990s, the Soviets probably will publicize actual production cutbacks relatively soon to demonstrate to Western audiences the seriousness of Gorbachev's intentions. For example, in March 1989 Western newsmen were given a tour of an aircraft plant in Moscow, which is said to be scheduled for at least partial shutdown.

The Soviets have not explained how reductions in weapon production will be implemented. They could phase out production of some older systems more rapidly than previously planned, replacing them with modern, more capable weapons on less than a one-for-one basis; stretch out procurement rates; and/or cancel some lower priority force modernization programs. Production cuts are likely to occur in larger proportions in the types of offensive systems mentioned by Gorbachev in his UN speech — T-72 and other tanks, aircraft,

Full-scale production of the MiG-29 Fulcrum, one of the USSR's newest supersonic air-superiority fighters, continues. More than 500 Fulcrums are now operational with Soviet air forces.

artillery, and bridging equipment. Furthermore, the Soviets probably will reduce output of at least some newer models to avoid charges that they are simply deactivating older equipment. At the same time, production of some defensive systems is likely to increase. For example, military leaders have indicated recently that antitank and air defense weapons in motorized rifle and tank divisions will be increased between 50-100 percent as part of the move toward a more defensive force posture.

In his UN speech, Gorbachev said that during 1989 the USSR will "draw up, as an experiment, conversion plans for two or three defense plants." Recent Soviet press articles have claimed a broader plan is under way for converting weapon production to civilian output. Igor Belousov, head of the Council of Ministers' Military-Industrial Commission (VPK), said in March 1989 that the Soviets intend to convert weapon plants by changing their "profile" — i.e., their production mix. Since most Soviet defense plants contain both military and civilian production lines, conversion may

involve reducing activities on individual military lines and transferring resources, such as energy, skilled labor, machinery and equipment, and electronics and other components, to the plant's civilian sections. The Soviets also have suggested they will convert some ongoing plant expansions from military to civil purposes, which could forestall the production of some new models of military materiel until later in the 1990s.

The effects of converting military to civilian production, however, remain to be seen. Belousov and other officials have announced seemingly impressive output goals for defense industry production of technically advanced consumer goods, medical equipment, and machinery for the textile and agro-industrial sectors. In March 1989 Prime Minister Ryzhkov claimed that 40 percent of current defense industrial output is nonmilitary, and that the Soviet goal is to raise this share to 50 percent in 1991 and 60 percent in 1995. Such a shift in civilian-military output shares could have a palpable effect on weapon production. However, the Soviets still have not provided enough information for

Throughout the 1980s, an entirely new generation of Soviet guided-missile cruisers and destroyers, such as this Sovremennyy-class destroyer, has continued to emerge from Soviet shipyards to equip an increasingly capable Soviet fleet.

Western observers to assess fully the impact on weapon output of these planned increases in civilian goods. For example, most of the civilian goods cited by the Soviets constitute such a small share of the defense industry's total production that a large percentage increase in their output would not substantially change the military-civilian production mix. It is also unclear whether the large amount of machinery and equipment produced by the defense industry for its own use in manufacturing weapons is included in the share of output Ryzhkov refers to as nonmilitary. Finally, plans to cut weapon production cannot be evaluated when the Soviets provide no data on past, current, or projected levels of military output.

Like other Soviet economic reforms, plans to convert from military to civilian production face many obstacles. The Soviet press has discussed the problems likely to impede extensive conversion. These include the current reliance of many defense plants on military-specific technologies and materials, the need to retrain workers and technicians, and potential labor discontent over loss of the premium wages paid for defense production. In addition, since priority resource allocation channels do not exist for most civilian manufacturing as they do for weapon production, defense enterprises could be required to adjust to a lower-priority status in obtaining resources. This will be difficult, given their lack of attention to conserving resources in the past. Another obstacle is the inertia and resistance of the defense industrial establishment, whose powerful role in the economic system has been based upon its primary mission of developing and producing military weapons and equipment.

THE MILITARY R&D BASE

Soviet leaders have long recognized the critical role of science and technology in economic growth and military power. Continuing improvements in the technological capabilities and mission performance of Soviet weapon systems are attributable to a research and development (R&D) establishment noted for its substantial and sustained funding growth and the long-range commitment of human and material resources to priority R&D projects. According to Soviet statistics, the USSR spent 33 billion rubles in 1988 on R&D, which was conducted by over four million scientists and engineers working in some 8,000 scientific institutions. The greatest share of R&D funding was devoted to military projects, which utilized the most capable personnel and the best equipment.

Recent Soviet military writings have argued that scientific-technological innovation has become the most dynamic factor affecting the East-West military balance. Although the USSR has succeeded in creating the world's largest R&D base, military leaders have expressed strong concern about the economy's long-term ability to compete in high-technology weapon systems development. The Soviets have continued to field weapon systems competitive with Western armaments. Marshal Sergey Akhromeyev has stated "the quality of both sides' weapons and equipment is comparable and approximately the same." Nevertheless, development lead times for Soviet weapons have lengthened in many cases and costs have grown rapidly. While the Soviets are among the world leaders in some technologies — for example, strategic metals and fabrication materials — they lag behind the West in other critical areas. Of particular concern are the latest Western technological advances in microelectronics, computers, and sophisticated design and manufacturing systems — areas where Soviet R&D and production capabilities are weakest. Soviet leaders are worried that increasingly lethal weapons and enhanced battle management systems that emerge from advanced Western technologies will erode past Soviet military gains.

The Soviets' concern has led to increasingly sharp criticism of military R&D shortcomings. In August 1988, the Soviet military newspaper *Krasnaya Zvezda* printed a highly critical assessment by Minister of Defense Dmitriy Yazov, who charged that the military R&D establishment is hobbled by a rigid bureaucracy that stifles initiative and innovation, promotes mediocrity, and fosters a lack of personal responsibility. According to Yazov, "departmentalism" has led to fragmented research efforts and the inefficient use of resources. He complained that R&D results have been introduced too slowly, and inadequate attention has been given to ensuring the quality and reliability of weaponry. Yazov's criticisms were echoed by General V. M. Shabanov, Deputy Minister of Defense for Armaments, who warned that "the introduction of new developments is generally a weak point in our country and in the armed forces in particular."

Soviet leaders have decided that both military and civilian R&D must be made more productive and efficient. Efforts are under way to reorganize the R&D structure, bring new blood into its leadership, and create closer links between research and application. Furthermore, R&D organizations may be required to operate increasingly on what the Soviets call a "self-financing" basis — i.e., cover their expenses through income and rely less on subsidies from the state budget. While military R&D institutes will continue to receive most of their funding through state orders for weapon development, they are likely to be under stronger pressure in the future to use human and material resources more efficiently, and to demonstrate the practical results of their work.

The Soviet decision to draw more upon military resources to assist economic modernization apparently also applies to R&D. Politburo member Lev Zaykov said in March 1989 that converting from military to civilian production "also touches on the cutting of budget appropriations for a number of scientific research, experimental, and design operations in the defense sphere, and the intellectual potential . . . thus freed will be used to resolve the most urgent national economic tasks." According to VPK Chairman Belousov, some 200 military design bureaus and research institutes and 250 military plants currently are involved in designing and manufacturing new equipment for the food-processing sector.

To bring military R&D priorities more into balance with the needs of the overall economy, the Soviets are likely in the future to engage less often in parallel development of similar weapon systems; be more selective in deciding which weapons to develop; and attempt to reduce redundancy in military research institutes, design bureaus, and test facilities. At the same time, however, they are unlikely to moderate their efforts to keep pace with rapid innovations in Western military technologies, and they will move ahead in those fields in which they are strongest. While funding for military R&D could come under increasing scrutiny, the Soviets are unlikely to make substantial reductions that would undercut their future technological capabilities.

SOVIET MILITARY MANPOWER

Human resources, which are as critical to Soviet national power as industrial and technological resources, are also a subject of increasing concern to the Soviet leadership. The predominantly Slavic European republics have experienced low birth rates and declining longevity while the traditionally Muslim regions — particularly the Central Asian republics — are seeing very high birth rates. The effect of the combination of these two trends has been a constraint in the overall population growth, a declining pool of new entrants into the labor force, and an altering of the USSR's ethnic composition. Ethnic Russians will soon lose their majority status in the population, although they will remain the dominant nationality — comprising 40 percent of the population as late as 2010. Slavic nationalities — Russians as well as Ukrainians and Belorussians — will still constitute a majority through 2050, but Central Asian nationalities will account for more than half the total population growth through 2010, and nearly two-thirds through 2050.

The Soviets responded to these trends by adopting a set of child-bearing incentives in 1981, which have

Gorbachev has targeted areas like computers, robotics, machine tools, and electronics plants, such as this one in Riga, for priority investment and development over the coming years.

helped to reverse declining birth rates in the European USSR. The higher fertility rates of the Central Asian nationalities have begun to stabilize — a trend typical of less-developed regions of the world as they begin to experience urbanization and industrialization — although the birth rate remains nearly three times higher than the rate in the European USSR. Even though a slightly larger overall manpower pool will emerge by 1999, demographic constraints and imbalances will persist.

These demographic trends have sharpened the trade-offs in allocating entrants into the labor force throughout the various military, civilian, and university sectors of society. Because Soviet Muslims prefer to live in their home republics — where religious, cultural, and family ties are strong — population growth does little to relieve labor constraints in the European USSR, where Soviet industry is concentrated. In education, the policy of *glasnost* has encouraged increasing complaints from academics and intellectuals that the tightening of student draft deferments in 1982 to help ease conscript shortages has conflicted with the wider needs of the scientific community, the economy, and Soviet society for university-trained professionals. Since there is a declining proportion of Slavic nationalities, ethnic Muslims and other non-Slavic nationalities comprise an increasing share of military conscripts. In a recent issue of the Soviet newspaper *Argumenty i Fakty*, Soviet Colonel Yuri Deriugin claimed that conscripts from Central Asia and Transcaucasian regions now constitute 37 percent of the total draft intake, compared to 28 percent in 1980.

Thirty-seven percent of the conscripts inducted into the Soviet armed forces in ceremonies such as this are now drafted from the Central Asian and Transcaucasian regions. Lower educational levels, poor technical skills, lack of Russian language training and morale problems among the non-Russian troops will present challenges for the military leadership into the foreseeable future.

The Soviet military press has published increasingly frank discussions of the manpower problems facing the armed forces. For example, educational levels among ethnic Muslims remain uneven, with marked deficiencies in technical skills, particularly among conscripts from rural areas. Muslim conscripts demonstrate a lower ability than Slavic conscripts to use sophisticated weapons and equipment. This lower proficiency is attributed primarily to their poor Russian language skills, which complicate training. The language barrier also complicates command by the predominantly Slavic officer corps, and exacerbates discipline and morale problems in multiethnic military units. For these reasons, the military has assigned Central Asian and other non-Slavic conscripts largely to noncombat, nontechnical units such as construction troops. The declining proportion of Slavic conscripts, however, is leading to an increasing ethnic mix in combat units. Although the Soviets have implemented measures to improve Russian language instruction in Central Asian secondary schools and have attempted to recruit more Muslims into the officer corps, neither strategy has enjoyed much success. This is due to the Muslims' strong ethnic identification and resistance to assimilation into the predominantly Slavic culture. In fact, the Soviet military press reports that the number of draftees with a poor knowledge of Russian is growing.

The December 1988 announcement of a 500,000-man reduction in military manpower will curtail the military's reliance on non-Slavic — particularly Central Asian — minorities. The reductions will buy the Soviet leadership time to reassess the role of non-Russians in the armed forces, and to improve upon methods to encourage Muslim integration into the military. This respite, however, is only temporary. The population's growth and changing ethnic composition will present challenges for Soviet leaders into the foreseeable future.

A 500,000-man reduction in the armed forces could help alleviate a number of other manpower-related problems, in addition to providing savings through reduced demand for weapon procurement and other military goods and services. The cut will provide unskilled labor to the civilian sector of the economy, supporting recent efforts to improve consumer welfare. According to the Soviets, the manpower reductions will also eliminate 100,000 officers, many of whom possess engineering and technical skills required by Soviet industry. In addition, the Soviets announced in March 1989 the reinstatement of university student deferments, a move they said was made possible by the scheduled troop cuts.

In February 1989, Chief of the General Staff Mikhail Moiseyev said the cuts already announced are "politically and strategically" justified, but he and other military leaders are concerned about recent calls by some Soviet intellectuals and activists for more drastic force reductions, a volunteer manning system, or territorial militias. He said the military must be "unambiguous" in its attitude toward such "unrealistic" recommendations. Territorial militias, or a policy of stationing conscripts within their home republics, could be a dangerous option given the increasingly vocal nationalist sentiment in Soviet republics. In addition, the military believes it needs full-time, well-trained personnel to operate modern, complex weapons and equipment. Nevertheless, the military manpower system appears to be under review, and some changes will probably occur, such as the enlargement of the corps of career noncommissioned officers, who currently constitute only a small percentage of the armed forces.

PROSPECTS

The Soviets must continue their program of economic modernization and reform in order to stem the industrial base's deteriorating capacity to support future economic and military requirements. Shorter-term objectives include boosting consumer welfare, bringing the state budget deficit under control, and creating a sense of order in the economy. Soviet leaders apparently intend to reduce defense spending over the next two years to support economic modernization. It is likely that a reduced level of defense spending will extend into the 13th Five-Year Plan, which covers the period 1991–95. Leonid Abalkin, Director of the Academy of Science's Economics Institute and economic adviser to Gorbachev, said in March 1989 that the government will adopt a tight financial policy for the 13th FYP that will require sharp cuts in military spending and in subsidies to other sectors of the economy. Soviet statements, however, far from provide a clear indication of the extent to which military spending and weapon production levels may actually be reduced. Spending is likely to remain at levels sufficient to continue weapon programs that are key to force modernization. Moreover, the recently announced troop and weapon reductions, in conjunction with the ongoing restructuring of Soviet military forces, should produce more up-to-date, streamlined forces that can be modernized at lower procurement rates.

The Soviet military, cognizant of the nature of future combat, acknowledges that larger quantities of outdated equipment do not compensate for high-quality weaponry, and recognizes the economic as well as the military necessity for a trade-off. Defense Minister Yazov, for example, wrote in October 1988 that "emphasizing quantitative features is not only becoming increasingly expensive, but increasingly ineffective, from both a military-political and the actual military point of view."

In the longer term, beyond 1995, Soviet decisions on military resource allocations are likely to depend upon the interaction of several factors: progress in the economic modernization program during the 13th FYP, and the leadership's perceptions of the status of their military force modernization, technological requirements, and Western military capabilities. If there is substantial improvement in productivity by the mid-1990s, the Soviets could proceed with, and possibly accelerate, military modernization without compromising economic modernization. If, as is more likely, the economy is still in a stage of transition, the Soviets will have to decide between two courses: postponing major military modernization by concentrating on projects requiring greater technological development and longer lead times, or accelerating military modernization programs despite the impact this would have on long-term economic and military progress. The leadership's answer to this dilemma will determine the future direction of the Soviet threat.

CHAPTER IV

Nuclear, Strategic Defense, and Space Programs

The Soviets continue to convert older Yankee ballistic missile submarines to the new Yankee Notch-class, seen here, which can threaten Europe or North America with its 3,000-km range sea-launched, nuclear-armed cruise missiles.

DOCTRINE

Despite public avowals that nuclear war is unwinnable and that strategic arms arsenals must be dismantled, the Soviets continue deploying new generations of intercontinental ballistic missiles, submarine-launched ballistic missiles, and manned strategic bombers. These new, far more capable strategic nuclear systems include:

- The highly accurate SS-18 Mod 5 ICBM, the road-mobile SS-25 ICBM, and the rail-mobile and silo-launched SS-24 ICBM;
- The Typhoon-class strategic ballistic missile subma-

rine with SS-N-20 SLBMs, and Delta IV-class SSBN with SS-N-23 SLBMs;
- The Blackjack and Bear H manned strategic bombers armed with 3,000-kilometer-range, air-launched cruise missiles; and
- Converted Yankee-class and other submarine platforms carrying sea-launched strategic land-attack cruise missiles.

Furthermore, Soviet plans for the employment of strategic nuclear weapons appear thus far to have changed little despite their claim to have adopted a defensive doctrine. These plans remain driven by two basic Soviet assessments: first, that the use of strategic nuclear weapons will most likely result from an escalation of battlefield nuclear weapon employment in Europe; and second, that the best way to limit damage in a strategic nuclear war is to initiate the attack.

Under their announced defensive doctrine, the Soviets appear to be continuing to seek a European theater posture relative to NATO that results in NATO being less likely to employ strategic nuclear weapons as provided in its strategic doctrine of flexible response. Thus one of their goals in signing the INF Treaty appears to have been the elimination of some nuclear weapons that, although designated for use in the European theater, could allow a battlefield nuclear exchange to spill over to the Soviet homeland. For the same reason, they also are continuing to seek the elimination of all short-range nuclear weapons in Europe as evidenced by Gorbachev's recent proposal to unilaterally cut short-range nuclear forces (SNF) in exchange for a US agreement to discuss SNF cuts.

By attempting to create conditions where a war between the alliances is restricted to Europe, the Soviets are increasing their emphasis on the deterrent aspect of their strategic offensive and defensive programs. This shift of focus, however, has not brought reductions in their nuclear weapon programs other than as a result of the INF Treaty. Indeed, while the Soviets recognize the deterring aspects of their nuclear forces, the basic tenet of their strategic nuclear doctrine is to have a strategic warfighting capability that can inflict a devastating nuclear strike against an adversary under all circumstances. Moreover, despite their announced defensive doctrine, the Soviets' preferred nuclear employment option, in circumstances in which the likelihood of enemy strategic nuclear weapon employment is considered high, remains a preemptive attack. This attack option involves launching Soviet nuclear weapons once convincing evidence has been received that an adversary is preparing to launch a nuclear attack against the Soviet Union. Although the Soviets argue that preemption is merely self-defense against an imminent attack, it is primarily designed to achieve strategic warfighting objectives and involves the Soviets launching their strategic missiles first.

The Soviets continue to develop and deploy strategic offensive forces based on force requirement decisions made ten to twenty years ago, and the general pace of this modernization has not been affected by the ongoing national security policy debates under Gorbachev. It remains to be seen how these debates will affect the future force structure. Systems being deployed today are increasingly accurate and survivable. Improved survivability is particularly evident in the deployment of the rail-mobile SS-24 and the road-mobile SS-25 ICBMs. The mobile systems enhance both the deterrent and warfighting capabilities of Soviet strategic offensive forces by increasing the likelihood that Soviet strategic nuclear weapons will be available for follow-on attacks after an initial exchange.

The Soviets have made START proposals to reduce the number of strategic nuclear systems available to both the Soviet Union and the United States. These proposals, however, do not in themselves confirm a change in Soviet employment policy, nor do they affect the Soviet capability to achieve its nuclear warfighting objectives.

COMMAND STRUCTURE AND ORGANIZATION

Soviet strategic nuclear forces consist of the land-based ballistic missiles and launchers of the Strategic Rocket Forces (SRF), the navy's ballistic missile and strategic land-attack cruise-missile submarines, and long-range aviation's intercontinental and medium-range bombers carrying air-launched cruise missiles and bombs. Historically, the Soviets have always favored the ballistic missile as a nuclear delivery system, and the bulk of Soviet nuclear weapons are mounted on SRF ballistic missiles. The Soviet SSBN force, however, has grown in the last twenty years, both in numbers of deliverable weapons and in SSBN and weapon capabilities. Soviet strategic aviation has received new systems with improved capabilities in the 1980s, but still remains a comparatively small portion of the Soviet strategic nuclear forces.

The Soviets combine the actions of these forces into an integrated, national-level plan for strategic force employment in wartime. In the event of war, the General Headquarters (or Stavka) of the Soviet Supreme High Command (VGK) would directly control the strategic nuclear forces through the General Staff's Main Operations Directorate. As General Secretary of the Communist Party and Supreme Commander-in-Chief of the Armed Forces, Gorbachev chairs the Defense Council and would head the Soviet Supreme High Command General Headquarters — the highest wartime military body. The order authorizing nuclear weapon employment would be passed from the VGK Stavka to the General Staff for implementation via its command, control, and communications system for the strategic nuclear forces. There are no indications that this organization or these command procedures are undergoing any changes.

The Soviets launched a sixth Delta IV SSBN in 1988 as well as deployed a modified version of the Delta IV's SS-N-23 missile.

Over a 40-year period the Soviets, through their wartime leadership continuity program, have made extensive, sustained investments in the direct protection of their top political leadership and key military command authorities. The program's intent is to ensure the survival and effective command function of these critical leadership elements under the full range of nuclear conflict contingencies, including protracted nuclear war. The Soviet program has resulted in the construction of highly survivable, readily accessible deep-underground command post facilities; the development of redundant communications systems and networks; and the deployment of an array of ground-mobile, trainborne, and airborne command platforms.

INTERCONTINENTAL FORCES

Missions and Operations

The Soviets have created and deployed a nuclear force structure designed to operate in a variety of nuclear exchange environments and still accomplish its mission of destroying a wide spectrum of enemy nuclear forces, military forces, and political and economic targets. They also have created a sophisticated intelligence organization that is adept at combining a wide variety of overt and covert collection and processing means to monitor strategic indicators. Should intelligence predict an imminent nuclear attack, the Soviets would likely try to preempt an enemy strike with a massive strategic nuclear strike of their own. They may see such an employment option as even more critical if a future environment arises in which there are fewer strategic weapons to conduct strategic tasks. In this case, signifi-

cant losses in its strategic forces may preclude Moscow from accomplishing critical warfighting missions.

In the event the Soviets fail to execute their preemptive option, they may have to launch while under attack. To deal with this contingency, they have established a complex system of launch detection satellites, over-the-horizon radars, and USSR-based large phased-array radars that will provide the Soviet high command with up to 30 minutes warning of an incoming attack. These systems are able to determine the general direction of the attack and conduct missile tracking.

Soviet military theorists have traditionally held that once an attack has been launched, a period of protracted nuclear operations would likely follow. To facilitate such operations, the Soviets have taken the following preparatory measures:

- Their nuclear force command and control system has been designed for maximum survivability. It combines hardened command posts and ground and air-mobile command post and communications assets.
- They have constructed extremely hardened silos and deployed increasing numbers of road- and rail-mobile launchers in the Strategic Rocket Forces; dispersed airfields for Long-Range Aviation; and dispersed basing and logistical sites for SSBNs to enhance nuclear force survivability.
- They are planning for their strategic forces to have a reload and refire capability.

Strategic Rocket Forces Development

Even as Gorbachev pushes for strategic arms negotiations, the Soviet Union continues to pursue the complete modernization of its ICBM arsenal. The latest round of modifications will provide the Soviets with a more lethal ICBM attack force. In some areas the Soviets are constructing new facilities, or renovating existing ones, for the purpose of expanding the mobile ICBM force. In other areas they are converting silos to house newer, more effective missiles that will enhance the fixed ICBM force.

The most significant current improvements to the SRF's ICBM force include greater accuracy, greater mobility, and a consolidated force in which seven unique missile systems will be reduced to just three classes of systems. However, in the absence of a START treaty, ICBM warheads are expected to increase as systems with greater reentry vehicle (RV) capacities come on line. The Soviets will likely maintain adequate weapons even under START constraints to cover current and anticipated future target sets. Silo conversion activity to

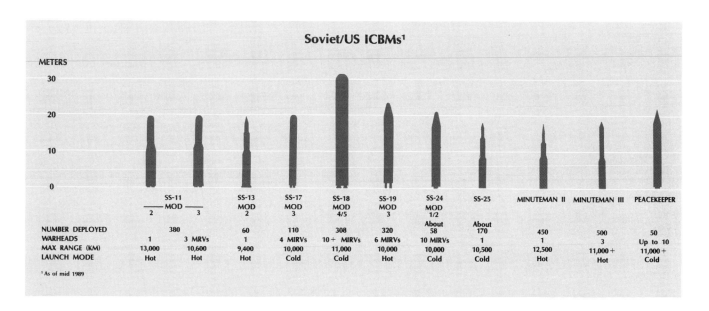

Soviet/US ICBMs¹

	SS-11 MOD 2	SS-11 MOD 3	SS-13 MOD 2	SS-17 MOD 3	SS-18 MOD 4/5	SS-19 MOD 3	SS-24 MOD 1/2	SS-25	MINUTEMAN II	MINUTEMAN III	PEACEKEEPER
NUMBER DEPLOYED	380		60	110	308	320	About 58	About 170	450	500	50
WARHEADS	1	3 MRVs	1	4 MIRVs	10 + MIRVs	6 MIRVs	10 MIRVs	1	1	3	Up to 10
MAX RANGE (KM)	13,000	10,600	9,400	10,000	11,000	10,000	10,000	10,500	12,500	11,000 +	11,000 +
LAUNCH MODE	Hot	Hot	Hot	Cold	Cold	Hot	Cold	Cold	Hot	Hot	Cold

¹ As of mid 1989

replace the current variant of the SS-18 Satan — which is the bulwark of the SRF's hard-target-kill capability — with a newer, more accurate version (the SS-18 Mod 5) is under way. The increase in the Mod 5's warhead yield, along with improved accuracy, would, under a START treaty, help allow the Soviets to maintain their hard-target-kill wartime requirements even with the 50 percent cut in heavy ICBMs START requires.

The deployment of both the road-mobile SS-25 in 1985 and the rail-mobile SS-24 Mod 1 in 1987 has significantly enhanced Soviet ICBM force survivability through these missile systems' dispersal and concealment capabilities. As the Soviets field more of these mobile systems, they are removing older missile systems, such as the SS-11 and the SS-17. Additionally, they are removing the SS-19 Stiletto from the SRF operational inventory and replacing it with a silo-deployed version of the SS-24. Conversion of selected SS-19 silos to SS-24 Mod 2 silos is currently under way, and some converted silos already house operational Mod 2 missiles. The dual-mode basing of the SS-24 provides a force mix of fixed and mobile ICBMs that meets Soviet requirements for survivability, responsiveness, and accuracy. Within several years the mobile SS-24 and SS-25 may comprise nearly 50 percent of the Soviet ICBM force.

This current series of modifications may take several years to complete and may face limitations under a START agreement. Nevertheless, the Soviet ICBM modernization program could be easily adapted to potential limits imposed by a START treaty. The Soviets probably will not allow strategic arms limitations to jeopardize their continued ability to meet targeting, survivability, and force responsiveness goals. The thrust of the program is clear: the Soviets are attempting to deploy an ICBM force that is capable of satisfying their wartime objectives with fewer, significantly more survivable missile systems.

The core of the Soviet Union's growing ICBM arsenal is the SS-18 with the hard-target-kill capability of 10 nuclear warheads on each missile. The silo-launched SS-18 Mod 5 and the fifth-generation road-mobile and rail-mobile ICBMs are shaping an ICBM force that is both more accurate and survivable.

Soviet/US Intercontinental Strike Aircraft

	Tu-95 BEAR	BACKFIRE	BLACKJACK	Tu-16 BADGER	Tu-22 BLINDER	FB-111	B-1B	B-52G/H
UNREFUELED COMBAT RADIUS (KM)	6,400[1]	4,000	7,300	3,100	2,400[1]	1,480	7,500	8,000
MAX SPEED (MACH)	0.8	2.0	2.0	.85	1.4	2.5	1.25	0.9

[1] Radius reassessed to reflect new information.

Strategic Aviation Force Developments

During the past decade, Soviet intercontinental bomber force modernization enhanced what had been the least effective element of the Soviet strategic triad. New aircraft and weapon systems, particularly the Bear H and Blackjack aircraft and the AS-15 long-range air-launched cruise missile (ALCM), represent a major effort to increase the bomber force's weapons delivery capability and improve its survivability to accomplish intercontinental nuclear strike missions.

The primary component of the intercontinental bomber force consists of Bear H AS-15 ALCM carriers. Prior to the Bear's introduction, older Soviet bombers (such as the Bison and older model Bears) had to penetrate Canadian or US airspace to launch their attacks. As recently as 1983, most of the intercontinental bomber force's air-delivered weapons were free-fall bombs. Today, the majority of the current strategic air-delivered weapons inventory comprises AS-15s that have a stand-off range of 3,000 kilometers. While Bear G and remaining older bombers could augment Bear H strike missions, their shorter-range weapons would make them vulnerable to North American air defenses. Midas and Bison tankers provide in-flight refueling support.

The Soviets' newest intercontinental bomber, the Blackjack, entered the operational inventory in 1988. Over 15 have been produced, and the first operational unit has begun forming at an airfield near Moscow. The world's largest and heaviest bomber, the Blackjack, is designed to carry either 12 AS-15s or 24 of the new AS-16 short-range attack missiles. The Blackjack can cruise subsonically over long distances, perform high-altitude supersonic dash, and attack using low-altitude, high-subsonic penetration maneuvers.

While the total number of Long-Range Aviation aircraft has remained relatively constant, the quality of deployed aircraft and the force weapons delivery capability has dramatically increased. The trend of the past decade has clearly been toward modernization and increased strategic strike capability. There is no current evidence to indicate a reversal of this trend.

SSBN/SLBM Developments

The Soviet Navy continues modernizing its strategic missile submarine force, even as it retires older systems. A sixth Delta IV SSBN put to sea in 1989 and a sixth Typhoon-class SSBN launched in early 1989 are

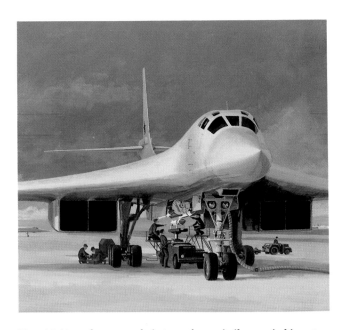

New AS-16 nuclear-armed air-to-surface missiles carried in rotary launchers aboard the Blackjack strategic bomber could be used against theater and intercontinental targets.

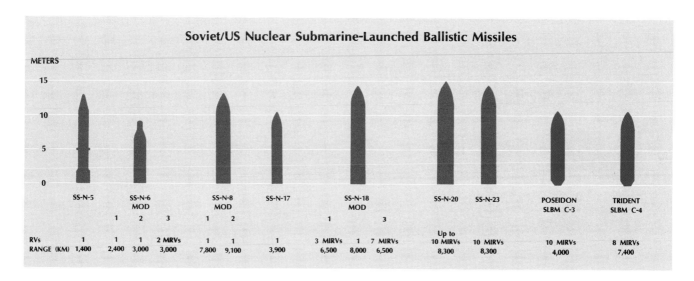

Soviet/US Nuclear Submarine-Launched Ballistic Missiles

expected to join the operational force later in the year. The Soviets also deployed a modified version of the Delta IV's SS-N-23 missile in 1988, and a modified version of the Typhoon's SS-N-20 missile may begin testing soon. Both programs are geared toward improving the accuracy and increasing the warhead yield of these systems in order to develop an SLBM hard-target-kill capability. Furthermore, the increased range of current SS-N-20 and SS-N-23 SLBMs allows Soviet SSBN patrols to remain close to or within USSR home waters, thus enhancing the survivability of their naval strategic assets.

The Soviets also have established an elaborate protection scheme whereby naval, air, and shore assets, in conjunction with the natural Arctic ice zone, protect SSBN bastion areas against US/NATO antisubmarine forces. Utilizing these combined arms assets, the Soviets hope to reduce significantly the vulnerability of their SSBNs.

Cruise Missile Developments

The Soviet Union has two versions of an operational long-range land-attack cruise missile: the SS-N-21 SLCM and the AS-15 ALCM. Both missiles give their respective launching platforms the ability to attack most North American and Eurasian targets. The SS-N-21 can probably be launched from any modern nuclear-powered class submarine. Specific candidates for employment are Yankee Notch-, Akula-, and Victor-class SSNs. The AS-15 is operationally deployed on Bear H and Blackjack intercontinental bombers. A new air-launched long-range cruise missile, the AS-X-19, is under development and when operational in the early 1990s could be deployed on the Bear H aircraft. Test activity for a sea-launched version, the SS-NX-24, is continuing at a slow pace.

Implications

As stated earlier, Soviet attempts to create conditions where a war between the alliances is restricted to Europe emphasize the deterrent aspects of their strategic offensive and defensive programs, but have not brought about reductions in these programs. Moreover, there is as yet no indication the Soviets will abandon their preferred strategic weapon employment policy of preemption and adopt the more defensive policy of retaliation.

A wide variety of issues including, but not limited to, arms control developments, the possible deployment of a US strategic defense system, and the potential for advances in future strategic weapons technology, will influence the Soviet leadership as it shapes the future Soviet strategic nuclear arsenal. Examples include:

■ START: It would be possible for the Soviets to sign a START treaty as currently envisioned and essentially retain the capability to conduct strikes against critical nuclear, other military, and political and economic targets. This capability would result from several factors, including a possible reduction in the number of US hardened targets the Soviets would have to attack; the improved capabilities of new Soviet nuclear systems such as the SS-18 Mod 5 (which potentially reduces the number of warheads that would be assigned to each target); and the improved survivability of new Soviet strategic systems.

■ SDI: Because US deployment of a strategic defense system with even limited effectiveness would seriously complicate Soviet strategic strike planning, such a US decision could lead the Soviets to reassess the effectiveness of their strategic war plans, and possibly modify their arms control proposals. According to Soviet statements, their response would involve both

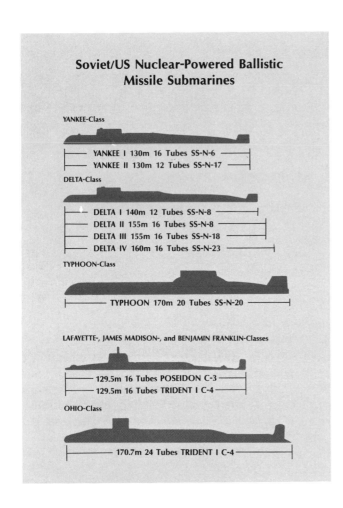

Soviet/US Nuclear-Powered Ballistic Missile Submarines

YANKEE-Class

YANKEE I 130m 16 Tubes SS-N-6
YANKEE II 130m 12 Tubes SS-N-17

DELTA-Class

DELTA I 140m 12 Tubes SS-N-8
DELTA II 155m 16 Tubes SS-N-8
DELTA III 155m 16 Tubes SS-N-18
DELTA IV 160m 16 Tubes SS-N-23

TYPHOON-Class

TYPHOON 170m 20 Tubes SS-N-20

LAFAYETTE-, JAMES MADISON-, and BENJAMIN FRANKLIN-Classes

129.5m 16 Tubes POSEIDON C-3
129.5m 16 Tubes TRIDENT I C-4

OHIO-Class

170.7m 24 Tubes TRIDENT I C-4

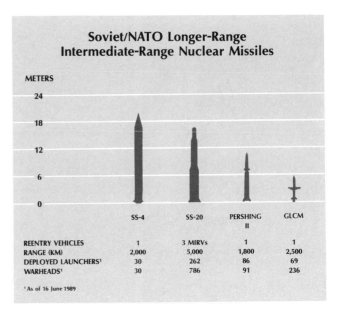

Soviet/NATO Longer-Range Intermediate-Range Nuclear Missiles

	SS-4	SS-20	PERSHING II	GLCM
REENTRY VEHICLES	1	3 MIRVs	1	1
RANGE (KM)	2,000	5,000	1,800	2,500
DEPLOYED LAUNCHERS[1]	30	262	86	69
WARHEADS[1]	30	786	91	236

[1] As of 16 June 1989

quantitative and qualitative measures. For example, at the extreme, the Soviets may deploy greater numbers of nuclear warheads as a means to saturate and overwhelm US defensive systems. Additionally, what the Soviets term "active measures," such as antisatellite weapons, and "passive measures," such as decoys and other penetration aids, could be deployed in an attempt to ensure the survivability of Soviet strategic forces conducting nuclear strikes.

THEATER NUCLEAR FORCES

Missions and Operations

The Soviets' intermediate-range nuclear systems — the road-transportable SS-4 Sandal MRBM and road-mobile SS-20 Saber IRBM — are currently integral components of the Soviet strategic nuclear forces. These systems have the capability to attack all European soft point or area targets.

Force Developments

The SS-20 and the SS-4 are among the missile systems being eliminated under the terms of the INF Treaty. The treaty, which became effective in June 1988, calls for both countries to eliminate over a three-year period all ground-launched nuclear force missiles (including cruise missiles) in the 500-5,500 kilometer range. The treaty also affects two shorter-range ballistic missile systems, the SS-12 and the SS-23; these systems are discussed in the Short-Range Nuclear Forces section of this chapter.

Current Status of the Soviet IRBM Forces Subject to the INF Treaty

	Treaty Entry into Force		Eliminated		Current 16 Jun 89	
	SS-20	SS-4	SS-20	SS-4	SS-20	SS-4
Total Missiles[1]	654	149	192	72	462	77

[1] Includes deployed and nondeployed.

The Soviets began eliminating INF Treaty-related missiles and launchers in July 1988. Prior to the INF drawdown, the SS-20 force comprised 48 bases that housed the regularly deployed force of 405 missiles and launchers. The SS-4 force consisted of 96 prepared launch positions supporting 60 deployed missiles.

Implications

Before negotiating the dismantlement of their SS-20 force, a system they developed in the early 1970s and began deploying in 1977, the Soviets weighed its value against the capabilities of US/NATO intermediate-range systems, and considered what systems were immediately available to compensate each side for its loss. Based on Soviet targeting goals and nuclear strike force missions

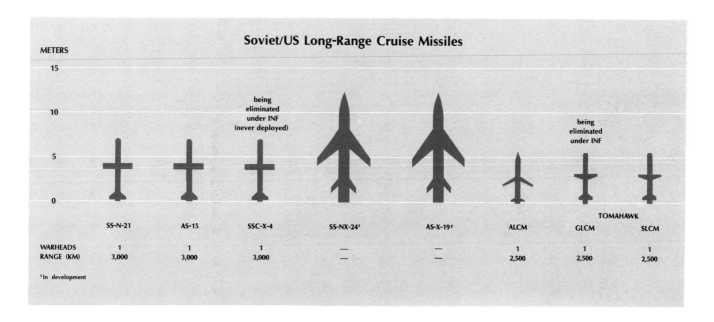

Soviet/US Long-Range Cruise Missiles

METERS		SS-N-21	AS-15	SSC-X-4	SS-NX-24[1]	AS-X-19[1]	ALCM	TOMAHAWK GLCM	SLCM
WARHEADS		1	1	1	—	—	1	1	1
RANGE (KM)		3,000	3,000	3,000	—	—	2,500	2,500	2,500

[1] In development

in Eurasia, it is likely that the Soviets determined they could compensate for the elimination of INF forces by retargeting other strategic and tactical nuclear delivery systems. Many of the SS-20's targets can be covered by ICBMs and SLBMs supplemented by aviation assets. The SS-11 and SS-19 ICBMs, as well as all SLBMs deployed in Soviet-protected bastions, will provide target coverage through the mid-1990s, with SS-24s and SS-25s potentially available as well. Even after INF and START treaty reductions, the Soviets will likely be able to satisfy their critical tactical, theater, and intercontinental targeting requirements as effectively as with their current arsenal due to the ongoing modernization of their strategic forces. The Soviets also recognize that the INF Treaty has caused some dissension within the NATO Alliance.

SHORT-RANGE NUCLEAR FORCES

Missions and Operations

The Soviet military also deploys a wide variety of nuclear delivery systems with a range of less than 1,000 kilometers. These include shorter-range intermediate range nuclear forces (SRINF) missiles, which are covered by the INF Treaty. Specifically, the SS-12 and SS-23 are currently being eliminated. The INF Treaty does not cover short-range nuclear missiles with a range of less than 500 kilometers, dual-capable aircraft, and artillery pieces. Thus, while the INF Treaty eliminates the most threatening Soviet nuclear systems, the Soviets will retain a more than adequate capability to provide tactical nuclear support for their ground forces.

Even though NATO's force modernization is in full

compliance with the INF agreement, General Secretary Gorbachev has characterized such force improvements as undercutting the Treaty. The Soviets are making such statements while they replace SS-23 missiles withdrawn under INF with SS-1 Scud missiles, which are not constrained.

Force Developments

The Soviet military has continued to improve the range and accuracy of its SNF. It has also, in some

The sixth Typhoon-class ballistic missile submarine, with its 20 multiple warhead SS-N-20 missile, will join the Soviets' growing fleet of modern nuclear submarines later this year.

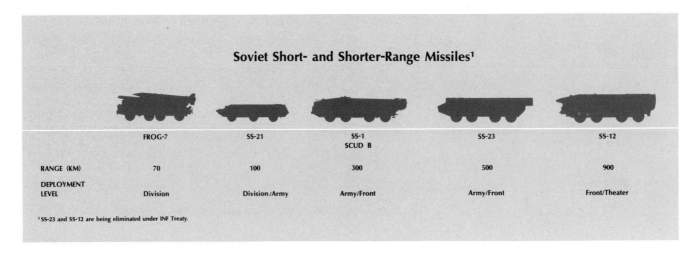

Soviet Short- and Shorter-Range Missiles[1]

	FROG-7	SS-21	SS-1 SCUD B	SS-23	SS-12
RANGE (KM)	70	100	300	500	900
DEPLOYMENT LEVEL	Division	Division/Army	Army/Front	Army/Front	Front/Theater

[1] SS-23 and SS-12 are being eliminated under INF Treaty.

cases, reorganized SNF units to ensure more centralized control and greater flexibility in their employment. The military, for example, has consolidated division level short-range ballistic missile (SRBM) battalions into brigades that are controlled at army level.

The Soviets also have declared plans to convert five missile bases vacated under the INF Treaty to bases supporting non-INF constrained SRBMs, as permitted by the treaty. Construction activities and training of new missile units have since occurred on or near several of these bases, including two in East Germany. Those actions are probably indicative of Soviet plans to compensate for the loss of their SS-12 and SS-23 systems, which should be completely eliminated by December 1989.

Current Status of the Soviet SRBM Forces Subject to the INF Treaty

	Treaty December 1987[1]		Treaty Entry into Force		Eliminated		Current[2] 15 May 89	
	SS-12	SS-23	SS-12	SS-23	SS-12	SS-23	SS-12	SS-23
Total Missiles	726	200	718	239	600	0	118	239

[1] Between the signing of the Treaty and entry-into-force, the Soviets eliminated eight SS-12 missiles, revealed an additional 39 SS-23 missiles, and moved some missiles from a deployed to a nondeployed status.
[2] All missiles have been moved to elimination sites and are considered nondeployed.

Implications

Even with Gorbachev's announced force reductions, the Warsaw Pact will retain a significant numerical advantage over NATO in SRBM launchers (a nearly 16:1 edge) and nuclear-capable artillery (a 4:1 advantage) in the Atlantic-to-the-Urals region. Improvements in the range and accuracy of these systems also have increased the quality of Soviet SNF.

STRATEGIC DEFENSE

Missions and Operations

In the Soviets' view, both active and passive strategic defenses are critical components of a military doctrine dedicated to wartime damage limitation to the Soviet Union. The strong continuing Soviet commitment to strategic defense programs can be measured by the variety of defensive weapon systems fielded or in development, and the scope of other active and passive defense capabilities. The Soviets have fielded a comprehensive air defense system and deployed ABM defenses around Moscow. They also are continuing impressive R&D efforts in traditional and advanced ballistic missile defense (BMD) technologies. The Soviets' extensive program of passive defense measures — including civil defense, mobility, hardening, and redundancy — is intended to limit the effects of enemy nuclear strikes on Soviet territory. Although not all of these programs have been proceeding at a rapid pace, funding support has been steady over the past two decades, indicating a long-term commitment to strategic defense efforts.

Air Defense Forces

The Soviets have been extensively modernizing and upgrading their air defense forces. In addition to integrating new weapon systems into these forces, a renewed emphasis on operational readiness has resulted after recent foreign incursions into Soviet airspace.

Surface-to-Air Missiles

Soviet strategic SAMs (the SA-2, SA-3, SA-5, and SA-10) provide barrier, area, and point air defense of the Soviet homeland. Since 1985 the number of strategic SAM sites and launchers has remained about the same; however, the engagement capability of strategic

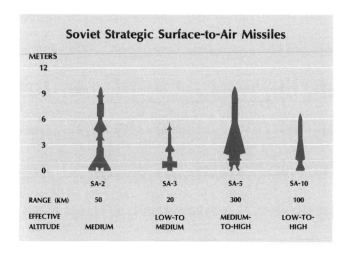

Soviet Strategic Surface-to-Air Missiles

	SA-2	SA-3	SA-5	SA-10
RANGE (KM)	50	20	300	100
EFFECTIVE ALTITUDE	MEDIUM	LOW-TO-MEDIUM	MEDIUM-TO-HIGH	LOW-TO-HIGH

SAMs has significantly increased with the deployment of the SA-10. The SA-10's ability to engage several targets simultaneously and its increased firepower (four missiles per transporter-erector-launcher, or TEL) have enhanced the Soviet Union's air defense capability. It also may have a limited capability to intercept some reentry vehicles (RVs) and cruise missiles. Presently, the SA-10 system comprises approximately 15 percent of all Soviet strategic SAM launchers.

Aircraft

As a result of the Soviet air and air defense reorganization that occurred in the mid-1980s, many interceptor aircraft were resubordinated and returned to the air defense forces. The Soviets deploy their newest and most sophisticated airborne surveillance and interceptor assets with these forces. For example, in the past year, the number of fourth-generation, lookdown/shoot-down-capable aircraft, such as the MiG-31 Foxhound and Su-27 Flanker, has increased by approximately 40 percent. While there are over 400 Foxhound and Flanker aircraft in the air defense force, the total number of fourth-generation aircraft remains small relative to the force of over 2,000 interceptors. By 1994 one-half of the air defense inventory will be made up of fourth-generation aircraft, and by 1999 all will be fourth generation or later. The Soviet air defense forces also are continuing to deploy their Mainstay AWACS to enhance their detection and tracking capabilities. The Soviets probably have at least 10 of these aircraft now operational.

Command, Control, and Communications (C^3)

The successful conduct of air defense operations depends, in part, on the speed and efficiency of C^3 systems as well as the air defense radar's ability to acquire accurate air-surveillance data. Recent developments indicate the Soviets are extensively using computer-assisted decisionmaking equipment, to include air and air defense battle management systems. The air defense surveillance network is assisted by passive detection systems located on the country's periphery that enhance overall early-warning capability.

Radars

Over the past decade, the Soviets have improved the capabilities of their air defense radars. New phased-array radars are better able to track and engage multiple air targets than their predecessors. Some new early-warning radars are capable of determining range, azimuth, and elevation, thus eliminating the need for separate height-finder radars. Some previous low-altitude radar gaps also are being closed, making undetected penetration by low-flying aircraft more difficult. Such improvements became more urgent in the wake of the

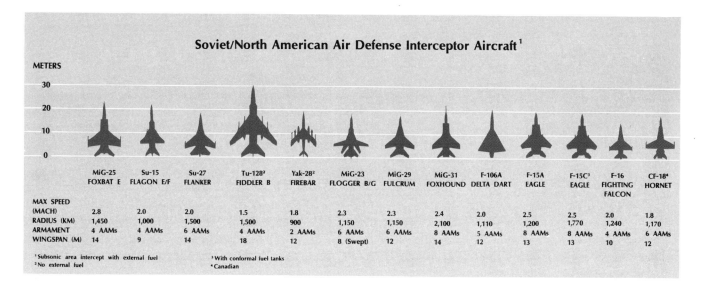

Soviet/North American Air Defense Interceptor Aircraft[1]

	MiG-25 FOXBAT E	Su-15 FLAGON E/F	Su-27 FLANKER	Tu-128[2] FIDDLER B	Yak-28[2] FIREBAR	MiG-23 FLOGGER B/G	MiG-29 FULCRUM	MiG-31 FOXHOUND	F-106A DELTA DART	F-15A EAGLE	F-15C[3] EAGLE	F-16 FIGHTING FALCON	CF-18[4] HORNET
MAX SPEED (MACH)	2.8	2.0	2.0	1.5	1.8	2.3	2.3	2.4	2.0	2.5	2.5	2.0	1.8
RADIUS (KM)	1,450	1,000	1,500	1,500	900	1,150	1,150	2,100	1,110	1,200	1,770	1,240	1,170
ARMAMENT	4 AAMs	4 AAMs	6 AAMs	4 AAMs	2 AAMs	6 AAMs	6 AAMs	8 AAMs	5 AAMs	8 AAMs	8 AAMs	4 AAMs	6 AAMs
WINGSPAN (M)	14	9	14	18	12	8 (Swept)	12	14	12	13	13	10	12

[1] Subsonic area intercept with external fuel
[2] No external fuel
[3] With conformal fuel tanks
[4] Canadian

air defense debacle involving the intruding Cessna that landed in Red Square in 1987.

Antiballistic Missile (ABM) Defense

Since the early 1980s the Soviets have been upgrading the world's only operational ABM system, located around Moscow. The upgraded system probably will be partly operational this year, and will provide the Soviets, for the first time, with a two-layered defense of high-value targets in the Moscow area.

The components of the new Moscow ABM system include two interceptor missiles: a long-range modified Galosh ABM designed to engage ballistic missile RVs outside of the atmosphere; and the Gazelle, a shorter-range, high-acceleration missile designed to engage RVs after they have reentered the earth's atmosphere. The ABM system also includes the new, large, multifunction Pillbox radar at Pushkino near Moscow. The radar provides 360-degree coverage against incoming missiles and is expected to become operational by 1990. This new system will allow the Soviets, for the first time, to engage ICBM and SLBM RVs accompanied by penetration aids, because the endoatmospheric interceptor can engage the RV after most penetration aids are stripped off by the atmosphere. In addition, the new system apparently will comprise the full 100 launchers permitted by the ABM Treaty. The system, however, has major weaknesses. With only 100 interceptor missiles, the system can be saturated, and with only the single Pillbox radar at Pushkino providing support to these missiles, the system is highly vulnerable to suppression.

In the mid-1970s, the Soviets began building a network of large phased-array radars (LPARs). Currently, there are nine LPARs, in various stages of construction. The entire network is expected to become operational by the mid-1990s. When fully operational, this network will provide highly redundant coverage of the main attack corridors into the USSR. Most of this coverage will also be redundant with the coverage of the Hen House ballistic missile detection and tracking radars. In addition, the LPARs can track far more objects than the older Hen House radars while providing improved impact prediction accuracy.

In October 1987 the Soviets declared a one-year moratorium on construction at the Krasnoyarsk LPAR, a facility that, because of its location and orientation, clearly violates the ABM Treaty. In fact, while there was some activity at the radar site last year, there was no apparent construction or electronics installation activity on the radar structure itself. Although the original moratorium was scheduled to end in October

1988, the Soviets announced that it will remain in effect indefinitely. In addition, in his speech before the United Nations, General Secretary Gorbachev announced that the military had turned over the Krasnoyarsk LPAR to the USSR Academy of Sciences for space-related research, and he suggested that an international space organization under UN auspices might eventually operate it. However, because the facility could be turned back to the Soviet military in a short period of time, and function as a ballistic missile detection and tracking radar, the United States continues to maintain that the Krasnoyarsk violation can only be corrected by the dismantlement of the facility.

Since the 1960s, the Soviets have been conducting a substantial research program in advanced technologies for ballistic missile defense. General Secretary Gorbachev acknowledged this effort in November 1987: "The Soviet Union is doing all the United States is doing, and I guess we are engaged in research, basic research, which relates to these aspects which are covered by the SDI of the United States." Although the Soviet programs cover many of the same technologies being explored by the US SDI, they involve a much greater investment of plant space, capital and manpower.

Passive Defense

The Soviet passive defense program is a major element in an integrated system of strategic defenses designed to lessen the effects of a nuclear attack. The principal objectives of the passive defense effort include: ensuring wartime leadership continuity; mobilizing the economy speedily and effectively; protecting the industrial base and essential work force; and developing a credible reconstitution capability. An extensive, redundant set of hardened command post and communications facilities and exurban relocation sites for all key echelons of command within the military and the Party-government apparatus constitutes the foundation of the Soviet passive defense program.

Wartime Leadership Facilities

For decades the Soviet Union has had a comprehensive program under way to ensure leadership survival and continuity of function in the event of nuclear war. This effort has involved the construction of deep underground command posts, secret subway lines, and other facilities beneath Moscow, major Soviet cities, and the sites of key military commands. These deep underground facilities today are, in some cases, hundreds of meters deep and can accommodate thousands of people. Their sole function is to protect the senior Soviet leadership from direct nuclear attack. As nuclear arsenals on both sides have become larger and more potent, these facilities have been expanded and excavated to greater depths.

In addition to deep underground facilities, the Soviets also have constructed near-surface bunkers and exurban relocation sites for military, Party, and government authorities, both in the Moscow area and throughout the Soviet Union. These would accommodate all key command and management staffs down to the local, territorial level in the Party-government hierarchy and the regimental-level in the Strategic Rocket Forces, Air Defense Forces, and Air Forces. The provision of leadership protection facilities for Party and state officials having no responsibilities for the conduct of military operations indicates that a major program goal is support of post-strike societal and economic reconstitution efforts.

The continued funding of improvements to the passive defense program indicates that it does not yet fully meet Soviet requirements. Nonetheless, the extensive preparations the Soviets have made give their leadership the potential to perform effectively in a nuclear war environment. The fact that the Soviets continue to build additional hardened command facilities and upgrade older ones suggests that the leadership continues to believe the program's benefits are well worth the cost.

Radio-Electronic Combat

Soviet planners use the term "radio-electronic combat" (REC) to refer to their integrated program to disrupt enemy military C^3 at all levels. Embodied in the Soviet doctrine for REC is an integrated effort centered on reconnaissance, electronic countermeasures (jamming), physical attack (destruction), and deception operations. Each of these elements contributes to the disruption of effective command and control at a critical decision point in battle. The Soviets vigorously pursue REC measures at strategic, operational, and tactical levels. At the strategic level, the Soviet REC effort may involve simultaneous operations to deceive Western intelligence collection programs and to jam strategic C^3. The Soviets are continuing to enhance their strategic REC mission capability.

Soviet attempts to counter enemy strategic command and control in wartime would involve disrupting the entire range of communication media available for strategic C^3. Using their concept of *Radioblokada* (Radio Blockade), the Soviets would attempt to isolate entire geographic regions and prevent deployed forces from communicating with their higher headquarters.

While the Soviets have recently stopped their routine jamming of foreign radio broadcasts directed at Soviet audiences, high-frequency jamming antennas are still located in all major Soviet urban areas. These civil broadcast antennas remain available for wartime or crisis use as a strategic countermeasures asset. The transmitter power and range capability associated with some of these systems make them suitable for employment against NATO high-frequency communications. The large number of high-power transmitters and long-range directional antennas under the Soviet Ministry of Communications constitutes an additional pool of strategic jamming assets. Used for the worldwide broadcast of such programs as Radio Moscow, these facilities could be employed effectively against US and NATO strategic high-frequency communications.

Implications

According to Soviet views on the nature of war, strategic defense operations are one of the basic forms of military action designed to repulse an enemy aerospace attack and limit its damage. While no single element of a layered defense need necessarily be highly effective, the Soviets seek to achieve defense with an overall significant effect through successive layers.

While the Soviets now insist that their military doctrine is defensive, they have made no specific statements as to how this relates to their strategic defense programs. The scope and nature of their programs indicate the overall capability of Soviet strategic defense continues to increase substantially.

SPACE FORCES

Glasnost has led to a variety of new public reports on the Soviet space program. These reports, however, have been highly selective and continue to downplay the largely military orientation of Soviet space systems and operations. Most information released by the USSR in recent years continues to portray the Soviet space program as nonmilitary, while extolling advances in technology and promoting Soviet efforts to penetrate the market for commercial space services. The Soviets apparently have made no effort to change their military space objectives as they maintain they are doing with some of their other military forces. The Soviets seek sufficient supremacy to provide optimal space-based support for their terrestrial military forces and the capability to deny the use of space to other states.

Missions and Operations

The Soviets currently operate about 50 types of space

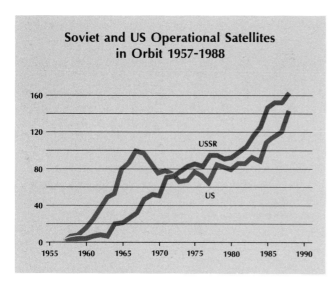

Soviet and US Operational Satellites in Orbit 1957-1988

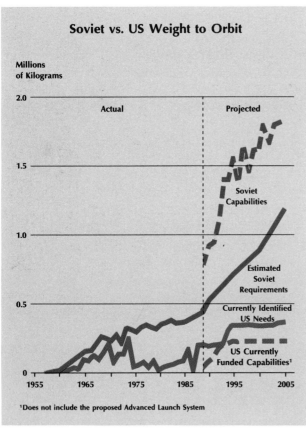

Soviet vs. US Weight to Orbit

Millions of Kilograms

Actual | Projected

Soviet Capabilities

Estimated Soviet Requirements

Currently Identified US Needs

US Currently Funded Capabilities[1]

[1]Does not include the proposed Advanced Launch System

systems, including numerous military satellites with missions such as reconnaissance and surveillance, launch detection and attack warning, support for strategic and tactical targeting, and the destruction of enemy spacecraft. Other satellites appear to have a variety of possible military-related missions, including radar calibration, atmospheric density modelling, and spacecraft technology experimentation. Most of the remaining Soviet satellite systems have dual military-civilian use.

These include all manned and man-related spacecraft as well as communications, navigational, meteorological, earth resources, and radar-carrying oceanographic satellites, and various other experimental or developmental payloads. By far the smallest category of Soviet satellites (about 5 percent) is assessed to be dedicated completely to civilian and/or scientific purposes. These include interplanetary probes and biological research, environmental, and materials processing (now called Foton) satellites.

Military Support from Space

The Soviets continue to maintain and improve their operational satellite networks dedicated to the support of terrestrial military forces, but particular satellites are never discussed in a military-related context. The Soviets are providing more data on some categories of these satellites, often in their launch announcements or occasionally in other press reports. The information reported is usually accurate, but is almost always selective and incomplete, and is designed to portray Soviet space activity as peaceful and nonmilitary in nature. Recently, however, the Soviet leadership has acknowledged that military space programs "enhance the combat efficiency of our armed forces by 1.5-2 times."

The Soviets generally attempt to present an unfavorable view of US military space activity, while emphasizing the peaceful and nonmilitary aspects of their space program. Yet, in fact, the Soviets provide dedicated military support from space. They possess and continue to operate unique space-based targeting systems that are designed to support combat operations. Satellites, such as the Radar Ocean and ELINT Ocean Reconnaissance Satellites (RORSAT and EORSAT), which are used to locate and target US and allied military forces, are clearly dedicated to support warfighting capabilities. The Soviets also have the world's largest and most responsive space launch infrastructure, including extensive booster and spacecraft production pipelines, which is optimized to support military operations. At the same time, their antisatellite capabilities allow the Soviets to deny or inhibit an enemy's use of vulnerable satellite systems. Such capabilities certainly reflect a military-oriented space program.

The Soviets describe their Global Navigation Satellite System (GLONASS), for example, as a space navigation system for Soviet civil aviation planes, merchant vessels, and fishing boats. Obviously, Soviet military aircraft, ships, and other equipment will find considerable utility in such a navigational system. In a similar vein, Soviet announcements of communication, meteorological, and geodetic satellite launches describe their missions solely

The multi-purpose rocket carrier *Energiya* and the reusable spaceship *Buran* are installed on the launching pad of Baikonur spaceport. The November 1988 launch, flight, and return of *Buran* demonstrated the Soviets' ability to conduct an unmanned shuttle mission — an impressive technical achievement. The *Buran* and the *Energiya* will provide the Soviets with an unparalleled ability to orbit and maintain large space structures.

Crew rotations for the *Mir* space station are accomplished via the Soyuz-TM capsule, shown here being launched from Tyuratam.

in terms of providing support to the Soviet Union's national economy and the interests of science and international cooperation. They never acknowledge the fact that the Soviet military directly benefits from these satellites for command and control, weather forecasting, and targeting purposes.

Antisatellite Systems

An important aspect of the Soviet space program is their antisatellite capability. Recognizing the significance of space-based support to terrestrial military missions, the Soviets long ago established a doctrinal objective of denying the use of space to other countries. They began testing a coorbital ASAT interceptor in the 1960s, which probably reached operational status

in 1971 and was last tested in space in 1982. On several occasions Soviet sources have claimed that work on ASAT systems halted with the August 1983 Soviet announcement of a unilateral moratorium on the launching of ASAT weapons. The Soviets maintain the operational readiness of their coorbital ASAT, however, by launching the booster used to orbit ASATs, the SL-11, with other payloads and testing other system components on the ground. They also have three other ASAT-capable systems: ABM missiles, ground-based lasers, and electronic warfare assets.

The Soviets recognize that their present ASAT capabilities are insufficient to deny completely the use of space to an opponent. Though they could physically attack, and possibly destroy, satellites in near-earth orbit,

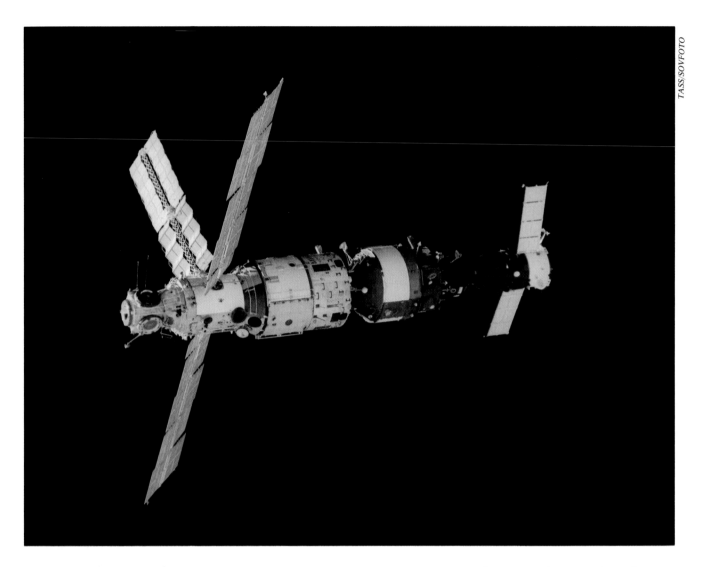

The *Mir* space station, shown here, is an impressive advancement over its predecessor, Salyut-7. In addition to enhanced solar energy and electrical power systems and greater computer capabilities, the *Mir* has six docking ports.

the Soviets are probably limited to using nondestructive methods such as electronic warfare against satellites in high orbits. Since the 1960s, the USSR has been engaged in research to develop directed-energy weapons, some of which will be based in space.

Manned Operations

The Soviets continued their very successful manned space program during 1988, concluding 27 months of continuous manned presence in orbit in April 1989. While the Soviets publicly emphasized the cost-saving implications of this development, a more important factor was the technical problems they encountered with the expansion modules they plan to launch to the *Mir* space station. This hiatus in manned space activity, which reportedly will continue until the fall of

1989, represents a minor setback for the Soviet space station program. It must be emphasized, however, that the Soviets have made great progress in manned-space activity during the past several years.

Space Launch Systems

The Soviets are heavily publicizing their space shuttle orbiter, the *Buran*, and its launch system, *Energiya*. The initial launch, flight, and return of *Buran*, conducted unmanned and entirely under automatic control on 15 November 1988, appeared successful. The demonstrated capability to conduct the mission unmanned, especially during landing, is an impressive technical achievement. When the shuttle system and the associated *Energiya* in the heavy-lift mode are fully operational, the Soviet Union will have a tremendous capacity

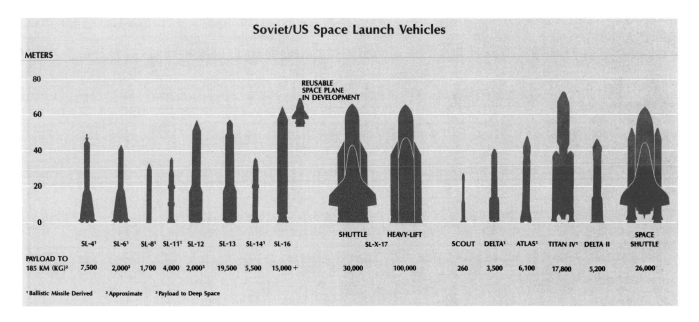

Soviet/US Space Launch Vehicles

METERS																		
	SL-4[1]	SL-6[1]	SL-8[1]	SL-11[1]	SL-12	SL-13	SL-14[1]	SL-16	SHUTTLE	HEAVY-LIFT SL-X-17	SCOUT	DELTA[1]	ATLAS[1]	TITAN IV[1]	DELTA II	SPACE SHUTTLE
PAYLOAD TO 185 KM (KG)[2]	7,500	2,000[3]	1,700	4,000	2,000[3]	19,500	5,500	15,000+	30,000	100,000	260	3,500	6,100	17,800	5,200	26,000

REUSABLE SPACE PLANE IN DEVELOPMENT

[1] Ballistic Missile Derived   [2] Approximate   [3] Payload to Deep Space

to assemble and maintain in orbit large spacecraft and space structures. The Soviets also will have greatly enhanced their ability to return large space station components, spacecraft, and significant amounts of materials to earth using their shuttle orbiter. In addition to space station support, the shuttle probably will serve as an alternate platform from which to conduct military and scientific research and development work.

Implications

The Soviet capability to provide space-based support to its terrestrial military forces continues to improve and expand, as does its capability to place payloads in orbit. The Soviet capability to conduct ASAT and ABM operations continues to be unrivaled, while research and development of even more capable systems is occurring in Soviet facilities. *Glasnost,* however, has yet to address the many significant military aspects of the Soviet space program. Soviet denials that they use cosmonauts for military purposes and possess systems for waging war in space are equivalent to the Soviet contention — prior to Gorbachev's admission in November 1987 — that the USSR was not conducting SDI-like research. Such discrepancies regarding Soviet military space programs and objectives leave their claims about a defensive military doctrine and reasonable sufficiency somewhat suspect.

PROSPECTS FOR CHANGE

The Soviet doctrinal requirement for a strategic posture that deters a strategic nuclear strike against the Soviet Union while, at the same time, providing a

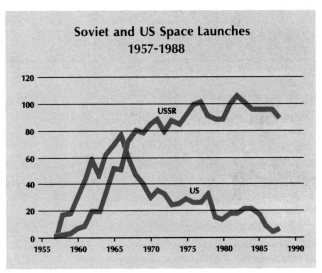

Soviet and US Space Launches 1957-1988

Soviet strategic warfighting capability will likely remain. However, developments within the various strategic programs may not proceed at the same rate as in the past decade. For example, the Soviets will continue to improve the effectiveness of their strategic weapons and deploy large numbers of land-mobile systems, but they appear to be serious about reducing the size of the overall force through mutual agreements with the West. Such reductions are expected to be consistent with reduced targeting requirements brought about by negotiated changes in Western forces. The Soviets have shown a similar willingness to make further reductions in shorter-range theater-nuclear weapons. In contrast, future developments in the Soviet defense and space forces, and in their passive defense programs, will probably show general continuity with past actions.

CHAPTER V

General Purpose Forces

GAMMA/BOUVET

Among the proposals announced by Gorbachev in his UN address was the withdrawal of six tank divisions from East Germany, Czechoslovakia, and Hungary by 1991. Here Soviet officers inspect the rail-car loading of T-64 tanks in April 1989, which form part of the tank division to be withdrawn from Hungary.

INTRODUCTION

In December 1988 the Soviet Union announced unilateral troop and conventional armament cuts over the next two years, including:

- A reduction in Soviet military personnel by 500,000 men.
- A reduction in Soviet armed forces in Eastern Europe and the European portion of the USSR (West of the Urals) totaling 10,000 tanks, 8,500 artillery

systems, and 800 combat aircraft. This will include a reduction of 50,000 men and 5,000 tanks from Eastern Europe, which will be accomplished in part by the withdrawal and disbanding of six tank divisions currently stationed in East Germany, Czechoslovakia, and Hungary.

- Substantial reductions in armed forces in Asian regions of the USSR, and the withdrawal of Soviet troops from Mongolia.

On 25 April 1989 the Soviets officially began their withdrawals with a well-publicized ceremony in Hungary, marking the beginning of the removal of a Soviet tank division from that country. Simultaneously, however, the Soviet Union has been reorganizing and modernizing its general purpose forces and is pushing ahead with research and development on new generations of weapons for those forces. Thus while unilateral reductions announced by the Soviet leadership are taking place, the implications of such reductions in terms of future capabilities of Soviet theater forces require careful assessment.

With the beginning of troop reductions, the Warsaw Pact has initiated a period of potentially far-reaching change in general purpose forces — changes that may well extend to the size, structure, and basic operational concepts of those forces. Traditionally, the Soviets have deployed their general purpose forces, along with those of their Warsaw Pact allies, in theaters of military operations (TVDs) along the Soviet Union's periphery, and have structured them to execute rapid, offensive operations to seize deep theater objectives in a conventional, chemical, or nuclear environment.

Since mid-1987, however, the Soviets have publicly proclaimed the "defensive orientation" of their forces and asserted that their military doctrine is based on "reasonable" or "defense sufficiency." The Soviets have depicted the force reductions now beginning as giving specific content to the defensive character of their military doctrine. This chapter will examine the structure and operations of Soviet general purpose forces in light of this defensive concept and assess the prospects for change.

Since the late 1960s, Soviet theater force structure has focused on establishing a capability to execute a theater-strategic operation — a massive, combined-arms offensive conducted under nuclear or nonnuclear conditions to a depth of 1,500 kilometers or more. This emphasis has resulted in dramatic growth in force size and combat capability. However, significant new challenges, along with some continuing old ones, are forcing Soviet leaders to reassess this structure as they plan for the 1990s. These challenges, discussed in previous chapters, are summarized below.

■ *Resource Limitations:* The Soviet leadership is seri-ously disturbed over the state of the USSR's economy. The most vexing problem is the long-term trend of declining economic growth rates. Announced military spending and production cuts stemming from growing economic difficulties may require Soviet force planners to face an environment of increasingly scarce defense resources. These planners will have to consider difficult new trade-offs between force size, equipment modernization, operations, readiness, and sustainability. In sum, the Soviets face the prospect of having to do more with less.

■ *US/NATO High Technology:* The Soviets are concerned that the United States and its allies are either maintaining or acquiring a distinct advantage in a number of critical technologies. For example, the Soviets view NATO stand-off weapons incorporating advanced technology as challenges to their ability to execute successfully a theater-strategic operation. They believe that they must meet this challenge by fielding expensive advanced-technology systems of their own, by preventing Western high-technology weapons deployment through arms control measures, and by projecting a nonthreatening image in order to erode public support in the West for development and deployment of such advanced weapons.

■ *Doctrinal Changes:* The Soviets publicly stated that their military doctrine is now based on the principle of war prevention and "reasonable sufficiency" and that they are restructuring their forces to reflect a defensive posture. What this actually means and what final form military restructuring will take are as yet uncertain. The Soviets are rethinking many doctrinal issues and attendant requirements for force size, structure, and equipment, as well as military strategies in the individual theaters of military operations. This is being done in the context of strategic force requirements and resource availability. Such rethinking of Soviet approaches to theater warfare will likely be a major factor in future changes.

■ *Qualitative Problems:* The growth of the Soviet ground forces has resulted in a force of uneven capabilities. Major components of Soviet forces, particularly those in the Western TVD opposite the NATO Central Region and selected units in other TVDs, have experienced impressive growth in combat capability. Within the USSR itself, however, there are numerous low-readiness formations with limited effectiveness due to often obsolescent equipment, inadequate cadre-level manning (some as low as 10-20 percent of wartime authorization), and significant training shortfalls. The Soviets plan to use most of these units later in a war as follow-on forces. While these units may be reasonably effective in this capacity against units which have suffered heavy losses, or against a poorly equipped enemy, their early employment against highly trained forces equipped with high-technology weapon systems could present significant risks.

Furthermore, long-standing problems with lower-level leadership and training, and morale and discipline in general, remain today. In the field, Soviet ground units often display mediocre tactical proficiency, and exercises are often stereotyped, set-piece affairs. Soviet Lieutenant General V. N. Khazikov, Deputy Chief of the Ground Forces Combat Training Directorate, recently complained that small unit tactical proficiency was poor, noting that the conduct of stereotyped exercises has made lower-level training worthless, and that restrictions on equipment usage prevent units from learning to utilize it properly. A significant disciplinary problem cited by the Soviets is the persistence of "non-regulation mutual relations," a euphemism for a brutal system of hazing and harassment of new recruits by older soldiers. In addition, concern is often expressed about the skill and professionalism of many officers, particularly the lack of initiative of many junior officers. Although these are largely traditional problems, in an era of declining human and material resources, the Soviets now believe they must correct them in order to forge the competent, modernized military necessary to meet the challenges of the 1990s.

Under the aegis of a program referred to as "military *perestroika*," the Soviets are initiating wide-ranging changes to improve the quality of their military forces. The Soviets expect a more modernized, competent, and professional military to emerge from changes they are implementing, even though its numerical strength may shrink. Army General Mikhail Moiseyev, newly appointed Chief of the Soviet General Staff, has recently observed that the "next two years will be especially crucial and tense for the armed forces and the General Staff." During that time there will be a fundamental restructuring of the armed forces, a restructuring of military training programs, and major organizational and technical changes in connection with announced force reductions. Moiseyev further indicated that they need to evaluate the entire system of combat readiness. He evidently was referring to the effect restructuring will have on peacetime manning levels, mobilization planning, reservist training, and the numbers and types of readiness exercises. He also indicated that the command and control system will be reorganized and "switched

decisively to a new automated technical base." Furthermore, strategy, operational art, and tactics will undergo radical changes. According to Moiseyev, "a new theory of military art is being created."

THEATER WARFIGHTING CONCEPTS

Soviet war planning provides for the use of general purpose forces to attain regional objectives in TVDs in, or adjacent to, the Eurasian landmass. The Soviets assign dedicated ground, air, air defense, and naval forces to the various TVDs to accomplish those regional missions. They also retain a large grouping of general purpose forces directly under control of the Supreme High Command (VGK). These centrally controlled forces include the air armies of the VGK, the airborne, ground, and air forces in certain interior military districts, and a large logistic support structure. The VGK will allocate those forces to theaters during the course of a war to influence operations. In addition, any strategic nuclear forces which may be employed in a TVD will remain under the control of the VGK.

While the Soviets appear to increasingly regard a major East-West conflict as both unlikely and undesirable, they nevertheless have put increased emphasis on the prolonged nature of a hypothetical conventional war in their current theater warfare concepts. The Soviets have asserted that the large military potentials of both the Warsaw Pact and NATO alliances make the possibility of obtaining victory in a short war unlikely, even if nuclear weapons are employed; therefore, prolonged costly operations featuring successive theater campaigns will be necessary to obtain victory. They also state that even if war can be kept at the conventional level, its lethality and destructiveness could approach that of nuclear operations. The Soviets believe that high-technology, deep-strike conventional systems now under development by both sides will be equivalent to low-yield nuclear weapons in their ability to inflict sudden, massive, and decisive losses.

During this decade in the critical Western TVD opposite the NATO Central Region, Soviet war planning has increased significantly its emphasis on defensive operations at the theater-strategic, operational, and tactical levels, which had been neglected for decades. At the theater-strategic level, Soviet planners operate from a conservative perspective that tends to ascribe worst-case capabilities to potential enemy forces. They are concerned that an enemy may be able to seize the initiative and conduct a theater offensive. In such a hypothetical situation, Soviet forces would repulse the enemy attack through a theater-strategic defensive operation involving defensive actions as well as a series of counterstrikes and counteroffensives intended to, at a minimum, restore their borders, destroy enemy forces, and create conditions for a possible transition to a theater offensive. In addition, the Soviet approach to theater warfare has moved away from emphasizing a quick attack by forward-based forces. The focus now is on large-scale reinforcement of the forward area in Eastern Europe through rapid mobilization and deployment of additional forces from the western USSR to ensure successful, sustained operations. This change in focus heightens Soviet concern over deep-strike systems that could dilute their reinforcement capability. Therefore, in war they will assign high-priority to locating and destroying these systems.

At the operational and tactical levels, the Soviets foresee a fluid battlefield in which highly mobile forces on both sides will strive to seize the initiative. Complementary offensive and defensive operations and maneuvers will be required at different times and places on the battlefield. A greater emphasis on defensive operations is the Soviet military planners' response to what they see as the conditions of current and future theater warfare. This does not represent any abandonment of capabilities for offensive operations, but rather reflects the view that they will have to defend against enemy attacks as well as stage offensive operations of their own.

The Soviets have pointed to the defensive themes and operations in their exercise and training programs as evidence that their doctrine is defensive. However, training for offensive operations also continues, even within defensive scenarios. The Soviets themselves indicate that the ability to conduct counterattacks and counteroffensives is an important element of their theater strategy conducted according to their defensive doctrine. The Soviets' dual-training program is a significant but inadequate indication of change. By itself, and in absence of major force structure changes, it does not constitute convincing proof that the Soviets have switched to a defensive strategy. Without changes, such as substantial reductions to correct the imbalances in ground and short-range nuclear missile forces or the withdrawal of much of their forward-deployed logistic stockpile, there will be insufficient evidence that the Soviets have abandoned the capability or intention to initiate an attack on NATO.

The unilateral troop reductions and force reorganization announced by Gorbachev and the non-Soviet Warsaw Pact (NSWP) countries will, when and if completed, provide some of the force structure and deployment changes indicative of a more defensively oriented strategy. They will constitute a reduction of Soviet military capability, particularly their unreinforced attack capability, against the NATO Central Region. However, the announcements also are designed to support one of the Soviet Union's most important long-standing foreign policy objectives: the eventual dissolution of NATO and the removal of US influence and military power from the European continent. Thus Moscow hopes its force cuts will:

- Generate public pressure in the West — especially in West Germany — for a similar force reduction pledge by either the NATO Alliance or individual members in the near future;
- Enhance its bargaining position in the conventional arms talks;
- Erode public support for NATO's development and deployment of high-technology, deep-strike weapons and derail the planned modernization of NATO's short-range nuclear forces;
- Improve opportunities for access to Western technology and capital.

These cuts, when completed, will diminish the capabilities of the Soviet armed forces to conduct a short-warning attack and prolong the preparation time required for Warsaw Pact ground forces to conduct offensive operations against NATO. However, in an extended build-up situation, the Soviets will have sufficient time to conduct the force mobilization, preparations, and forward deployment to a reinforced posture from which they can launch a sustained offensive. The large stockpile of supplies already in place in the forward area will be available for reinforcing forces from the USSR.

In addition, Gorbachev has announced unilateral short-range nuclear forces (SNF) reductions. These cuts, however, would result in a reduction of only about 5 percent of the Soviets' total SNF warhead inventory and do not match the cuts made by NATO since the 1970s. The ratio of Soviet warheads to US warheads in Europe would still be 12 to 1. Thus, SNF reductions the Soviets have announced so far would only begin to address existing US-Soviet SNF asymmetries and would make only a small dent in Soviet short-range nuclear capability.

Gorbachev also has announced large-scale conventional force reductions on the Sino-Soviet border and in Soviet forces in Mongolia. These reductions went a long way toward answering Beijing's demands that the Soviets reduce their troops along the Sino-Soviet border, and contributed to the normalization of relations between the two countries at the May 1989 Sino-Soviet summit — the first in three decades.

Warsaw Pact Announced Force Reductions

During his United Nations speech on 7 December 1988, Gorbachev announced major unilateral Soviet force reductions. He and other Warsaw Pact political and military leaders have subsequently provided additional details on these unilateral reductions, with five of the Soviet Union's six Warsaw Pact allies announcing their own packages of force cuts. These Pact announcements are summarized below:

- *Personnel:* A total of 500,000 personnel, including 100,000 officers, are to be cut from the Soviet armed forces. Of these, 190,000 are to be removed from the European part of the USSR; 50,000 from Soviet forces in Eastern Europe; 200,000 from the Asian part of the USSR; and 60,000 from the southern USSR.

- *Force Structure:* Elements to be withdrawn from Eastern Europe include six tank divisions, and air assault and assault river-crossing units. Four of the divisions will come from Soviet forces in Eastern Germany, and one each from Hungary and Czechoslovakia. The Pact will disband these divisions, and reorganize and reduce the tank forces of those remaining in Eastern Europe, establishing them as "clearly defensive" forces. Tanks will be cut by 40 percent in motorized rifle divisions and by 20 percent in tank divisions. In addition, about three quarters of the Soviet forces in Mongolia are to be withdrawn to the USSR, and the Soviet air force there is to be "liquidated." At the Beijing summit meeting, Gorbachev promised the reduction of 12 divisions and 11 aviation regiments in the Far East. Soviet Minister of Defense Yazov also stated that in the eastern and southern parts of the USSR, some motorized rifle divisions will be converted to machine gun and artillery units structured primarily for static defensive operations. He also stated that the restructuring of

the armed forces would result in cutting the number of combined-arms divisions by almost half.

Soviet Union

- *Tanks:* Ten thousand tanks will be removed from the European USSR and Eastern Europe. Of these, 5,300 are to come from Soviet forces in Eastern Europe. Gorbachev pledged that the tanks will be destroyed, converted to tractors for civilian use, or used as training vehicles.

- *Aircraft:* Eight hundred aircraft will be removed from the European part of the USSR and Eastern Europe. Senior Soviet air force officers have promised that these aircraft will, in some cases, be superior to corresponding Western aircraft. The aircraft will be destroyed or dismantled for spare parts.

- *Artillery:* Eight thousand five hundred artillery systems will be removed from the European USSR and Eastern Europe.

- *Short-Range Nuclear Systems:* The Soviets have promised that the nuclear systems associated with the six tank divisions being withdrawn will also be removed. These will include 24 missiles — most likely FROG or SS-21 systems, as well as their nuclear-capable artillery. In addition, in May 1989, Gorbachev announced that the Soviets will unilaterally withdraw 500 "tactical nuclear weapons" from Europe including 284 missile warheads, 166 bombs, and 50 artillery shells.

Eastern Europe

- *East Germany:* East Germany announced its intention to reduce its forces by 10,000 troops, six tank regiments, and an air force wing. Altogether, reductions will amount to 10,000 personnel, 600 tanks, and 50 combat aircraft.

- *Poland:* Poland announced the deactivation of four divisions which will be maintained as inactive, unmanned mobilization base sets of equipment. Two other divisions will be reduced to cadre manning with 10-15 percent of wartime-authorized personnel. Between 10 and 20 armored and artillery regiments will be deactivated, and remaining divisions will be restructured. Additionally, the air forces and air defense forces commands will be consolidated, resulting in an unspecified reduction in aviation regiments. Cuts will amount to 40,000 troops, 850 tanks, 900 guns and mortars, 700 other armored vehicles, and 80 aircraft.

- *Czechoslovakia:* Prague will reduce manpower in combat units by 12,000, but will increase its construction troops by 20,000. In addition, 850 tanks, 165 armored vehicles, and 51 aircraft will be eliminated. Three divisions will be deactivated and maintained as mobilization bases, and an unspecified number of tank regiments and air force regiments will be eliminated.

- *Hungary:* One tank brigade, one fighter squadron of nine aircraft, 251 tanks, 30 armored vehicles, 430 artillery, six tactical missiles, and 9,300 personnel will be eliminated.

- *Bulgaria:* Sofia announced cuts amounting to 10,000 troops, 200 tanks, 200 artillery systems, 20 aircraft, and five ships.

In summary, the Soviet/Warsaw Pact countries have pledged themselves to reductions totalling 581,300 personnel, 12,751 tanks, and 1,010 aircraft by 1991. While key ambiguities concerning the status of remaining forces and the disposition of reduced equipment remain, these announced, unilateral reductions will represent a step in the direction of reducing Warsaw Pact imbalances in conventional forces.

The structure, numbers, and capabilities of Soviet theater forces are described below. Since force reductions are only now beginning and the final status and disposition of Soviet forces after reductions remain uncertain, the description will, of necessity, focus on force status as of early 1989, just before reductions began.

THEATER COMMAND STRUCTURE AND LOGISTICS

Command Structure

Soviet war planners have long been concerned with the possibility of a multitheater war in which Soviet forces would confront enemy coalitions in TVDs at opposite ends of the Soviet Union. Consequently, Soviet forces designated for operations in Europe, the Far East, and Southwest Asia are designed to operate without major reinforcement from other theaters. Beginning in the late 1970s, with the formation of high commands for controlling the ground, tactical air, air defense, and general purpose naval forces in each of the theaters on the Soviet periphery, the Soviets have developed the ability to conduct simultaneous, independent campaigns in several widely separated regions. The regional high commands would act as extensions of the Headquarters, Supreme High Command, centralizing control over the theater operations. Their formation as permanent peacetime command authorities enhances the Soviet military command, control, and communication (C^3) system's potential to cope with the demands of a multitheater war.

Fronts would comprise the bulk of the forces that each high command would control in wartime. Fronts are large formations with organic air forces that are roughly equivalent to NATO army groups. They would be formed from forces currently located in border military districts in the Soviet Union and from both Soviet and non-Soviet Warsaw Pact forces in Eastern Europe. Once activated, fronts would relocate, leaving the military district structure intact to perform internal territorial administration, military support, and recovery management functions.

To direct complex theater-strategic operations effectively, the Soviets and their allies have established a comprehensive, redundant network of bunkered command posts (CPs) and supporting communications facilities. The current C^3 infrastructure for theater warfare began to take shape almost 20 years ago, when the first theater-level command facilities were constructed along the Soviet Union's periphery. Having under-

gone steady expansion (which still continues), the fixed command post system now includes a variety of hardened facilities for the regional high command staffs and their principal subordinates. Theater-wide fixed communications networks incorporating a variety of redundant communication means link the bunkered command posts with General Staff facilities and those in adjacent theaters. These networks are being upgraded through the construction of additional communication sites, especially in the key Western and Southwestern TVDs. To enhance network survivability, all major command posts are equipped with buried antennas and separate, bunkered radio transmitter facilities.

Despite their comprehensive C^3 hardening program, the Soviets expect the fixed components of their theater C^3 system to suffer extensive damage in wartime, particularly if nuclear weapons are employed. As a result, they have deployed an array of field-mobile and airborne command posts and communication units for theater forces. At higher levels of command, field-mobile CPs would be used primarily to supplement the system of large bunkers from which staffs would direct operations, and to replace damaged or destroyed CPs. At lower levels, command functions would be exercised from field-mobile CPs once force mobilization was completed. These CPs would relocate regularly with the forces themselves. Small airborne battle staffs add an additional layer of redundancy at each echelon, although they are inherently less capable than the larger ground-based CPs.

The theater command system also employs a complex and redundant communications system that includes mobile satellite, tropospheric scatter, high-frequency radio, line-of-sight radio relay, and cable systems. The KGB also operates separate, parallel communications at key echelons of command within Soviet theater forces.

The Soviets expect enhancements in C^3 coupled with weapons modernization to be a key element of their future force development. They believe, for example, that deep-strike missile and artillery systems teamed together with advanced surveillance and target-acquisition systems and an automated command and control system will provide them the capability to accomplish military objectives with significantly decreased numbers of forces and expenditure of munitions. Against possibly less dense and more mobile Western forces in a post-conventional arms control treaty environment, short Pact response requirements will necessitate almost instantaneous C^3 support. Additionally, if a strenuous wartime situation demands the commitment into Europe of Soviet forces from TVDs not opposite NATO, then effective C^3 will be essential for managing the rapid redeployment and formation of combat groupings of troops.

Logistics

Soviet planners have devoted significant attention to developing a logistics force structure and management system capable of sustaining simultaneous strategic offensives by coalition armed forces in multiple theaters of military operations. This has involved establishing echeloned reserves of critical supply items and equipment throughout the Warsaw Pact, and introducing increasingly capable logistics transport means, mobile repair shops, pipeline-laying vehicles, materiel-handling equipment, and other specialized rear service items. The Soviets also have restructured their logistic support units. These units, which are tasked to provide ammunition, fuel, repair parts, food, clothing, and other materiel to theater forces, were modified to improve mobility and control. The Soviets also upgraded their transport base with high-capacity motor vehicles. To enhance the management of their logistic assets, they combined supply resources and transport assets under a single commander responsible to the Deputy Commander for Rear Services. Finally, they created powerful theater-level rear-service control and planning headquarters within the high commands of forces.

During a war, supplies from strategic stockpiles in the Soviet Union will be sent forward to supplement the large prepositioned stocks in each theater. Hardware, including tanks, armored personnel carriers, field artillery, and air defense systems, are also stockpiled throughout the Soviet Union. These supplies and materiel will be transported over a road and rail network that, at least in the Western TVD, is highly developed and affords a

Modern Soviet ground forces' assault river-crossing equipment has long been of concern to NATO planners, as it facilitates high-speed offensive operations.

number of alternate routes often necessary in wartime. In the past decade, the amount of prestocked military supplies has increased substantially. The ammunition stockpile which the Pact has augmented over the past decade comprises over three million tons in the Western TVD alone and is still growing, although the rate of growth has slackened over the past few years. This probably has more to do with the Soviets attaining their stockpile objectives than with any decision by Gorbachev. These levels will likely remain, since Gorbachev's announced troop reductions did not address cuts in Soviet operational-strategic logistical stocks.

GROUND FORCES

Although Gorbachev has announced dramatic reductions in Soviet ground forces, Soviet offensive capabilities have been qualitatively enhanced during his first four years in office through continued ground forces modernization. This has included the introduction of late-model tanks, self-propelled artillery, multiple rocket launchers, and infantry fighting vehicles. The emphasis on mobility continued with self-propelled artillery and heavy mortars replacing older but still capable towed systems. The air defense forces received equal attention with deployment of a new self-propelled gun (probably the 30mm 2S6) replacing the ZSU-23-4, and with the SA-16 replacing or supplementing the SA-7 and SA-14 systems. At the army level, SA-11 and SA-X-12B surface-to-air missile (SAM) systems began to replace SA-4 systems, while improved versions of the divisional SA-6 and SA-8 systems were fielded. The SA-X-12B Giant variant has some capability against certain types of ballistic missiles.

Prior to the beginning of announced reductions, Soviet ground forces comprised 214 active divisions, three additional inactive wartime mobilization bases, and numerous independent regiments and brigades. These divisions have been structured to conduct high-speed, deep-striking offensive operations.

In peacetime Soviet divisions vary greatly according to readiness, equipment, and manning. In general the Soviets maintain about 40 percent of their divisions at what they consider a ready status. These are manned at more than 50 percent of wartime authorization, are assigned late models of equipment, and train up to division level. The Soviets consider the rest as not-ready divisions. These consist of cadre divisions that are manned at less than 50 percent of wartime authorization, are often assigned older equipment, rarely train above the company or battalion level, and are dependent on extensive mobilization and preparation before they are committed to combat. Unmanned, inac-

Vast ammunition storage depots in Eastern Europe, such as the one shown here, contain millions of tons of arms and ammunition to sustain Soviet ground force operations in the forward area.

tive, mobilization-base divisions consisting of equipment configured in unit sets are also in the not-ready category of divisions.

As part of their announced unilateral reductions, the Soviets have promised to restructure their divisions to make them "clearly defensive." They have indicated that the number of tanks in tank divisions in the forward area will be cut more than 20 percent and in motorized rifle divisions 40 percent. In addition, they will increase the numbers of antitank, antiaircraft, and engineer obstacle creation systems in divisions. It is debatable, however, whether these changes will make Soviet divisions "clearly defensive." They will remain formidable, combined-arms maneuver formations well-suited to conducting the complementary offensive and defensive operations the Soviets believe will be required on the fluid battlefield of the future.

It is expected that the manpower reductions an-

nounced by Gorbachev may result in downgrading the readiness of a number of divisions in the USSR. Some may be deactivated and held as mobilization-base units. The formation of Unified Army Corps (UACs) — offensively oriented forces structured primarily to operate as front operational maneuver groups (OMGs)

Soviet Divisions: Equipment and Personnel Holdings

	Tank Division	Motorized Rifle Division
Tanks	330	220[1]
APC/IFV	225	439
Artillery	165	215
Personnel (fully mobilized)	11,100	13,500

[1] MRDs assigned to Groups of Forces (GOF) traditionally have 270 tanks assigned.

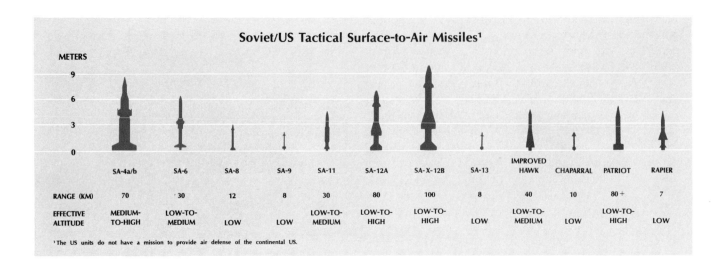

Soviet/US Tactical Surface-to-Air Missiles[1]

	SA-4a/b	SA-6	SA-8	SA-9	SA-11	SA-12A	SA-X-12B	SA-13	IMPROVED HAWK	CHAPARRAL	PATRIOT	RAPIER
RANGE (KM)	70	30	12	8	30	80	100	8	40	10	80 +	7
EFFECTIVE ALTITUDE	MEDIUM-TO-HIGH	LOW-TO-MEDIUM	LOW	LOW	LOW-TO-MEDIUM	LOW-TO-HIGH	LOW-TO-HIGH	LOW	LOW-TO-MEDIUM	LOW	LOW-TO-HIGH	LOW

[1] The US units do not have a mission to provide air defense of the continental US.

— appears to have ended. The Soviets had established two such corps structures, one each in the Western and Far Eastern TVDs in the early 1980s. While roughly equal in equipment and personnel to a combined tank and motorized rifle division, the UACs were equipped with the latest weapons, including some not found at division level. Interest in OMGs continues, but reduced employment of this organizational structure may indicate an increasingly defensive orientation. On the other hand, the Soviets may have concluded that they were not viable or effective military units.

Equipment

Prior to Gorbachev's announced reductions, the ground forces of the USSR deployed over 53,000 main battle tanks; 61,000 APC/IFVs; 49,000 artillery pieces, mortars, and multiple rocket launchers (MRLs) with a caliber 100mm or greater; 4,900 SAM launchers (excluding handheld systems); 12,000 antiaircraft artillery (AAA) pieces; 1,460 surface-to-surface missile (SSMs) launchers; 4,300 helicopters; and nearly two million personnel. Thus, the announced force reduction will amount to 19 percent of the tanks, 17 percent of the artillery, and 1.6 percent of the SSMs now possessed by the Soviet ground forces.

Newer main battle tanks — the T-64A/B, T-72 variants, and T-80 — continue to enter the force. The Soviets have more than 20,000 of these newer tanks, and their number constitutes about 40 percent of the Soviet tank inventory. Many of the newer models have reactive armor packages, wrap-around armor and side skirts, as well as bolt-on armor on upper surfaces to protect turret tops and engine compartments. The Pact has upgraded its older tank fleet to extend its service life. Weapon, automotive, and fire control improvements, when added to increased armor protection, will extend the useful life of these older models into the next century.

Artillery modernization and expansion remain a high priority throughout the Warsaw Pact, with emphasis on achieving a high volume of fire and improving range and mobility. Soviet artillery units are receiving a new, heavy multiple rocket launcher, the M1983 MRL. In addition, some Soviet divisions in the forward area are

Soviet/US Main Battle Tanks

	T-54/55	T-62	T-64 A/B	T-72 M1	T-80	M-60A1/3	M-1/M-1A1 ABRAMS
WEIGHT (MT)	36	37	35	41	42	51	55
SPEED (KM/HR)[1]	40	40	50	50	55	50	65
MAIN ARMAMENT	100-mm	115-mm	125-mm	125-mm	125-mm	105-mm	105-mm/120-mm
MUZZLE VELOCITY (MPS)	1,500	1,600	1,750	1,750	1,750	1,500	1,500/1,660

[1] Revised to reflect new information.

increasing their numbers of 100mm MT-12 antitank guns by about 40 percent. Soviet artillery modernization continues with new towed and self-propelled 152mm gun/howitzers, self-propelled 203mm 2S7 guns, 240mm 2S4 mortars, and 120mm SP 2S9 howitzers. The Soviets also have made great strides in improved conventional munitions, fuel-air explosives, enhanced blast technology, and sub-projectile warheads. All new systems also can fire chemical warfare rounds, and weapons 152mm and above are nuclear capable. Newer 122mm howitzers may have a nuclear capability as well.

Not covered by the reductions mandated by the INF Treaty are short-range ballistic missiles and rockets with ranges of less than 500 kilometers. The Soviets continue building these systems. The inaccurate FROG artillery, with a range of about 70 kilometers, is being replaced by SS-21 systems, with vastly improved reliability, accuracy, and range. Older Scud systems are assigned to front and army surface-to-surface missile brigades and also are being assigned to units that gave up the SS-23 under the INF Treaty.

Effects of Troop Reductions

Moscow's unilateral troop reductions now under way represent a significant and substantial cut in Warsaw Pact military capability. However, the USSR and Warsaw Pact will retain significant advantages against NATO. The numerical superiority in short-range ballistic missiles, in particular, will provide a major advantage if war escalates to the nuclear level. The reductions announced for the forward area amount to 20 percent of the maneuver divisions, 8 percent of the manpower, and about 50 percent of the tanks assigned to Soviet forces in Eastern Europe. Twenty-four Soviet divisions in the forward area will remain, however, with over 5,000 tanks and an extensive logistics and command and control structure. The cuts announced for the European part of the USSR and Eastern Europe amount to more

Soviet offensive capabilities have been qualitatively enhanced during Gorbachev's four years in office through continued modernization of ground forces with systems like the T-80 main battle tank. The Soviets have more than 20,000 of these newer tanks in their current inventory.

than 10 percent of the personnel, over a quarter of the tanks, and more than 7 percent of the Soviet combat aircraft in the Atlantic-to-the-Urals zone.

CHEMICAL AND BIOLOGICAL WARFARE

The USSR has the most extensive chemical warfare (CW) capability in the world. The Soviets can deliver chemical agents with almost all of their conventional weapon systems, from mortars to long-range tactical missiles to high performance aircraft. In 1987, the Soviets admitted for the first time that they maintain a chemical weapons stockpile. They acknowledged an aggregation of 50,000 agent tons, which is by far the largest in the world. It is believed, however, that this Soviet figure greatly understates the USSR's total offensive chemical weapons stockpile. The Soviets have

	2S1	2S3	2S5	2A36	2S7	2S4	M109A2/A3	M110A2	M198
TOWED/ SELF-PROPELLED	Self-Propelled	Self-Propelled	Self-Propelled	Towed	Self-Propelled	Self-Propelled	Self-Propelled	Self-Propelled	Towed
CALIBER/TYPE	122-mm Howitzer	152-mm Howitzer	152-mm Gun	152-mm Gun	203-mm Gun	240-mm Mortar	155-mm Howitzer	203-mm Howitzer	155-mm Howitzer
MAXIMUM RANGE¹ (M)	15,000	18,000	28,500	28,500	35,000	9,700	18,100	21,300	18,100
NUCLEAR-CAPABLE	No	Yes	Yes	Yes	Yes	Yes	Yes	Yes	Yes

¹ Ranges can be extended by the use of rocket-assisted projectiles.

Soviet/US Selected Artillery

admitted these weapons include persistent and non-persistent nerve agents, blister agents, and thickened versions of both blister and nerve agents. The Soviet chemical industry could rapidly produce other agents, as well as larger amounts of the acknowledged agents. The variety and diversity of agents and weapons available to the Soviets allow them to select weapon systems that can effectively attack and neutralize virtually any target at any range.

Soviet abilities to initiate chemical warfare are enhanced by their extensive ability to protect themselves in a contaminated environment using specially trained and equipped units. The Soviets have over 60,000 dedicated personnel who specialize in support operations in contaminated areas and over 30,000 special vehicles for CBW operations. The readiness of these troops has been enhanced through reorganization to better support offensive operations, and has been further improved by continuous emphasis on training for operations in contaminated areas. The extent of this capability is far greater than that required by the limited CW capability of any potential opponent of the Soviet Union.

Research, development, and testing of new chemical weapon systems has continued with funding and emphasis from the highest levels of the Soviet government. The Soviets have evaluated thousands of toxic compounds for use as chemical warfare agents and have also conducted parallel research on new methods of dissemination and weapon configurations. This research program is directed at the defeat of NATO's protective measures.

The Soviets have attempted to deflect world attention from their enormous chemical warfare establishment by emphasizing in public statements the construction of their demilitarization pilot facility at Chapayevsk. A Soviet destruction facility would have been necessary to destroy leaking and obsolete munitions in any case, regardless of the provisions in any chemical treaty. Many munitions declared as part of the current stockpile by the Soviets at Shikany in 1987 were clearly obsolete and ready for destruction.

The Soviets continue to improve their ability to use biological agents. New biological technologies, including genetic engineering, are being harnessed to improve the toxicity, stability, and military potential of the Soviet biological warfare (BW) stocks.

The Soviets continue to deny that they have an offensive BW program, but there has been evidence not only to support the existence of research and development but also weaponized agents. The Sverdlovsk biological agent accident of 1979 that resulted in the release of anthrax from a bacteriological warfare institute provided such evidence and a strong indication that the Soviets have violated the Biological Weapons Convention of 1972.

CONVENTIONAL AIR FORCES

Three major elements comprise the Soviet Air Force (SAF) — the Air Armies of the Supreme High Command (VGK), Air Forces of the Military Districts and Groups of Forces (AF MD/GOF), and Military Transport Aviation (VTA). The Soviets are improving these conventional air elements by introducing late-generation aircraft and weapons to support offensive operations. While the replacements have generally been on a less than one-for-one basis with limited net growth to the force, quality has improved significantly. Shortfalls in range, weapon loads, and avionics are steadily being overcome with late-generation aircraft. The Soviets also are improving and consolidating their command and control of the air forces, especially at the theater level.

Air Armies of the VGK

The Soviets have medium bombers assigned to the Air Armies of the VGK located in both the eastern and western USSR. They are continuing to modernize their intermediate-range bomber forces at a steady pace, as they upgraded an additional Badger regiment to Backfire systems in 1988. Sustained Backfire production of about 30 per year indicates that all Badger strike aircraft left in the force will eventually be replaced.

The remaining Badger and Blinder force consists of 220 weapon carriers and 210 specialized reconnaissance and electronic countermeasures (ECM) aircraft. While Badger strike aircraft are being phased out, the Soviets have retained and enhanced their reconnaissance and ECM capabilities by modifying existing Badger and Blinder variants. Retention of these variants emphasizes the importance attached to these assets' projected wartime role to support strike operations. At present, there is no Backfire variant configured for reconnaissance or ECM missions.

The continuing modernization of the medium-bomber-equipped air armies underscores their importance to the success of Soviet wartime theater operations. In particular, the substantially greater combat radius and weapon-carrying capacity of the Backfire provide capabilities critically needed in wartime. Backfire can strike effectively theater targets that are beyond the range of air army Fencers and the fighter-bombers of the air forces of the military districts and groups of

Soviet/US Tactical Aircraft

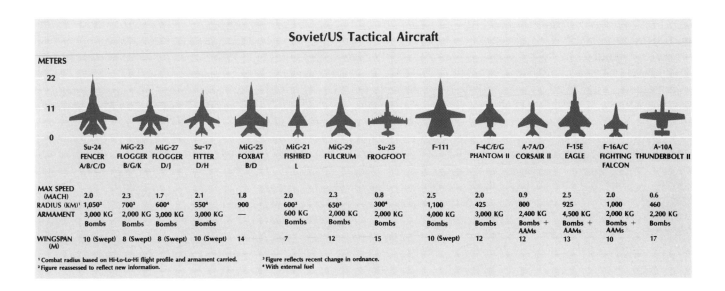

	Su-24 FENCER A/B/C/D	MiG-23 FLOGGER B/G/K	MiG-27 FLOGGER D/J	Su-17 FITTER D/H	MiG-25 FOXBAT B/D	MiG-21 FISHBED L	MiG-29 FULCRUM	Su-25 FROGFOOT	F-111	F-4C/E/G PHANTOM II	A-7A/D CORSAIR II	F-15E EAGLE	F-16A/C FIGHTING FALCON	A-10A THUNDERBOLT II
MAX SPEED (MACH)	2.0	2.3	1.7	2.1	1.8	2.0	2.3	0.8	2.5	2.0	0.9	2.5	2.0	0.6
RADIUS (KM)[1]	1,050[2]	700[3]	600[4]	550[4]	900	600[3]	650[3]	300[4]	1,100	425	800	925	1,000	460
ARMAMENT	3,000 KG Bombs	2,000 KG Bombs	3,000 KG Bombs	3,000 KG Bombs	—	600 KG Bombs	2,000 KG Bombs	2,000 KG Bombs	4,000 KG Bombs	3,000 KG Bombs	2,400 KG Bombs + AAMs	4,500 KG Bombs + AAMs	2,000 KG Bombs + AAMs	2,200 KG Bombs
WINGSPAN (M)	10 (Swept)	8 (Swept)	8 (Swept)	10 (Swept)	14	7	12	15	10 (Swept)	12	12	13	10	17

[1] Combat radius based on Hi-Lo-Lo-Hi flight profile and armament carried.
[2] Figure reassessed to reflect new information.
[3] Figure reflects recent change in ordnance.
[4] With external fuel

forces. Badger and Blinder ECM assets also provide capabilities indispensable to the success of Soviet air operations.

The strike component of other air armies consists almost exclusively of Su-24 Fencer light bombers. They are receiving an air-refuelable Fencer variant that has the capability to conduct attacks to a greater depth into enemy territory with increased payloads and loiter time. Currently, the Soviets have over 500 Fencers deployed. In addition, they have 270 fighters including the MiG-21 Fishbed, MiG-23 Flogger, and Su-27 Flanker, and 120 reconnaissance/ECM aircraft, including some elements resubordinated from frontal aviation. The fighters' primary mission is to escort Fencer strike aircraft. The fighter components of both air armies are in the process of converting over to the Flanker for strike support because of its longer range and advanced avionics.

Besides the two Fencer air armies, Fencer organizations are forming in two other TVDs. The formation of these two organizations would give the Soviets a dedicated Fencer strike force in four of the five continental TVDs. Consolidating all of the Soviet Union-based Fencers into VGK-subordinate air armies enhances both responsiveness and the ability to meet theater requirements.

Frontal Aviation

When Soviet forces assume wartime organizations, the AF MD/GOF will be assigned to various wartime fronts to support ground operations and achieve frontal objectives. Due to continued growth in Army Aviation, combat helicopter units will provide an increasing proportion of the direct air support to ground forces. Helicopters will be supplemented by Frontal Aviation's Su-25 Frogfoot units.

The strike components of two of the Soviet air armies consist almost exclusively of Su-24 Fencer light bombers. The formation of two new Fencer organizations will give the Soviets a dedicated Fencer strike force in four of its five continental TVDs.

The supersonic Su-27 Flanker is a fighter-interceptor that entered series production in the mid-1980s. With look-down/shoot-down radar and advanced air-to-air missiles, it can operate against low-flying aircraft and cruise missiles.

A dedicated ground support fighter, the Su-25/Frogfoot is armed with rockets, antitank missiles, and cannon for its close air support mission.

The world's largest transport aircraft, the An-225, with a payload of 250 metric tons, is one of five transport models with military applications being produced today in the USSR.

The majority of AF MD/GOF strike assets consists of Su-17 Fitter and MiG-27 Flogger fighter-bombers. These aircraft will be tasked to support the majority of the tactical defense suppression and interdiction missions. To complement the fighter-bombers, Fencers assigned to the AF MD/GOFs will provide deep interdiction capability. The MiG-25 Foxbat F will provide dedicated stand-off defense suppression with the AS-11 missile. Finally, the Frogfoot, which is being fielded in both the Soviet and NSWP inventories, will provide close air support and conduct battlefield air interdiction-type missions.

Older tactical fighters assigned to the AF MD/GOF, consisting of the aging Fishbed and Flogger, are being replaced by the MiG-29 Fulcrum. Over 500 Fulcrums are now deployed with the Soviet Air Force, and several NSWP countries have started to introduce the aircraft into their active inventories. Reconnaissance and ECM assets include the Fishbed, Foxbat, Fitter, Fencer, and Yak-28 Brewer.

Military Transport Aviation

Over the past decade, the Soviets have continued to modernize their Military Transport Aviation (Voyenno Transportnaya Aviatsiya or VTA) with the addition of the Il-76 Candid and An-124 Condor. This has significantly increased VTA's payload and range capabilities. The long-range Il-76 Candid is now the VTA's primary workhorse, comprising 70 percent of its inventory. The An-124 Condor is becoming increasingly

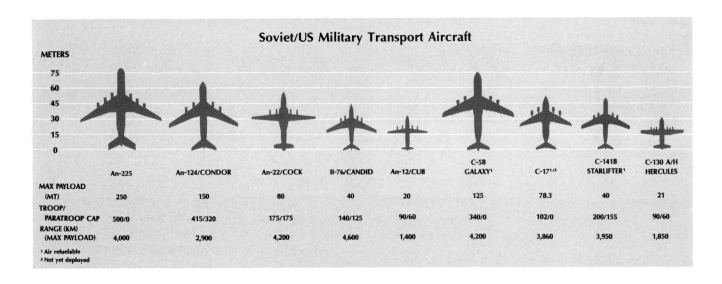

Soviet/US Military Transport Aircraft

METERS	An-225	An-124/CONDOR	An-22/COCK	Il-76/CANDID	An-12/CUB	C-5B GALAXY[1]	C-17[1/2]	C-141B STARLIFTER[1]	C-130 A/H HERCULES
MAX PAYLOAD (MT)	250	150	80	40	20	125	78.3	40	21
TROOP/ PARATROOP CAP	500/0	415/320	175/175	140/125	90/60	340/0	102/0	200/155	90/60
RANGE (KM) (MAX PAYLOAD)	4,000	2,900	4,200	4,600	1,400	4,200	3,860	3,950	1,850

[1] Air refuelable
[2] Not yet deployed

active in VTA heavy-lift operations. Very similar to the US C-5 transport, the Condor has twice the lift capacity of the aging An-22 Cock. The An-22 remains active in the VTA inventory but most likely will be replaced by the Condor. The An-22 and An-124 together represent approximately 25 percent of VTA's lift capacity and can transport wide and bulky — or "outsized" — cargo. The An-22 can lift 80 metric tons, and the An-124 has lifted a record-breaking 170 metric tons.

The Condor enjoyed a brief reign as the world's largest transport aircraft. In November 1988 the Soviets unveiled the An-225 *Mechta*, or "Dream," the largest and heaviest airplane ever made. Based largely on Condor technology, the An-225 has six engines, can carry a maximum payload of 250 metric tons almost 4,000 kilometers, and also can carry large items mounted on top of the fuselage. Although it is capable of carrying tanks and other outsized military and civil cargo, its primary mission will be to transport Soviet space shuttle components, replacing the aging modified Bison now used. It is expected that the Soviets will produce only a limited number of An-225s and that their roles will be highly specialized.

Army Aviation

The army aviation forces of the Soviet Union and most of its Warsaw Pact allies consist primarily of combat support helicopters with battlefield applications in defensive as well as offensive warfare. The Pact's standard attack helicopter, the Mi-24 Hind, can employ a variety of guns, rockets, antitank-guided missiles and bombs, and constitutes a significant mobile firepower reserve to support counterattacks or contain enemy penetrations. The Mi-8 Hip E and Mi-17 Hip H assault helicopters also would be useful in landing forces behind enemy lines or rapidly reinforcing positions and sectors under attack. These combat helicopters are backed up by a range of transport (Hip C, Mi-6 Hook and Mi-26 Halo), electronic warfare (Hip H/J/K), and command/control (Hook B, Hip D/G) helicopters performing important rear-area tasks.

Two new combat helicopters expected to enter service in the near future will enhance Army Aviation's offensive and defensive capabilities. The Mi-28 Havoc will supplement and eventually replace the Hind in its battlefield fire-support missions. The Hokum is assessed as fulfilling a new helicopter mission, battlefield air defense, against opposing antitank helicopters and lower performance fixed-wing ground attack aircraft. The Hokum, like other army aviation elements, can be used in a variety of roles, including countering enemy attacks, preparing for and executing counteroffensives, and sup-

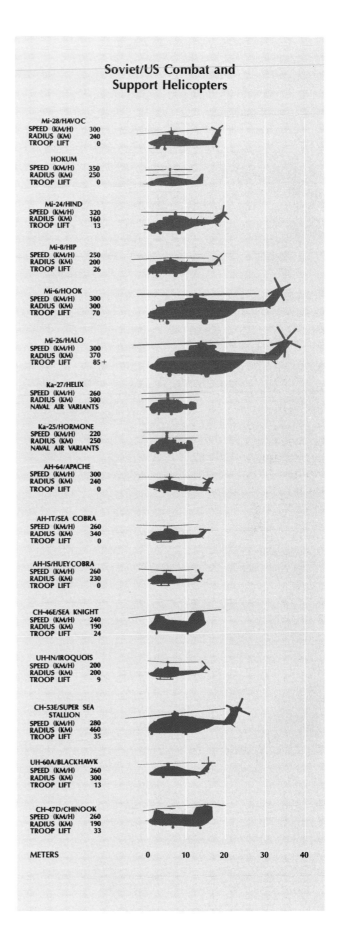

Soviet/US Combat and Support Helicopters

Mi-28/HAVOC
SPEED (KM/H) 300
RADIUS (KM) 240
TROOP LIFT 0

HOKUM
SPEED (KM/H) 350
RADIUS (KM) 250
TROOP LIFT 0

Mi-24/HIND
SPEED (KM/H) 320
RADIUS (KM) 160
TROOP LIFT 13

Mi-8/HIP
SPEED (KM/H) 250
RADIUS (KM) 200
TROOP LIFT 26

Mi-6/HOOK
SPEED (KM/H) 300
RADIUS (KM) 300
TROOP LIFT 70

Mi-26/HALO
SPEED (KM/H) 300
RADIUS (KM) 370
TROOP LIFT 85+

Ka-27/HELIX
SPEED (KM/H) 260
RADIUS (KM) 300
NAVAL AIR VARIANTS

Ka-25/HORMONE
SPEED (KM/H) 220
RADIUS (KM) 250
NAVAL AIR VARIANTS

AH-64/APACHE
SPEED (KM/H) 300
RADIUS (KM) 240
TROOP LIFT 0

AH-IT/SEA COBRA
SPEED (KM/H) 260
RADIUS (KM) 340
TROOP LIFT 0

AH-IS/HUEY COBRA
SPEED (KM/H) 260
RADIUS (KM) 230
TROOP LIFT 0

CH-46E/SEA KNIGHT
SPEED (KM/H) 240
RADIUS (KM) 190
TROOP LIFT 24

UH-IN/IROQUOIS
SPEED (KM/H) 200
RADIUS (KM) 200
TROOP LIFT 9

CH-53E/SUPER SEA STALLION
SPEED (KM/H) 280
RADIUS (KM) 460
TROOP LIFT 35

UH-60A/BLACKHAWK
SPEED (KM/H) 260
RADIUS (KM) 300
TROOP LIFT 13

CH-47D/CHINOOK
SPEED (KM/H) 260
RADIUS (KM) 190
TROOP LIFT 33

METERS   0   10   20   30   40

The Mi-28 Havoc, armed with antitank guided missiles, unguided rockets, and a single-barrel gun mounted beneath its forward fuselage, is the USSR's newest attack helicopter.

The Hokum, now in flight test, will have an air-to-air combat role but could be used in a number of roles including combined-arms offensives and counteroffensives.

porting combined-arms offensives into an opponent's territory.

Prospects for Change

If carried out, General Secretary Gorbachev's recent pledge to cut 800 aircraft from Soviet air forces west-of-the-Urals and to "liquidate" the Soviet air forces deployed in Mongolia constitutes a potentially significant cut in combat capability. However, the magnitude of the change and the combat capability of the air force after reduction will depend on what aircraft are reduced and what is done with them. If only excess or older aircraft are eliminated, the effect will be minimal. On the other hand, if large numbers of deep-strike aircraft such as Fencers and Backfires are actually removed from the inventory, destroyed, or placed in nonflyable storage (and not just rebased), the Soviet ability to conduct offensive operations will be reduced significantly. Recent statements by senior Soviet officers indicate that some modern aircraft will be eliminated, and that a large proportion of these will be ground-attack aircraft. However, the West has yet to see major changes in the structure or operational deployment of the Soviet air forces or significant changes in procurement trends.

There have been no indications of reductions in the prestocked air logistics assets such as aviation fuel, ammunition, and spare parts. In fact, during the past decade aviation fuel stocks have been substantially increased and runways lengthened at the Western Group of Forces airfields. Ammunition stocks have also increased, but to a lesser extent. These logistics improvements should enhance the Soviets' Forward Area air sustainability capabilities while operating with a reduced number of aircraft.

There have been changes under the military *perestroika* program, however, that may enhance significantly Soviet operational capabilities. These changes are now being reflected in Soviet air forces training. They are particularly obvious in the air-to-air environment where Soviet fighter pilots have started conducting dogfight maneuvers with reduced reliance on strict control and scripted tactics. Current air-to-ground training also reflects increased realism, including the use of lower ingress/egress altitudes; multidirectional axes of attack on targets; and an emphasis on large-scale, integrated air operations training involving fighter protection, and reconnaissance, ECM, and attack formations. Furthermore, as a result of operations in Afghanistan, most tactical combat aircraft are being equipped with active ECM suites and routinely practice anti-SAM maneuvers while ingressing or egressing from the target area.

NAVAL FORCES

In the decades following World War II, Soviet maritime forces have evolved from what was essentially a coastal defense force into an ocean-going fleet capable of executing a broad range of missions. The evolution of the Soviet Navy into a more technologically sophisticated and capable force has continued since Gorbachev assumed leadership of the Soviet Union in March 1985. There also have been discernible changes in Soviet naval operational patterns. Nearly all of these changes represent the continuation of long-term trends which antedate the Gorbachev rise to power.

Current Soviet naval forces have developed over an extended period of time and have evolved in the context of uniquely Soviet historical experiences, geopolitical realities, and perceptions of need. Compared to the US Navy, the Soviet Navy has had a substantially different set of general purpose force missions competing for resources. There have been few overseas Soviet allies, no global sea lines of communication to protect, and at least until the mid-1960s, there was no need for naval forces to routinely operate beyond Soviet coastal areas.

Geography and climate also have had significant influence on the development of the Soviet Navy. With the exception of Arctic coast ports and the port of Petropavlovsk in the Soviet Far East, maritime forces must conduct transits to the open ocean via non-Soviet controlled straits and constricted waters. Consequently, during times of increased political tensions or conflict, Soviet access to open oceans could be imperiled. Some Soviet ports located in the northern latitudes, moreover, are inaccessible for much of the year due to severe ice conditions. Current Soviet naval organization and force composition have been developed partially in response to these factors, and are divided into mission-oriented entities. These two entities are the ballistic missile submarine force, and the general purpose forces assigned to the four widely separated, largely autonomous fleets — the Northern, Baltic, Black Sea, and Pacific Ocean. Subordinate fleet air forces, naval infantry elements, and an associated logistics infrastructure ashore also are components of the general purpose force structure.

Naval Missions

The Soviet Navy, armed with many weapon systems both conventional and nuclear capable, is an important element of the Soviet armed forces. One of the Navy's highest wartime mission priorities is ensuring the availability of its ballistic missile submarines (SSBNs) for strategic strikes against intercontinental and theater targets. This requires protection of the SSBNs from attack conducted by Western antisubmarine warfare (ASW) forces. The later-generation Delta- and Typhoon-class SSBNs are armed with longer-range and more accurate submarine-launched ballistic missiles (SLBMs) equipped with a greater number of missiles/reentry vehicles that can reach North America from Soviet ports and coastal waters. This offers the Soviets the option of deploying such platforms in sea areas close to the Soviet homeland where general purpose ships, submarines, and aircraft can provide greater protection. Moscow fully expects Western ASW forces to target the Soviet SSBN force vigorously early in a major conflict. Consequently, Soviet ASW and antisurface (ASUW)-capable platforms are considered vital to SSBN defense during conventional or nuclear conflict.

The Soviet Navy also is responsible for neutralizing enemy naval forces that may threaten the Soviet Union, its allies, or its SSBN force. It relies on a mix of aircraft, surface combatants, and submarine platforms to accomplish this mission. The Soviets view enemy carrier battle groups, amphibious forces, and sea-launched cruise missile (SLCM)-carrying surface ships as the primary surface threats, while their primary ASW focus is on Western SSBNs, SLCM-equipped SSNs, and ASW-oriented SSNs.

The support of Soviet or Warsaw Pact ground forces also remains an important mission. It entails protecting the ground forces' flanks from attack by enemy naval

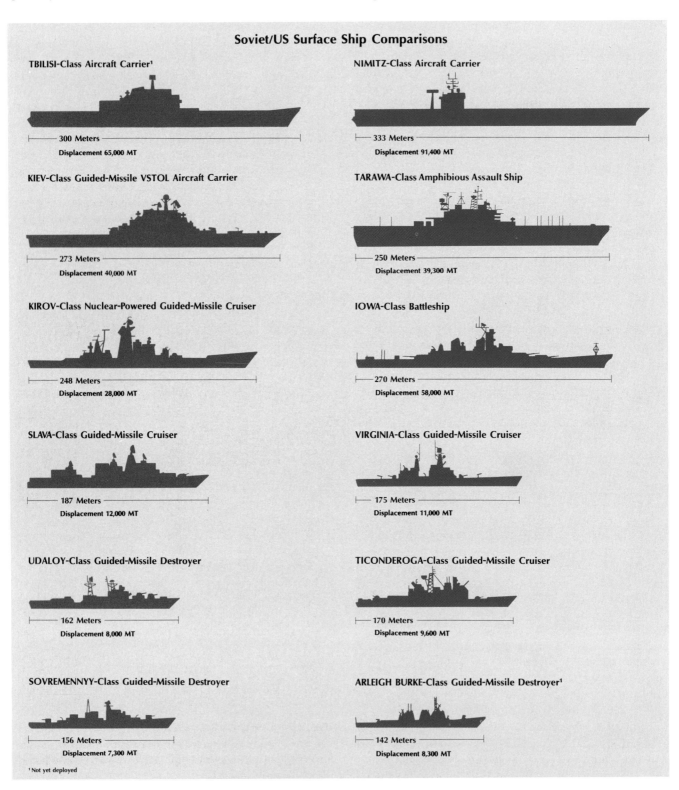

Soviet/US Surface Ship Comparisons

TBILISI-Class Aircraft Carrier[1]
300 Meters
Displacement 65,000 MT

NIMITZ-Class Aircraft Carrier
333 Meters
Displacement 91,400 MT

KIEV-Class Guided-Missile VSTOL Aircraft Carrier
273 Meters
Displacement 40,000 MT

TARAWA-Class Amphibious Assault Ship
250 Meters
Displacement 39,300 MT

KIROV-Class Nuclear-Powered Guided-Missile Cruiser
248 Meters
Displacement 28,000 MT

IOWA-Class Battleship
270 Meters
Displacement 58,000 MT

SLAVA-Class Guided-Missile Cruiser
187 Meters
Displacement 12,000 MT

VIRGINIA-Class Guided-Missile Cruiser
175 Meters
Displacement 11,000 MT

UDALOY-Class Guided-Missile Destroyer
162 Meters
Displacement 8,000 MT

TICONDEROGA-Class Guided-Missile Cruiser
170 Meters
Displacement 9,600 MT

SOVREMENNYY-Class Guided-Missile Destroyer
156 Meters
Displacement 7,300 MT

ARLEIGH BURKE-Class Guided-Missile Destroyer[1]
142 Meters
Displacement 8,300 MT

[1] Not yet deployed

and amphibious forces and providing naval gunfire, amphibious, and logistics support to land operations.

The interdiction of Western sea lines of communication (SLOCs) has been a long-standing mission of the Soviet Navy. In the early phase of a NATO-Warsaw Pact conventional war, however, we expect the Soviets to assign a lower priority to disrupting the flow of reinforcements and supplies to Europe. They will probably be engaged in higher-priority tasks, such as protecting SSBNs and destroying enemy sea-based strike forces. If such a war evolved into an extended conflict, and the US reinforcement and resupply effort became a decisive factor, additional Soviet naval forces could increase the interdiction of NATO's strategic shipping. The Soviets, primarily motivated by the lessons learned from the German World War II U-boat effort in the Atlantic, and by inherent military resource constraints, would probably concentrate attacks at the SLOC termini. A total Soviet SLOC interdiction effort would probably include attacks on NATO ports of embarkation and debarkation, mining of close-in transit routes and harbor approaches, as well as attacks against merchant shipping in coastal and open areas.

A major peacetime mission of the Soviet Navy is to support Soviet political-military interests through naval presence operations. Today Soviet naval forces are deployed around the globe but at reduced levels as compared to the early 1980s. In 1988, for example, Soviet Navy ships — including auxiliaries and research ships — conducted port visits to over 40 countries. This naval presence is designed to assert Soviet rights in international waters, protect Soviet merchant and fishing fleet interests, show support for Soviet client states, and counterbalance Western naval presence.

The Soviet Navy has served as a highly visible instrument of the Soviet Union's foreign policy. For example, the Soviet Indian Ocean Squadron (SOVINDRON) has been highly responsive to regional political and military developments. In recent years, SOVINDRON surface combatants have escorted Soviet bloc merchant ships operating in the troubled Persian Gulf region.

Soviet Naval Developments in the Gorbachev Era

Over the past four years the Soviet Navy has experienced leadership and structural change. For example, within six months of Gorbachev's rise to power, the Soviet Navy's leadership changed hands from Fleet Admiral of the Soviet Union Gorshkov — Commander in Chief of the Soviet Navy since 1956 — to Fleet Admiral Chernavin. Due to Gorshkov's advanced age and long service, a change in Soviet naval leadership

was probably inevitable. In addition, the Soviet Navy has responded not only to political pressures resulting from *perestroika* but also to what it views as a changing operational environment characterized by its perception of the US Navy's offensively oriented maritime strategy and the US deployment of Tomahawk land-attack cruise missiles. This has involved a continuing reassessment of its force structure.

A large percentage of the Soviet Navy's order of battle constructed in the 1950s and 1960s — including over 200 major combatants and submarines — is facing block obsolescence. Since 1987, 20 major Soviet Navy surface combatants (4 cruisers and 16 destroyers) have been either scrapped or stripped of weapons and electronics while awaiting scrapping; reportedly, dozens of over-age attack submarines are also candidates for scrapping. It should be noted, however, that while modern naval units are not replacing older units on a one-for-one basis, qualitative improvements in these

The Soviets have now launched a fourth unit of the 28,000-metric-ton Kirov-class nuclear-powered guided-missile cruiser, which carries 20 SS-N-19 500-km range surface-to-surface missiles as part of its weapons suite.

newer units have resulted in a more capable force. The Soviet Navy, moreover, could afford to decommission even greater numbers of obsolete platforms without significantly affecting combat effectiveness.

Shipbuilding

Over the past four years the Soviets have continued their impressive naval construction efforts at about 150,000 standard displacement tons per year. Most of this impressive naval building program, however, was well under way by the time Gorbachev came to power.

Surface Combatants

Although it is often said that the Soviets consider the submarine to be their capital ship, they also have assigned important roles to their surface combatants and have invested considerable R&D effort and resources in their development. In peacetime, surface combatants provide the Soviets with a visible presence in support of their client states and a force-in-being to react to Third World crises. In wartime, the major Soviet surface warships generally would operate close to Soviet home waters. Their missions would include coordinating surface, air, and subsurface operations; extending the land-based air defense network by providing early warning and some area defense capability against enemy aircraft and cruise missiles; and performing antisubmarine and antisurface warfare missions against threatening surface and submarine forces that have penetrated through Soviet forward-deployed maritime defenses.

The trend in Soviet major surface warship construction has been toward larger units incorporating increased firepower, including improved naval guns, and surface-to-air and surface-to-surface missiles, enhancing their capability to fight in a prolonged conventional war while maintaining a potent nuclear reserve. There also has been an emphasis on producing more sophisticated weapons and sensors, including phased-array radars, improved sonars, and electronic warfare support measures (ESM) sensors. As of 30 June 1989, an ambitious building program resulted in the construction of 17 warships of destroyer size or larger since March 1985. The Soviets also have continued to construct or acquire smaller naval combatants, amphibious ships, and auxiliaries to conduct operations in sea areas contiguous to the Soviet Union and to support amphibious, logistic, and intelligence collection missions.

Submarines

Historically, the Soviet Navy has focused considerable energies on developing its general purpose sub-

marine force. This emphasis has continued during the Gorbachev era. With some 275 active submarines, nearly one-half of which are nuclear-powered, the Soviet general purpose submarine force is the world's largest.

The development of the SS-N-21 SLCM, a nuclear land-attack cruise missile which became operational in 1987, is one of the most significant Soviet submarine-related developments in recent years. The SS-N-21, which is launched from torpedo tubes, may be carried by specific classes of properly equipped current-generation or reconfigured submarines. This complicates Western threat assessments since some newer-generation SSNs are more versatile and can also function as strategic strike platforms.

Soviet Naval Aviation

Naval aviation forces, along with general purpose submarine forces, are the Soviet Navy's primary tactical strike elements. Naval aviation missions include antisubmarine warfare, reconnaissance, C^3, and ground attack. Soviet Naval Aviation (SNA) accomplishes these missions through a variety of fixed wing aircraft: bombers, fighters, ground attack, reconnaissance, antisubmarine (ASW) and electronic warfare, and airborne early warning variants. Additionally, a wide assortment of helicopters used in mine warfare, attack, ASW, and transport roles is part of the operational order of battle. During the past four years, SNA has continued its long-term development into an increasingly modern and more capable force. Indeed, with the 1988 assignment of Backfire C bombers to the Northern Fleet Air Force, all four Soviet fleets are now equipped with this modern

The Soviet Navy's one-of-a-kind Mike-class nuclear-powered attack submarine caught fire and sank while on patrol in the Northern Norwegian Sea on 7 April 1989.

air-to-surface, missile-equipped bomber. Furthermore, since March 1985 SNA has increased its aircraft order of battle by approximately 6 percent.

Other than the late 1988 assignment of Backfire C bombers to the Northern Fleet, little SNA deploy-ment activity occurred during the year. No new air-craft types were introduced, and only modest increases in the strength of SNA Bear J very-low-frequency-communications relay aircraft, shipboard-capable Helix ASW helicopters, and Forger VSTOL aircraft were noted.

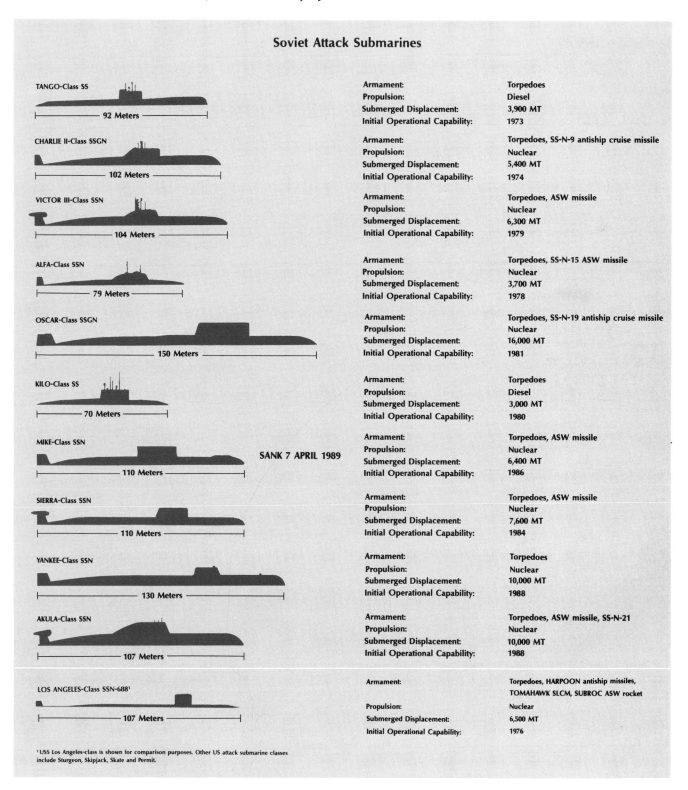

Soviet Attack Submarines

TANGO-Class SS — 92 Meters

Armament:	Torpedoes
Propulsion:	Diesel
Submerged Displacement:	3,900 MT
Initial Operational Capability:	1973

CHARLIE II-Class SSGN — 102 Meters

Armament:	Torpedoes, SS-N-9 antiship cruise missile
Propulsion:	Nuclear
Submerged Displacement:	5,400 MT
Initial Operational Capability:	1974

VICTOR III-Class SSN — 104 Meters

Armament:	Torpedoes, ASW missile
Propulsion:	Nuclear
Submerged Displacement:	6,300 MT
Initial Operational Capability:	1979

ALFA-Class SSN — 79 Meters

Armament:	Torpedoes, SS-N-15 ASW missile
Propulsion:	Nuclear
Submerged Displacement:	3,700 MT
Initial Operational Capability:	1978

OSCAR-Class SSGN — 150 Meters

Armament:	Torpedoes, SS-N-19 antiship cruise missile
Propulsion:	Nuclear
Submerged Displacement:	16,000 MT
Initial Operational Capability:	1981

KILO-Class SS — 70 Meters

Armament:	Torpedoes
Propulsion:	Diesel
Submerged Displacement:	3,000 MT
Initial Operational Capability:	1980

MIKE-Class SSN — 110 Meters — SANK 7 APRIL 1989

Armament:	Torpedoes, ASW missile
Propulsion:	Nuclear
Submerged Displacement:	6,400 MT
Initial Operational Capability:	1986

SIERRA-Class SSN — 110 Meters

Armament:	Torpedoes, ASW missile
Propulsion:	Nuclear
Submerged Displacement:	7,600 MT
Initial Operational Capability:	1984

YANKEE-Class SSN — 130 Meters

Armament:	Torpedoes
Propulsion:	Nuclear
Submerged Displacement:	10,000 MT
Initial Operational Capability:	1988

AKULA-Class SSN — 107 Meters

Armament:	Torpedoes, ASW missile, SS-N-21
Propulsion:	Nuclear
Submerged Displacement:	10,000 MT
Initial Operational Capability:	1988

LOS ANGELES-Class SSN-688[1] — 107 Meters

Armament:	Torpedoes, HARPOON antiship missiles, TOMAHAWK SLCM, SUBROC ASW rocket
Propulsion:	Nuclear
Submerged Displacement:	6,500 MT
Initial Operational Capability:	1976

[1] USS Los Angeles-class is shown for comparison purposes. Other US attack submarine classes include Sturgeon, Skipjack, Skate and Permit.

The first unit of the Soviet Union's new 65,000-metric-ton Tbilisi-class aircraft carriers will mark a significant evolutionary advance over the Kiev-class carriers. Candidate aircraft for its intended airwing include the new Yak-41 VSTOL fighter interceptor now in flight test, as well as the Su-27 Flanker. The first Tbilisi-class carrier may begin sea trials this year.

While SNA is projected to remain primarily a land-based force during the foreseeable future, pilot training and aircraft-carrier-associated test and development activities involving the Su-27 Flanker point to a Soviet intention to deploy that aircraft, or a derivative thereof, aboard their new class of aircraft carriers.

Recent Trends in Soviet Naval Operating Patterns

In recent years, there have been discernible changes in Soviet naval operating patterns. In part, these recent changes are rooted in the Soviets' unique approach to naval readiness. To maintain a high degree of responsiveness in home waters, the Soviets, in marked contrast to the US Navy, historically have maintained a relatively small proportion of their forces operationally deployed in distant areas. Soviet naval forces at home and overseas operate at a much lower activity level than US naval forces, but this is consistent with their mission priorities and wartime force employment. Another factor strongly influencing recent Soviet naval operational patterns is the perceived threat to their homeland from the US Navy's pronouncements of its maritime strategy and the proliferation of Western land-attack cruise missiles on air- and sea-based systems.

The most significant trend in Soviet naval operating patterns over the past four years has been the reduction in naval activity beyond Soviet home waters. The presence of such deployed forces, and their capability to respond quickly to developing crises, has dropped approximately 15 percent from the high levels of the 1980-85 timeframe. Principal factors in this decline appear to be the Soviets' need for what they term enhanced combined-arms training (the close integration of the Navy with other military services) in anticipated wartime operating areas, and the increased naval commitment to combined-arms warfare and offshore air defense of the Soviet Union against the expanding US sea- and air-launched cruise missile capability. Another factor is the requirement to economize on fuel and husband progressively aging elements of the fleet.

Soviet naval exercises are dominated by the recurring

themes of protecting their sea-based strategic strike submarines and defending against sea-based attack along the maritime approaches to the Soviet Union. Recent changes involve the integration of new platforms, increased combined-arms play, and more intense, realistic training scenarios.

NAVAL WARFARE AREAS

ASW Forces

Antisubmarine warfare (ASW) forces, the largest single component of the Soviet Navy's major surface and submarine forces and a major element of SNA, have been tasked with a major portion of deployment requirements. From the Soviet perspective, ASW forces are expected to protect Soviet SSBNs, defend the USSR against Western submarine strategic strike assets, and protect Soviet SLOCs.

The Soviets' emphasis on improving their ASW capabilities is reflected by the introduction in recent years of two new classes of SSNs (Akula, Sierra) and by the increasing numbers of improved ASW aircraft and surface ships. New Soviet SSNs have demonstrated marked improvement in quieting at specific operating profiles that approaches that of some later-generation US SSNs. New ASW surface ships, such as the Udaloy DDG, as well as new multimission combatants like the Kiev CVHG and Kirov CGN, combine better ASW weapons and sensors with the long-range ASW search

Baku, the fourth unit of the Kiev-class carriers, which carries more sophisticated target acquisition and tracking radars than the other ships of the class, joined the Northern Fleet in 1988.

The Akula-class nuclear-powered attack submarine incorporates substantial advances in sound quieting and warfighting capabilities, demonstrating reductions in noise levels the US had not projected the Soviets to attain until the early 1990s.

capabilities of the new Helix A ASW helicopter. Continued production of these platforms, along with ongoing research to improve their capabilities, could challenge the West's lead in this vital naval warfare environment.

ASUW Forces

Antisurface warfare (ASUW) — the ability to attack and sink surface forces — is a critical requirement of Soviet maritime strategy. Consequently, the Soviet Navy has a wide variety of ASUW weapon systems employing both conventional and nuclear warheads, including antiship cruise missiles (ASCMs), tactical air-to-surface missiles (ASMs), guns, torpedoes, and mines.

Soviet ASUW doctrine includes their concept of "combined forces," i.e., coordinated operations among surface ships, submarines, and aircraft. The Soviets plan to mass firepower on an enemy with coordinated strikes by torpedo attack submarines, cruise missile-equipped submarines, aircraft, and, where possible, surface combatants. These strikes will be either simultaneous or staggered with a second attack closely following the first to take advantage of degraded defenses. The Soviets are developing the necessary command, control, and communications to manage such coordinated strikes. Except for a small proportion of ships deployed in forward areas, such as the Mediterranean and the Indian Ocean, surface combatants will be primarily reserved for operations in areas close to the Soviet Union under the protective umbrella of land-based aircraft and the coastal missile artillery force. These ships will serve largely as an extension to the land-based air defense network in an early warning and command, control and communications role.

Amphibious Warfare

Soviet Naval Infantry (SNI), with contingents in all four fleets, constitutes the primary Soviet amphibious warfare capability. With an estimated peacetime strength of 18,000, this elite, well-trained body has the mission of spearheading amphibious assaults in support of ground-force operations, providing coastal defense in critical areas, and conducting small-scale landings and specialized raids in lightly defended areas. Due to limited force strength, insufficient assault lift capabilities, and the absence of a Soviet sea-based air power capability to support an amphibious landing against significant opposition, the SNI is not capable of being employed as a major distant power-projection combat force.

Nevertheless, even a few hundred Soviet marines afloat could provide the Soviet Union with a valu-able political-military instrument during a Third World crisis. Such forces conduct routine deployments off Angola and in the Indian Ocean. Small SNI security detachments are stationed on the Dahlak Archipelago, Ethiopia, and at Cam Ranh Bay, Vietnam.

Naval Logistics

Compared to most Western navies, the Soviet Navy traditionally has received relatively little logistics support afloat. The capability to conduct under way at-sea replenishment remains a low priority for the Soviets and consequently some of their methods are rather slow and primitive. The capability for transferring munitions while under way is considered even more limited to the point that in a war, the ability of surface combatants to fight for prolonged periods would probably be directly affected.

Shortfalls in indigenous Navy logistics support have been minimized in peacetime through the heavy employment of the merchant fleet. Merchant vessels call in many Western ports (particularly those in the Mediterranean) to obtain supplies for naval combatants. By providing logistic support to the Navy with their merchant fleet, the Soviets have maintained their capability to support and sustain out-of-area naval operations. Merchant tankers, however, cannot provide high-speed under way replenishment, and stores transfer is normally done at anchor.

If the Soviets reduce the size of their navy, their naval logistics infrastructure may be able to support remaining units more effectively. The scrapping and selling of older vessels, in addition to providing positive political reaction and much-needed foreign exchange from the West, would lessen the burden on Soviet maintenance and repair facilities while increasing pier space, which is now at a premium.

NAVAL SUMMARY

The Soviet Navy has continued to evolve as an increasingly modern force capable of meeting the requirements of conventional or nuclear war at virtually any level. It is true that fewer numbers of the current generation of major surface and submarine combatants are being built than in past decades, signifying a declining force structure trend in the 1990s. However, the increased individual capabilities of the new vessels will more than offset the numerical reductions in some — but not all — missions. These production rate reductions undoubtedly predate General Secretary Gorachev's announced initiatives, however, and future rates are uncertain.

RADIO-ELECTRONIC COMBAT

The Soviets continue to augment their capability to degrade command and control of Western military forces. Embodied in the doctrine known as radio-electronic combat (REC) is an integrated effort centered around reconnaissance, electronic countermeasures (jamming), physical attack (destruction), and deception operations. Each element contributes to the disruption of effective command and control at a critical decision point in battle.

At the operational (front/army) and tactical (division and below) levels, the Soviets can deploy a comprehensive and effective array of equipment to execute REC missions. Soviet hardware is modern, sophisticated, and, increasingly, mounted in armored vehicles to facilitate operations in close proximity to the forward line of troops. For example, over the past several years the Soviets have widely deployed a tactical communications jammer in their MTLB armored personnel carrier, which provides the advantages of mobility and survivability required for operations. Continuing this trend, the Soviets have now modified the MTLB to carry several variations of communication-intercept and direction-finding equipment and deployed it with divisions in the forward area. As a result, these divisions now possess an organic capability to degrade NATO tactical communications. The addition of communication jammers at division level potentially doubles the jamming capability of a Soviet front.

THEATER FORCES: PROSPECTS FOR CHANGE

The Soviets have large, impressive general purpose forces currently structured primarily for offensive operations. The Soviets, however, have stated their intention to effect far-reaching changes that will see their forces restructured to adopt a defensive posture. The initiation of unilateral troop reductions could be the first step in this process.

At the same time, the Soviets are calling for mutual Pact and NATO force reductions through the arms control process as the means by which their defensive doctrine will be fully realized. They have publicly advanced a staged approach that will culminate in

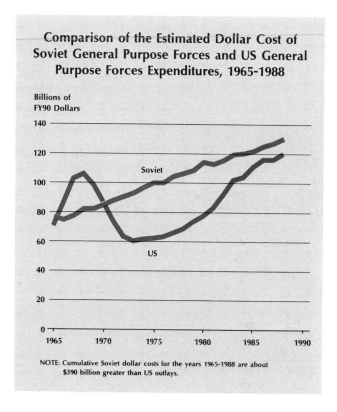

Comparison of the Estimated Dollar Cost of Soviet General Purpose Forces and US General Purpose Forces Expenditures, 1965-1988

NOTE: Cumulative Soviet dollar costs for the years 1965-1988 are about $390 billion greater than US outlays.

both Pact and NATO forces being deeply reduced and structured so that neither side, according to them, poses a significant offensive threat to the other.

The Soviets believe their unilateral reductions will act as a catalyst for reducing NATO military efforts and for achieving the large force reductions called for in their arms control proposals. Whether or not the Soviets are willing, during the CFE talks, to accept deeply asymmetric reductions and to address conventional force imbalances in Europe will be a key indicator of how serious the Soviets are about structuring their forces into a defensive posture.

Currently, the Soviets are initiating changes designed to produce a Soviet force significantly reduced in size but with its combat capability maintained or even improved. They hope to achieve this capability through continuous equipment modernization, qualitative improvements in training, leadership, morale, and discipline, and enhancement of command and control capabilities.

PART

2

An Assessment of the Balance

2

CHAPTER VI

The Military Balance

Deployment of the world's largest supersonic bomber, the Blackjack, is but one indication of the Soviets' commitment to the continued modernization of their strategic nuclear forces.

INTRODUCTION

Soviet military power does not exist in isolation. Indeed, to appreciate fully the formidable aggregation of military might possessed by Moscow, it is necessary to evaluate it in comparison with the military forces of the Western coalition of nations arrayed against it.

If deterrence ever fails, it will likely occur in large measure because of conclusions the Soviet leadership has reached concerning the military balance — or trends in the balance — between its forces and those of the Western democracies. In that event, the Soviet armed forces will be judged by their ability to achieve Moscow's wartime objectives over the opposition of the United States and its allies. Therefore, to place Soviet military power in perspective this chapter provides a general assessment of the US and allied military capability to deter Soviet aggression, or, if deterrence fails, to deny the Soviet armed forces their wartime objectives.

Unfortunately, there is no single measure of merit

that provides an assessment of the global military balance. National security objectives vary from region to region, and the number of other variables, contingencies, and inherent uncertainties increase dramatically as the focus of an assessment is widened. Consequently, this chapter examines the overall military balance by assessing the balances in a number of significant regional and functional areas, while keeping in mind the relationships that exist among the various balances.

THE STRATEGIC NUCLEAR BALANCE

The purpose of US strategic nuclear forces is to deter aggression, particularly nuclear attacks, against the United States and its allies. To fulfill their mission, these forces must, in the aggregate, possess a number of attributes. They must be effective, flexible, survivable, and enduring. The Soviet Union must perceive that the United States will employ these forces if necessary, and that the costs to Moscow of US retaliation far outweigh any potential gains of aggression. Additionally, it is important that US strategic forces promote a condition of "strategic stability" — a condition whereby deterrence is assured and neither the United States nor the Soviet Union feel pressured to use nuclear weapons preemptively or suddenly.

Measuring strategic stability requires an evaluation of the Soviet leadership's perceptions and an understanding of how they weigh the various factors involved in calculating stability. However, because the Soviets are not open about their own judgments, and because they appear to hold very different views about nuclear war than does the United States, measuring strategic stability is very difficult. Consequently, analysts must rely on measuring "the strategic balance," comparing easily quantifiable and roughly equivalent aspects of each superpower's forces. While these "static" comparisons are of some value, they do not reveal the entire story. Therefore, while this section addresses static measures, it also discusses less quantifiable factors and their impact upon deterrence and stability.

Static Measures

Today both the United States and the Soviet Union deploy approximately equal numbers of strategic nuclear weapons, although the composition of each side's arsenal is different. The United States, reflecting its

historic interest in maintaining a balanced triad of delivery systems, possesses a more varied set of forces than does the USSR. The Soviets have traditionally favored ICBMs, both for historical reasons (the Soviet Strategic Rocket Forces are an outgrowth of their artillery, which has long dominated Soviet military thinking) and for doctrinal purposes (the fast time-of-flight and large number of MIRVs carried by Soviet ICBMs provide the preemptive capabilities favored by Soviet military planners).

A number of important points, however, are lost by these comparisons. For example:

■ The Soviets' emphasis on land-based ballistic missiles gives them more warheads available for an attack on a day-to-day basis than the United States.
■ While the Soviets continue deploying large numbers of MIRVed ICBMs, during the 1980s they have further diversified their strategic forces by introducing MIRVed SLBMs, by deploying two new bombers capable of carrying air-launched cruise missiles, and by deploying mobile ICBMs.
■ The relative parity that currently exists between the two sides is not reflected in the pace of their development and modernization efforts. Indeed, over the years the Soviets have deployed more types of strategic nuclear systems and modernized them more frequently than has the United States. American efforts have been much more restrained.
■ The throw-weight — or payload capability — of the Soviet ballistic missile force is vastly larger than that of the US force.

Asymmetries Not Revealed by Static Measures

Comparing missiles against missiles and bombers against bombers, however, misses the mark in assessing the strategic balance. For example, bombers fly not against other bombers, but against air defenses; and strategic forces threaten targets and installations (which include, but are not limited to, other strategic forces). Significant asymmetries exist between the United States and the Soviet Union in their strategic defenses and target bases. For example:

■ The Soviet Union deploys the world's most extensive air defense system and the world's only antiballistic missile system. United States air defenses, by compar-

Strategic Offensive Forces

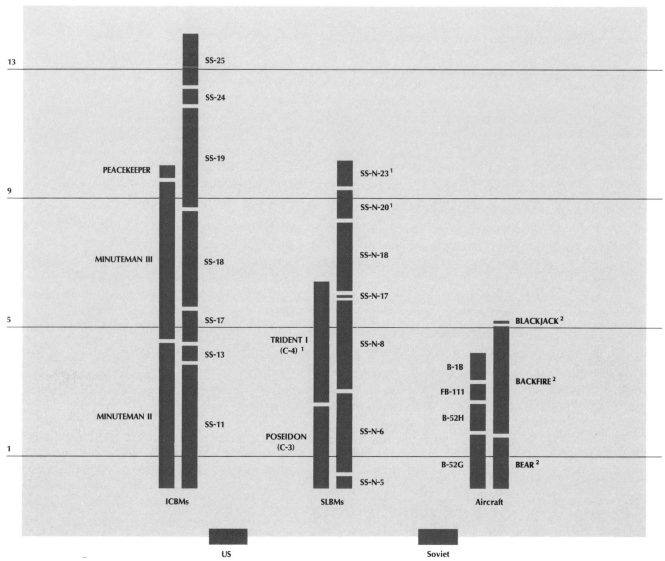

[1] Includes SLBMs potentially carried on Trident, Typhoon, and Delta-IV submarines on sea trials.

[2] Includes Backfires assigned to Soviet Naval Aviation and other training aircraft.

ison, are much smaller, and are dedicated largely to providing warning and attack assessment.

- The USSR places great emphasis on passive defenses to protect many of its key assets from US retaliation. Important examples in this regard are hardened Soviet missile silos, the majority of which are several times harder than their US counterparts, and their system of deep underground bunkers across the Soviet Union for key leadership personnel and their support cadres.
- There is a significant asymmetry in the US and Soviet target bases. The Soviet Union has a target base approximately twice as large as the US base Soviet nuclear planners have to cover. This means that

the Soviets can, by having roughly the same number of warheads as the United States, plan on having more warheads than the United States after a nuclear exchange.

Finally, there are profound doctrinal differences between the United States and the Soviet Union, and mirror imaging in this context is very dangerous. While both sides maintain military establishments to deter aggression, the focus of Soviet doctrine and force procurement has consistently been on achieving the most credible capability to fight a nuclear war should deterrence fail. Soviet strategic nuclear doctrine continues

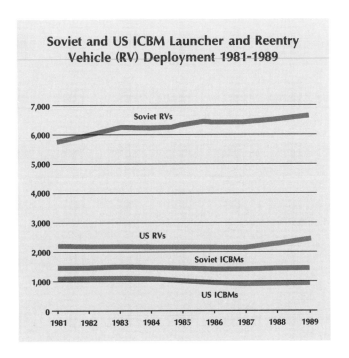

Soviet and US ICBM Launcher and Reentry Vehicle (RV) Deployment 1981-1989

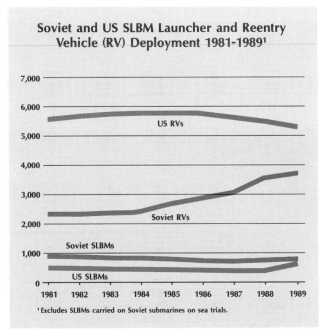

Soviet and US SLBM Launcher and Reentry Vehicle (RV) Deployment 1981-1989[1]

[1] Excludes SLBMs carried on Soviet submarines on sea trials.

The B-1B bomber is emerging as the backbone of the US strategic bomber force, and has significantly improved the force's capability to penetrate heavily defended areas and hold critical strategic targets at risk.

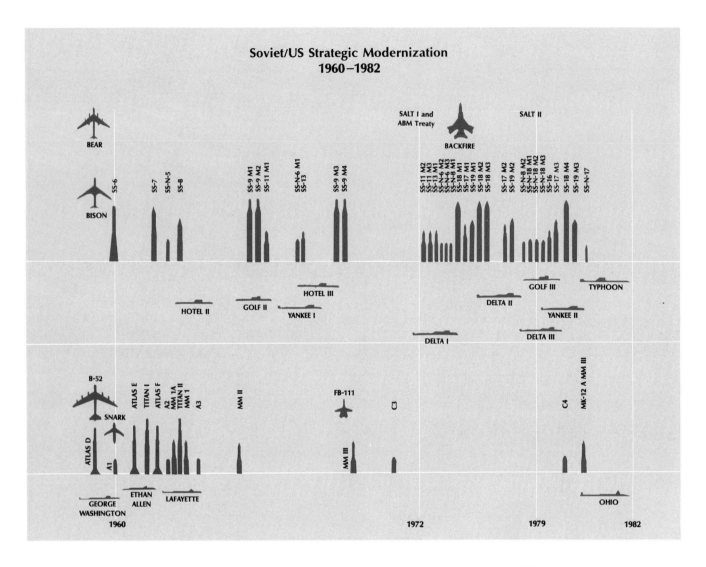

Soviet/US Strategic Modernization 1960–1982

to posit that preemptive strikes should be used when judged necessary. Indeed, although the Soviets claim that they have adopted a new defensive doctrine, a restructuring of Soviet strategic forces — to include major programmatic changes and a major reallocation of resources away from strategic nuclear programs — will likely require some years to effect, if it is undertaken at all. While the future remains uncertain, it appears that the Soviet military leadership retains its belief that "strategic sufficiency" at the level of strategic nuclear forces rests on their ability to maintain a military advantage over their potential adversaries.

In summary, three factors affect the balance and the stability of deterrence: first, the significant differences within the forces deployed by each side; second, the defenses and targets against which they would be employed; and third, the military doctrines and rationales supporting their existence and governing their use.

In the final analysis, maintaining strategic deterrence rests on the United States' ability to convince the Soviets that it has both the means and the will to respond effectively to any Soviet attack on the United States or its allies. However, as the history of the last two decades demonstrates, deterrence is a dynamic concept. Given Moscow's long-term and persistent modernization of its strategic forces, it is reasonable to assume that the Soviets will continue trying to weaken the US nuclear deterrent. Consequently, the United States must be prepared to respond with appropriate programs, and to develop capabilities, as necessary, to maintain its strategic deterrent.

THE BALANCE IN SPACE

Both the United States and the Soviet Union have become dependent on space systems for support of military operations, whether in the theater or strategic arena. While US military space capabilities are adequate in peacetime or a short-term crisis, they are inadequate

88

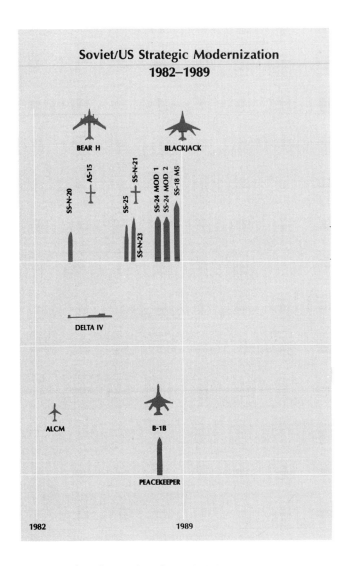

Soviet/US Strategic Modernization 1982–1989

BEAR H

BLACKJACK

SS-N-20

AS-15

SS-25   SS-N-21

SS-N-23

SS-24 MOD 1
SS-24 MOD 2
SS-18 M5

DELTA IV

ALCM

B-1B

PEACEKEEPER

1982   1989

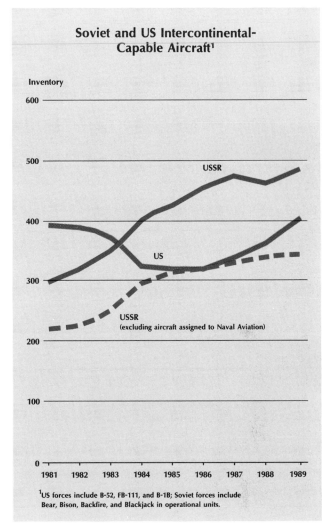

Soviet and US Intercontinental-Capable Aircraft[1]

Inventory

USSR

US

USSR
(excluding aircraft assigned to Naval Aviation)

1981 1982 1983 1984 1985 1986 1987 1988 1989

[1]US forces include B-52, FB-111, and B-1B; Soviet forces include Bear, Bison, Backfire, and Blackjack in operational units.

to meet the demands of warfighting forces during a NATO-Warsaw Pact conflict.

Considerable asymmetries exist in US and Soviet military space infrastructures. The US military space structure, as well as its infrastructure, has evolved with a peacetime orientation. In contrast, Soviet space systems, rapid launch capability, and space system production capability are prioritized for wartime operations. The Soviet infrastructure will continue to provide the Soviets with a significant advantage in space support responsiveness. Soviet space systems enhance support for their terrestrial forces and also pose a threat to US forces deployed in various theaters around the globe.

To provide effective space support for terrestrial forces in time of conflict, the United States must be able to ensure its freedom of action in space. At present, the Soviets possess the world's only operational ASAT weapon, as well as several other systems with ASAT capability. This capability provides the Soviets with

the option to degrade the performance of US space systems in time of crisis or low-level conflict, and to destroy some critical US systems at low altitudes as the crisis or conflict worsens. Current US plans to develop such capabilities must continue in order to overcome this glaring deficiency in the US military posture. This threat to US freedom of action in space will persist if the United States does not also develop the capability to replace quickly critical space capabilities that are damaged or destroyed in a conflict.

In summary, the Soviet Union holds an advantage over the United States because of the Soviets' unique ASAT capability and robust space support infrastructure. United States on-orbit systems provide superior capabilities for peacetime operations. Nevertheless, in order to ensure their ability to continue functioning effectively in a conflict, the United States must continue to pursue an operational ASAT capability, a more responsive space system reconstitution capability, and a more survivable space support infrastructure.

STRATEGIC ARMS
REDUCTION TALKS (START)

The United States does not regard arms control as an end in itself but, rather, as an important complement to its strategy of deterrence. Thus the United States seeks to reach an agreement with the Soviet Union on a START Treaty that will codify deep reductions in the strategic arms of both sides. The US objective is to enhance strategic stability through equal and verifiable limitations on the two sides' forces.

Significant progress has been made toward achieving these goals. For example, both sides have agreed to a limit of 6,000 accountable warheads that either side may place on its deployed strategic offensive delivery systems. These systems are, themselves, subject to a deployment limit of 1,600.

With regard to enhancing strategic stability, the United States and the Soviet Union also agreed to a limit of 4,900 warheads on ballistic missiles, and to a reduction of approximately 50 percent in Soviet ballistic missile throw-weight. They also have agreed on a 50 percent reduction in the number of Soviet heavy ICBMs, and on the number of warheads they will be permitted to deploy. These reductions and limitations are important because land-based ballistic missiles — characterized by high alert rates, high accuracy and short flight times — are particularly suited to a first-strike role. Despite these successes, both sides must resolve some key issues before the United States can agree to a START Treaty. These issues are discussed below.

Heavy ICBMs

As noted above, the United States views Soviet heavy ICBMs as destabilizing first-strike weapons. Consequently, the United States wants an agreement to prohibit the production, flight testing or modernization of new or existing types of heavy ICBMs. The US objective is to bring about the eventual elimination of this most destabilizing strategic weapon. Soviet proposals, on the other hand, specifically permit the production, flight testing and modernization of existing heavy ICBMs, but would prohibit the same activities for new types of heavy ICBMs. The Soviet approach would, in effect, codify a Soviet monopoly in heavy ICBMs rather than eliminate them.

Mobile ICBMs

The United States has proposed to ban mobile ICBMs because of the verification problems they pose. However, if a regime that meets US criteria can be identified, then the United States would reconsider its position.

Sublimits

The United States and the Soviet Union also disagree over how ICBMs and manned air-breathing weapon systems affect the strategic balance. The United States has proposed a sublimit of 3,000–3,300 on the number of ICBM warheads to reduce reliance on this vulnerable, destabilizing type of weapon system. The Soviets hold that all nuclear weapons are equally destabilizing. Hence, they reject a special sublimit on ICBM warheads unless the sides also agree to impose the same sublimit on warheads carried by SLBMs on board submarines.

Similarly, the Soviets propose a sublimit of 1,100 on bomber-carried weapons. In this regard the Soviet approach seeks to have United States ALCM-carrying bombers counted as having roughly twice the 10 warheads attributed to the Soviets' first-strike heavy ICBM, the SS-18. The Soviet approach also is contrary to the US "one-way freedom to mix" position which seeks to place the most restrictive limitations on the most destabilizing weapon systems. The United States places the least restriction on heavy bombers because they are slow-flying, can be recalled, and therefore are not well-suited for a first strike.

SLCMs

Sea-launched cruise missiles (SLCMs) represent another difficult issue in START. Due to their small size, SLCMs are all but impossible to verify. In addition, the United States has not yet identified a verification regime that is workable, that

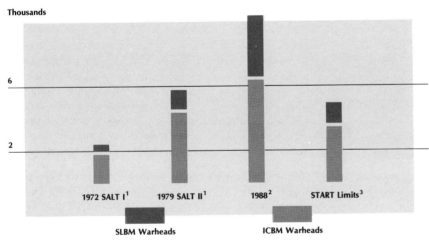

Growth in Soviet Strategic Offensive Warheads

Thousands

1972 SALT I[1]   1979 SALT II[1]   1988[2]   START Limits[3]

SLBM Warheads   ICBM Warheads

[1]Neither SALT I nor SALT II placed limits on ballistic missile warheads. Data reflect Soviet ballistic missile warheads on these dates.

[2]As of 30 November 1988.

[3]The United States and Soviet Union have agreed to a sublimit ceiling of 4,900 on the aggregate number of ICBM plus SLBM warheads. The United States has proposed a 3,000-3,300 limit on ICBM warheads under the 4,900 limit.

The US Triad's sea-based leg — its ballistic missile submarines — is considered the most survivable. The Ohio-class *USS Michigan* SSBN shown here carries 24 ballistic missiles, incorporates significant advances in survivability and effectiveness, and will preserve the US advantage over the USSR in SSBN forces.

The deployment of the Peacekeeper ICBM has significantly improved the responsiveness and hard-target-kill capability of the US strategic land-based missile force.

does not place unacceptable constraints on US general purpose naval forces, and that does not compromise the long-standing US policy neither to confirm nor deny the presence of nuclear weapons at a particular location. Due to these considerations the United States has proposed that both sides make nonbinding declarations regarding their nuclear SLCM inventories.

Compliance

Soviet cheating on existing arms control commitments remains a source of continuing concern for the United States. There have been some 16 instances of clear Soviet violations of a number of agreements, including the ABM Treaty, SALT I and II, the Biological Weapons Convention, and the Geneva Protocol on Chemical Weapons. In response to US protests, the Soviet Union has corrected some but not all of its noncompliant activities. Of particular concern is the illegally sited radar at Krasnoyarsk, a clear violation of the ABM treaty.

If arms control is to have meaning — if it is to contribute to national security and to global and regional stability — all parties must comply fully with the agreements they make. This fundamental precept underlies US arms control policy. For this reason, the United States has informed the Soviet Union that no further agreements in the START or Defense and Space areas are possible until Moscow corrects its violation of the ABM Treaty involving the Krasnoyarsk radar in a verifiable manner that meets US criteria.

REGIONAL AND FUNCTIONAL BALANCES

Since the end of World War II, the United States has followed a national security strategy requiring forward-based military forces to aid its friends and allies against the threat of Soviet aggression and encroachment. To determine whether US and allied forces can preserve deterrence, or prevail should deterrence fail, comparative analyses of the various regional and functional military balances must be undertaken.

The primary components of the military balance are qualitative and quantitative in nature. While relative numbers of forces do not constitute the only measure of military effectiveness, they do provide the basic pa-

The Soviet SL-16 booster, now operational, is capable of placing a payload of more than 15,000 kilograms into low Earth orbit, filling a gap in the current inventory for launching medium-weight payloads. With new launch vehicles like the SL-16 and SL-X-17 in the inventory, the Soviets can double their annual payload capability during the next five years.

rameters within which a more comprehensive assessment can occur. On the other hand, further examination and comparison of nonquantifiable aspects of the military balance, including opposing strategies and operational concepts, are also necessary. With this approach in mind, the following sections focus on the relevant military capabilities of the US and Soviet military forces and those of allies and friends within key geographic areas and along functional lines.

THE MILITARY BALANCE IN EUROPE

Introduction

The full effect of the political and military changes now occurring in the Soviet Union and other Warsaw Pact countries is as yet unknown. These changes may result in conventional arms cuts that significantly reduce the Pact advantage in the region, but it would be imprudent to count the cuts before they occur. Consequently, this section will address current, not anticipated force structures. With this consideration in mind, the first step in analyzing the military balance in Europe is to compare the strategies and objectives of NATO and the Warsaw Pact against the military forces available to implement those strategies.

Pact Objectives

Although the long-term political and military goals of the Soviets and their Warsaw Pact allies are not easily discernible, their primary peacetime objective has long been to exploit the fissures within the NATO Alliance. During the last several years the Soviets have embarked on a skillful and sophisticated public relations campaign to reduce the West's perception of the Warsaw Pact threat. They have announced unilateral arms and spending cuts, along with a new defensive military doctrine. In addition defensive operations are played frequently in Soviet exercises.

Soviet military planning has yet to match Moscow's rhetoric. Sufficient time, however, has not elapsed to produce a significant decrease in Soviet defense spending, force structure, or Soviet/Warsaw Pact military capability. If Gorbachev's announcements become reality, and the military does not reorganize its reduced forces to maintain its current relative combat power, the Soviet/Warsaw Pact threat upon which the whole security structure of the NATO Alliance rests will have diminished significantly. Even with these cuts, however, Pact forces will still outnumber NATO's forces in the critical Central Region by a better than 2:1 ratio in tanks, artillery, and divisions.

The Delta II shown here, and the Titan IV, are the newest expendable launch vehicles in the US booster inventory. These boosters will help the United States maintain access to the operational environment of space.

NATO Regions and Soviet Theaters of Military Operation

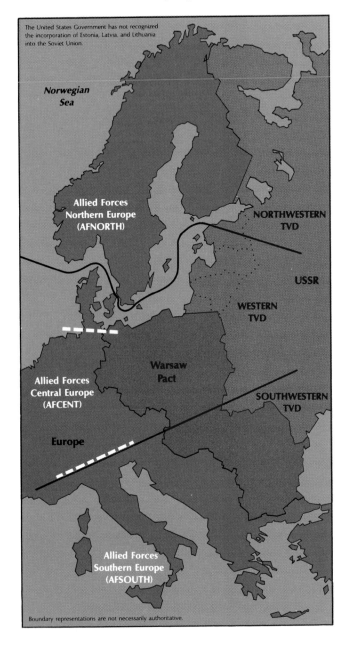

The United States Government has not recognized the incorporation of Estonia, Latvia, and Lithuania into the Soviet Union.

Norwegian Sea

Allied Forces Northern Europe (AFNORTH)

NORTHWESTERN TVD

USSR

WESTERN TVD

Warsaw Pact

Allied Forces Central Europe (AFCENT)

SOUTHWESTERN TVD

Europe

Allied Forces Southern Europe (AFSOUTH)

Boundary representations are not necessarily authoritative.

At present, the Soviets do not seem to anticipate war in Europe in the near future, and are stressing political, diplomatic, and economic alternatives to achieve their strategic goals. If, however, these alternatives fail to protect Soviet vital interests and war becomes, in their view, unavoidable, they would probably strive to keep it conventional for fear of the potential devastation to their nation should the conflict escalate to the use of nuclear weapons.

Although the Soviets are better prepared for a long-term conflict than is NATO, they would much prefer a victory in what they call the initial period; that is, before NATO can fully mobilize and reinforce itself. Even though the Pact has proclaimed that its military doctrine is based on "defense" or "reasonable sufficiency," and that its military posture is defensively oriented, it continues to maintain a force capable of sustained offensive operations. In offensive operations, Pact forces can be expected to concentrate along NATO's Central Front on narrow axes of attack to break through what they consider to be the most vulnerable sectors of NATO's forward defenses. This will be followed by operations designed to encircle and trap NATO forces, and capture key objectives in NATO's rear. By attacking with overwhelming strength and making maximum use of surprise, the Soviet objective would be to win quickly, and thus preclude a cohesive and reinforced defense and the capability for large-scale use of nuclear weapons by NATO. The Soviets hope to avoid a protracted war for several reasons. First, they would have to face significant NATO reinforcements from America, Britain, and Canada. Second, NATO's greater economic strength would become increasingly important. Third, the Soviets' hold on their Warsaw Pact allies may weaken as the loose bonds holding that alliance together succumb to the tremendous stress of a prolonged conflict. Further, US and allied worldwide military capabilities and the current conventional force asymmetries at sea pose additional challenges to Soviet military strategy, and in a protracted conflict, the Soviets would find themselves increasingly isolated from the rest of the world community.

NATO Objectives

Since 1967, NATO has followed the strategic doctrine of flexible response, which is designed to deter aggression against the Alliance and successfully defend it should deterrence fail. Thus NATO maintains a mix of conventional and theater nuclear forces that, along with US strategic nuclear forces, will allow an appropriate response to Warsaw Pact aggression across the spectrum of conflict. The Alliance requires strong military capabilities to ensure that it can resist political and military intimidation from the Soviet Union during periods of increased tension. Should war come, NATO plans to respond directly to military aggression by defending Alliance territory as far forward as possible, and as necessary, deliberately escalating to the level considered appropriate to reestablish the status quo ante or provide for the Alliance's defense.

As a defensive alliance, NATO has never sought the capability for rapid, aggressive war against the Warsaw Pact. The structure, size, and logistics of NATO's forces make them incapable of launching any large-scale

Possible Warsaw Pact Attack Axes in NATO's Central Region

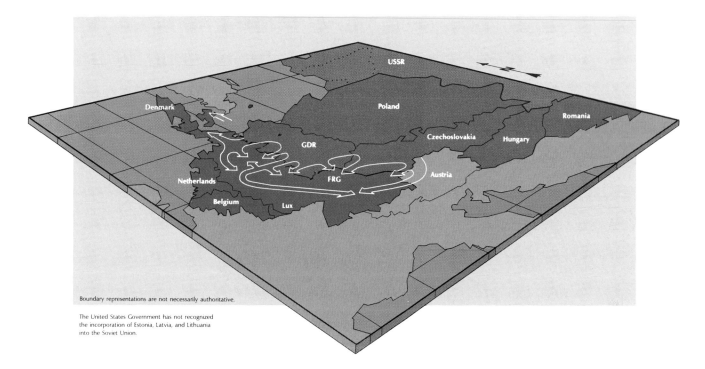

Boundary representations are not necessarily authoritative.

The United States Government has not recognized
the incorporation of Estonia, Latvia, and Lithuania
into the Soviet Union.

offensive operations. Rather, they are designed to defend the forward area, improve their capability to attack Pact reinforcements before they arrive at the front (primarily through air interdiction against the follow-on forces), and maintain the option for nuclear escalation if it becomes necessary. Historically, NATO has relied on the quality of its conventional forces to offset the Warsaw Pact's quantitative force advantage. However, while the Alliance still retains a significant qualitative edge in tactical aircraft and certain fields of defense electronics, the Soviets have seriously eroded the broad qualitative superiority NATO once enjoyed.

The Central Region

Defeating NATO's forces in the Central Region is the most important objective of any Warsaw Pact conventional operation in Europe. The Pact has organized, trained, equipped, and deployed forward Soviet, East German, Czech, Hungarian, and Polish forces in peacetime for a combined arms operation against West German, US, British, Dutch, Belgian, Canadian, and Danish ground, air, and naval forces. The NATO Northern Army Group (NORTHAG) provides four corps (I Netherlands, I German, I British, and I Belgian) to defend the area south of the Elbe to the Gottingen Corridor, while Central Army Group defends with four corps (III German, V US, VII US, and II German, and a Canadian brigade group) south of Gottingen to the Austrian border. This "layer cake"

arrangement presents serious problems for NATO's defensive forces. Differences in equipment, doctrine, language, munitions, and command networks create seams along the NATO front which constitute serious obstacles to a coherent defensive effort. Furthermore, the shallow strategic depth available (particularly in the NORTHAG sector) for NATO's forces makes it very difficult to trade space for time. Conversely, while the terrain of the North German Plain was considered good tank country in the years following World War II, suitable for rapid Soviet armored advances, the sprawling urbanization that occurred in the following decades will now hinder large-scale armored offensives or counteroffensives.

On the Warsaw Pact side, 19 highly trained Soviet maneuver divisions (and one artillery division) comprise the Western Group of Forces (WGF), with two more divisions in Poland and five in Czechoslovakia. Supplementing these forces are 37 divisions in the western USSR and perhaps an additional four divisions in Hungary. The non-Soviet Warsaw Pact (NSWP) allies contribute approximately 29 divisions and 15 brigades to the alliance. These forces have the advantage of common doctrine, equipment, and command and control networks, but the readiness of Pact units varies. Few are close to 100 percent strength and most will require time for manning, and in some cases, training. Most have older Soviet equipment, small unit leadership problems, and an inadequate non-commissioned officer

These Blackhawk helicopters provide US ground forces with tactical airlift and air assault capabilities, enabling them to maneuver rapidly on today's battlefield.

(NCO) corps. Language problems also may be a factor, but they are no more serious than those faced by NATO.

NATO's forces in the Central Region, in turn, suffer from maldeployment. In the broadest sense, analysts generally concede that CENTAG not only has the strongest NATO forces but also has the more defensible terrain and faces less capable Warsaw Pact forces. NORTHAG, on the other hand, faces the strongest Soviet and NSWP forces in the Warsaw Pact. Since the Pact will have the initiative, it will have the luxury of choosing when and where to attack. Furthermore, since the Pact has far more of its forces closer to the border than does NATO during peacetime, NATO could conceivably find itself unable — due to unheeded warnings and indications of an attack, or political delays — to mobilize and deploy forces forward as quickly as the Pact. Unfortunately, some NATO countries are highly dependent on time to mobilize "in-place" forces forward to defensive positions, including defensive units that must deploy from their home countries. Follow-on Pact forces are also much closer to their foward positions than North American-based US and Canadian follow-on forces.

In Central Europe, assessments indicate that US and allied ground, air, and naval forces should be able to mount a strong defense that might frustrate the Soviet Union and its allies from achieving their objectives. Primarily as a result of combat force modernization, US warfighting capability has improved in the last five years, and should continue to improve in the near term. However, deficiencies in US and allied force numbers and their sustainability remain, and many of the improvements are offset by Soviet and Warsaw Pact quantitative and qualitative advances.

Should deterrence fail, NATO faces a dilemma. If the initial defense falters, the coalition will face the unpalatable prospect of losing considerable European territory or resorting to the employment of theater-nuclear weapons. A determined Soviet campaign would severely stress the alliance's conventional defense capability. This is of great concern, as is the danger that the Alliance's members will not continue to invest in a credible conventional defense.

However, even with the current favorable force asymmetries in Central Europe, the Soviets would face a significant dilemma as well. If Warsaw Pact conventional forces are successful, the Soviets risk a nuclear response that would negate their initial gains and threaten the very fabric of their society. Alternatively, if NATO elects to pursue a conventional defense, the Warsaw Pact would still confront the prospect of long-term conflict against the now mobilized military and industrial might of the world's most powerful economies.

NATO's Northern and Southern Regions

Although the Soviets would direct the bulk of their military operations against NATO's Central Region, the Alliance's northern and southern regions figure prominently in Soviet strategy.

Northern Europe

The Soviet threat to NATO's Northern Region is most acute across an arc running from Greenland through Iceland to Norway and Denmark. This area shields the northern approaches to the Atlantic and the sea lines of communication that would provide a vital lifeline between NATO Europe and North America in wartime.

The balance of land forces in the region significantly favors the Soviets. Furthermore, the Norwegian and Danish prohibition against the stationing of foreign troops or nuclear weapons on their soil during peacetime complicates NATO's defense. These constraints make advance warning of a Pact attack critical, since NATO reinforcements involved in defending the area must be deployed from outside the region. In addition, indigenous military manning is limited. Norway, for example, relies upon reservists for over 80 percent of its wartime strength and maintains only a small land force for defense in peacetime. Training deployments and prepositioned stocks for a US Marine Expeditionary Brigade in Norway will bolster the area's defense.

The Soviets have positioned land forces, along with land-based air and Soviet Naval Infantry assets, to

Possible Soviet Operations in Northern Norway and the Baltic

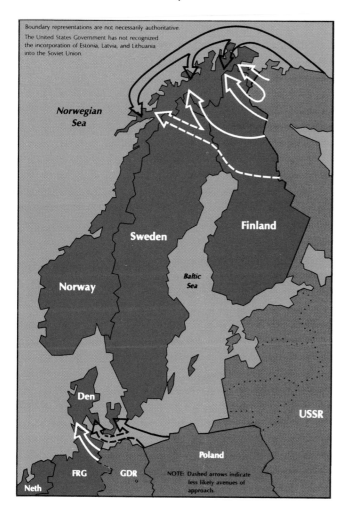

threaten in-place Norwegian forces, seize airfields in northern Norway, and destroy vital early warning and communication sites. Loss of access to the North Cape of Norway would seriously hinder allied efforts to contain Soviet naval forces. Soviet control of the area, in turn, would facilitate attacks on southern Norway, Iceland, the United Kingdom, and the flow of reinforcements to Europe from North America. The Soviets can be expected to attack Denmark, and thus split NATO's Northern and Central Regions, and secure control of the Danish Straits. With Denmark under their control, the Soviets would then be able to conduct offensive air operations well into NATO's vital logistical rear areas in the Netherlands and Belgium, and the United Kingdom would become more vulnerable to attack. Nevertheless, the difficult Norwegian terrain, NATO Baltic naval forces, and the Soviets' relatively limited amphibious capability would make a Warsaw Pact seizure of the north cape and the Baltic Straits a difficult operation.

The Soviets also would undertake operations to roll back the significant NATO air-breathing and naval threats to its forces. The Soviets have greatly improved the Kola Peninsula air defenses in recent years with modern interceptors such as the MiG-31 Foxhound and the Su-27 Flanker supported by Mainstay AWACS aircraft. They intend to protect their Northern Fleet SSBN forces by using long-range Soviet naval aviation aircraft to attack NATO antisubmarine warfare and surface strike groups. Fighter-bombers will attack NATO airbases in northern Norway, while Soviet Northern Fleet nuclear attack submarines would engage NATO submarines and surface combatants in the Barents and Norwegian Seas as part of the battle for control of the air and sea around Norway. Should the Soviets establish control, they could then attempt to control the North Atlantic.

Southern Region

The Southern Region has several potential subtheaters: the Mediterranean Sea; Turkey, the Turkish Straits and Thrace; and the Balkans and northern Italy. Soviet long-range aviation will probably initially attack NATO nuclear forces and sea power in the eastern Mediterranean. Warsaw Pact success in this theater will depend on long-range power projection through the air and via amphibious operations. Unlike the Central Region, NATO countries in the Southern Region depend almost totally on their own resources for defense. The most significant link between these countries is a maritime one. The key to the balance of power in the region lies in controlling the Mediterranean, the Black Sea, and the connecting Bosporus/Dardanelles-Aegean passage. For NATO the Mediterranean is the key reinforcement route, while for the Pact the Black Sea guards access to the Soviet Union, provides the vital sea lines of communication to Bulgaria, and supports the movement of Soviet land forces into Greece and Turkey.

While NATO enjoys a manpower advantage over the Pact in the region, the Pact forces have qualitatively superior equipment and hold an advantage in the number of combat divisions, tanks, antitank missiles, surface-to-air missiles, and surface-to-surface missiles. Ten Greek and Turkish divisions deployed in Thrace around the Bosporus/Dardanelles passage represent the highest concentration of land forces in NATO's forward defenses. However, the slow pace of modernization and the lack of such key weapons as antitank systems will limit these forces' effectiveness. In addition, these forces could be augmented by one or more US Army divisions and a Marine Air-Ground Task Force (MAGTF). While it is true that both NATO and NSWP countries in

The MiG-31 Foxhound, a fourth-generation Soviet fighter interceptor with a look-down/shoot-down capability, has significantly increased the quality of Soviet air defense forces.

the region have been relatively slow to modernize their forces, the Soviets have improved considerably the quality of their forces in the area.

NATO has a significant advantage in naval forces forward deployed in the Mediterranean. In fact, the most significant improvements within the Southern Region have been at sea. The US 6th Fleet currently deploys one or two aircraft carriers and nine to ten other supporting surface combatants, four submarines, four or five amphibious ships, and a variety of other supporting ships. The French Mediterranean Squadron and the Italian Navy also now operate jointly to maximize their combat effectiveness. Spain and Italy are modernizing their forces with the acquisition of vertical take-off and landing (VTOL)-equipped antisubmarine aircraft carriers, while the United States and nations in western Europe are providing the Greek and Turkish navies surface warfare ships. The Soviets have, on average, 31–42 ships in their Mediterranean Flotilla. Due to reinforcement problems during wartime, the flotilla would probably withdraw to help defend the Black Sea.

The Pact has more in-place air forces in the region than NATO. Deployment of long-range, sophisticated strike aircraft, such as the Su-24 Fencer, can threaten key NATO targets including C³ facilities and nuclear forces. Soviet Backfire bombers, based in the Crimea and armed with long-range cruise missiles, also threaten NATO land and naval forces. The Soviets reportedly deployed modern MiG-29 Fulcrum fighters to their forces in Czechoslovakia, while both Bulgaria and Hungary now have squadrons of Frogfoot direct air support aircraft as well as the latest variants of the MiG-23 Flogger.

NATO, however, also is upgrading its air forces in the region. Turkey and Greece are in the process of replacing older fighters, including the F-104, with modern F-16s (Greece is also buying the Mirage 2000) which will improve significantly NATO's ability to counter the Soviet air threat. The Italian Air Force is modernizing its older F-104s and adding Tornados and the AMX to its strike/attack force. In the western Mediterranean, Spain and Portugal are deploying the F-18 and the F-16, respectively. NATO will further bolster its in-place air forces by deploying approximately 17 US fighter squadrons (available for deployment to Turkey, Italy, and Greece), and possibly the aviation combat element of a MAGTF, and carrier-based naval aviation. Unfortunately, problems may exist in NATO air defense coordination between Greece, Turkey, NATO naval forces, and deploying US squadrons. Greek forces, for example, do not routinely participate in air defense exercises or operational planning with other NATO air defense elements in the region.

Operational Concepts

Today both NATO and the Warsaw Pact declare themselves to be defensive alliances whose main purpose is to deter aggression. For the last 40 years, however, each has followed a different approach to achieve this purpose.

Warsaw Pact

The Pact subscribes to concepts of offensive warfare that have shaped Soviet warfighting since Tsarist times. The doctrine of "defense through offense" began appearing in Soviet military writings in the 1930s and stressed the idea that effective defense meant conducting operations on the territory of the aggressor. This notion, which appeared in the 1936 Field Manual for the Soviet Army, stated that the destruction of enemy forces must take place on enemy territory, not Soviet territory. These doctrinal imperatives were reinforced by historical experience in World War II, when the Germans destroyed much of the Soviet Union in the wake of their 1941 invasion. Soviet military writings following the war held that this must never happen again.

The Soviets have created a force structure that reflects the Pact's operational concepts of defense through offense. Pact ground forces outnumber NATO forces in tanks, artillery, and infantry fighting vehicles (IFVs)

SOVIET FORCE DATA

In March 1988, NATO's Heads of State and Government stated, "The Soviet Union's military presence in Europe, at a level far in excess of its needs for self-defense, directly challenges our security as well as our hopes for change in the political situation in Europe. Thus the conventional imbalance in Europe remains at the core of Europe's security concerns." These concerns were documented in *Conventional Forces in Europe: The Facts,* NATO's force comparisons published in November 1988, which showed an overwhelming superiority in Warsaw Pact conventional forces. (These data were not intended for use in negotiations, where definitions and counting rules will differ in scope and detail.)

In January 1989, the Soviets printed a lengthy article in *Pravda* providing data on Warsaw Pact and NATO military forces in Europe and adjoining waters. Its purpose was to respond to Western claims of overwhelming Soviet/Warsaw Pact offensive forces in Europe. The article observed that " . . . while the [NATO and Pact] ground forces and air forces are roughly equal the North Atlantic Treaty has a twofold superiority over the Warsaw Pact in naval strength." The article claims that NATO also has superiority in the number of "strike" aircraft, naval aviation, combat helicopters, and antitank missile systems. It goes on to admit Warsaw Pact superiority in tanks, tactical missile launchers, air defense interceptors, infantry combat vehicles, armored personnel carriers, and artillery.

A Comparison of Warsaw Pact and NATO Data on Military Forces in Europe

	Warsaw Pact Count	NATO Count[1]
Tanks		
Warsaw Pact	59,470	51,500
NATO	30,690	16,424
Armored Troop Carriers		
Warsaw Pact	70,330	55,100[2]
NATO	46,900	23,340[2]
Artillery		
Warsaw Pact	71,560	43,400
NATO	57,060	14,458
Combat Aircraft		
Warsaw Pact	7,876	8,250[3]
NATO	7,130	3,977[3]
Helicopters		
Warsaw Pact	2,785	3,700[3]
NATO	5,270	2,419[3]
Ground Forces		
Warsaw Pact	3,573,100	3,090,000
NATO	3,660,200	2,213,593

[1] NATO count includes only equipment in fully or partially manned units. NATO has the following equipment levels in storage: tanks — 5800; ATCs — 5260; artillery — 2870; combat aircraft — 530; and combat helicopters — 180. NATO estimates that Warsaw Pact stored equipment levels are in excess of NATO stored equipment levels in all categories.
[2] Figures were released by NATO in May 1989.
[3] Figures do not include trainer combat aircraft, and are not based on the same definitions used in determining the ceilings on combat aircraft and combat helicopters that NATO proposed in CFE negotiations in July 1989.

There are major differences between the NATO and Soviet figures (which are reprinted in abbreviated form here) in terms of how each side categorizes equipment. This complicates severely any direct comparison between the two sets of figures. In particular, there are discrepancies in the two sides' definitions and counting rules. For example, the Soviet category of "strike" aircraft includes nearly all NATO aircraft but very few Pact aircraft. The Soviets also appear to have applied those rules inconsistently, in some cases counting nearly all possible NATO systems, and omitting many of those in Warsaw Pact inventories. The *Pravda* data also included some naval forces, despite the fact that these are global forces that cannot be ascribed to any particular region.

Nevertheless, the *Pravda* publication of data on Warsaw Pact forces indicated a willingness on Moscow's part to begin resolving inconsistencies in military balance data. Resolving differences in definitions and counting rules will also be a major element in current Conventional Armed Forces in Europe (CFE) negotiations taking place in Vienna among NATO and Warsaw Pact members.

by huge ratios. Over the last decade, Soviet forces in East Germany alone have increased their strength in IFVs and armored personnel carriers by 70 percent, in artillery by over 85 percent, and in attack helicopters by over 200 percent. Such superiority in armor, firepower, and mobility clearly supports an offensive doctrine. Over the past 20 years, Pact air forces have evolved from a force of relatively unsophisticated point-defense interceptors to a balanced force of highly capable air-superiority fighters and ground-attack aircraft. The result is that the offensive potential of Pact air forces today is greatly increased over what it was even 10 years ago.

Today the Soviets and the Warsaw Pact appear to be in the midst of conceptual change, at least at the political level. Pact leaders addressed NATO's fears of a sudden surprise attack through a 1987 declaration that proposed mutual force reductions to levels at which neither side would be capable of a surprise attack. This has now become a major Soviet theme in the current round of arms-reduction talks. In addition, some Soviet statements declare that they now will attempt to defeat NATO on Pact territory and imply that they will not violate the border.

These indicators of change, however, are ambiguous. For example, Soviet Defense Minister Yazov wrote in 1987 that Soviet doctrine must be designed to secure the destruction of the invading forces, but that it was impossible to destroy the aggressor only through effective defense; forces must be capable of decisive offensive

The US Army's Multiple-Launch Rocket System (MLRS) is capable of striking targets beyond cannon range to complement NATO's follow-on forces attack (FOFA) concept.

Missile Production: USSR and NATO[1]

Equipment Type	USSR 1986	USSR 1987	USSR 1988	US 1986	NUSN[2] 1986	US 1987	NUSN 1987	US 1988	NUSN 1988
ICBMs	75	125	150	11	0	26	0	19	0
SLBMs	100	100	100	33	10	5	10	0	10
LRINF	25	75	50	200	5	130	5	0	5
SRBMs	600	500	450	0	0	0	0	0	0
Long-Range SLCMs[3]	200	200	200	200	0	170	0	280	0
Short-Range SLCMs	900	900	900	520	150	200	150	400	150

[1] Revised to reflect current total production information, NATO figures include France and Spain.
[2] Non-US NATO
[3] SLCMs divided at 600 kilometers.

operations. Although the US military and many others also recognize the value of seizing the initiative, only the Soviets have the forces to conduct offensive operations throughout the theater. This, combined with NATO's assumption that the Pact will initiate conflict at a place and time of its choosing, complicates NATO's defense. Despite the ongoing unilateral force reductions, little substantive change has yet occurred in the Pact forces facing NATO. Since the Pact depends on large numbers of tanks, IFVs, and artillery to pierce NATO's defenses and achieve its goal of a rapid victory, significant reductions in these forces could mean that the Pact is seriously moving toward a defensive military posture along NATO lines. Until this occurs, however, the Pact will retain a significant military advantage.

NATO

Since 1967 NATO has responded to the Pact's "offensive defense" doctrine with the strategic doctrine of flexible response and a forward defense posture. By the early 1980s NATO's concepts for warfighting began to shift from linear to maneuver defense. Linear defense was to hold as much territory as possible through set-piece battles in which NATO forces would attrit the Pact's tanks and artillery in large numbers by concentrated firepower. In addition, NATO sought to exploit the advantage of being the defender by capitalizing on heavy firepower from defensive strong points. Thus NATO optimized its force structure to defend across the breadth of the battle area. However, since NATO reserves were few, there was little operational flexibility.

NATO's approach began to change in 1982 when the US Army promulgated a new doctrine, AirLand Battle, based on the concept of maneuvering and fighting deep in the enemy's rear area, as well as along forward lines

of defense. While NATO has not formally adopted the AirLand Battle doctrine, it has incorporated many of its ideas into its warfighting concepts. As a result, NATO now plans to maneuver and counterattack vulnerable Pact forces as well as operate from fixed defenses. NATO ground forces have fielded tanks and fighting vehicles capable of high speeds for rapid maneuver, while the air forces have deployed more multi-role aircraft capable of carrying a variety of highly specialized munitions. Unlike the Pact, however, NATO does not have sufficient forces to execute this strategy theater wide.

New concepts that exploit the West's advanced technologies have also begun to appear. The prime example is the follow-on forces attack (FOFA) concept first espoused in 1984. Under this concept, NATO's forces

NATO's Airborne Early Warning Force E-3A AWACS aircraft provide Alliance commanders with the data necessary to conduct a successful defense of Western Europe's airspace.

THE IMPACT OF GORBACHEV'S ANNOUNCED REDUCTIONS

On 7 December 1988 General Secretary Gorbachev addressed the United Nations and announced his intention to reduce unilaterally Soviet forces by a significant margin before the end of 1990. Following Gorbachev's lead, many NSWP states also announced force reductions.

If these cuts do take place as scheduled, the short-warning threat to NATO could be significantly reduced. Furthermore, these cuts would represent an encouraging first step in moderating the Pact military threat to NATO. It is important to note that these unilateral reductions in manpower are 20 percent more ambitious than any previously proposed in negotiations on conventional forces. For example, the announced size of the Soviet tank withdrawals is greater than the US Army's entire active duty tank assets stationed in Europe, and will return the Pact to roughly the level of active tank forces it fielded in the late 1960s. These reductions are unquestionably important not only in political terms, but in military terms as well. It is important to note, however, that unless the Pact destroys the tanks it withdraws, it could mobilize and redeploy them to Eastern Europe in a crisis.

NATO should exercise great caution regarding any unilateral reductions that are not bound by mutual treaty constraints. Thirty years ago, Khrushchev made significant unilateral cuts that were even more drastic than those announced by Gorbachev. He reduced the size of the Soviet armed forces by over one million men, which accounted for over 36 divisions. In addition, he withdrew 14 divisions from NSWP countries. Even a reduction of this magnitude, however, left his successor, Leonid Brezhnev, with a force of over 3.3 million men under arms and an army consisting of over 140 divisions and 35,000 tanks. In the ensuing decades following the unilateral cuts, the Soviets quietly rebuilt their forces. Consequently, by December 1988 Gorbachev commanded a force comprising over 5.5

Warsaw Pact Announced Cuts In Eastern Europe

WESTERN GROUP OF FORCES (WGF)[1]	EAST GERMANY
4 Tank Divisions	6 Tank Regiments
3,300 Tanks (est)	600 Tanks
1 Air Assault Brigade	50 Aircraft
5 Tank Training Regiments	10,000 Troops
8 Independent Battalions	

SOUTHERN GROUP OF FORCES (SGF)	HUNGARY
1 Tank Division	251 Tanks
1 Tank Training Regiment	9,300 Troops
1 Air Assault Battalion	9 Aircraft
1 Chemical Defense Battalion	430 Artillery Pieces
1 MiG-29 Regiment	30 APCs
450 Tanks	
10,500 Troops	

NORTHERN GROUP OF FORCES (NGF)	POLAND
1 Tank Training Regiment	2 Tank Divisions
1 SAM Regiment	2 Tank Regiments
1 Independent Assault Brigade	1 Battlefield Tactical Missile Brigade
	1 Training Regiment
	80 Aircraft

CENTRAL GROUP OF FORCES (CGF)	CZECHOSLOVAKIA
1 Tank Division	3 Divisions
2 Independent Battalions	850 Tanks
1 Combat Engineer Regiment	12,000 Troops
1 Landing Assault Battalion	51 Aircraft
	165 Armored Vehicles

BULGARIA	
200 Tanks	20 Aircraft
10,000 Troops	200 Artillery Pieces

[1] Formerly Group of Soviet Forces Germany (GSFG).

million men organized into 214 divisions with some 53,000 tanks.

Gorbachev's announced reductions, while substantial, will not establish a balance of forces in Europe. For example, the Pact will retain a 2.5:1 advantage in tanks over NATO, and a 2.8:1 advantage in the number of divisions. Even when considering the larger size and greater firepower of most NATO divisions, the Pact advantage in number of divisions exceeds 2 to 1. Furthermore, although Moscow has announced that it will move to exact a 19.5 percent reduction in its output of military equipment and weapons, production of tanks, ships, and combat aircraft continues at previous rates. As an example, at current rates of production, the Soviets can build 7,000 modern tanks, 4,000 artillery pieces, and 1,400 fighters and fighter bombers in 24 months. The fact that Moscow announced unilateral cuts resulting in a reduction in current force structure does not prevent Soviet leaders from reversing the trend at a later date. While the United States is optimistic that Gorbachev's announced cuts will occur, it prefers to engage in mutual reductions announced by President Bush as part of a conventional arms limitation agreement. Indeed, the President's proposed cuts, if adopted, would involve significantly greater reductions than unilateral Pact reductions.

would shift their focus from attacking fixed targets in the enemy's rear, such as bridges and buildings, to striking echeloned mobile formations on the move. To accomplish this, NATO would use airborne platforms to look deep into the Pact's rear areas and to identify and target vulnerable enemy forces located on predictable routes of advance. These attacks would require sophisticated, tactical surface-to-surface and air-to-surface missiles, and advanced tactical aircraft and weapons. Furthermore, NATO corps and army group plans now include counterattacks to exploit opportunities created by successful FOFA campaigns. While Soviet analysts describe these plans as offensive, NATO has designed them to respond to a large-scale Pact attack, not as part of an offensive designed to initiate conflict.

Deterrence

The effectiveness of NATO's deterrence strategy must be evaluated on the basis of Soviet perceptions of NATO's capabilities and intent. The Pact appears to base its assessments on the perception of NATO as an unpredictable, technologically sophisticated alliance that is encouraged by the United States to adopt more threatening postures. Still, Soviet near-term assessments of the military balance tend to reflect confidence that if the conflict can be held to the conventional level, they will likely prevail. Soviet assessments, however, also reflect little confidence that they can keep such a conflict conventional. The prime element of uncertainty for the Soviets (and, therefore, of deterrence for NATO) is the escalatory linkage between conventional and nuclear weapons inherent in flexible response.

Soviet assessments of future trends in the conventional balance are somewhat pessimistic. They are concerned about NATO's development of extremely sophisticated warfighting systems such as the family of FOFA weapon systems designed for "deep attack." These developments and other NATO modernization trends appear to have convinced the Soviets that any nonnuclear war in Europe will be more prolonged and far more destructive than previously envisioned. Soviet writings indicate that the optimism of the 1970s is waning and that the future is fraught with formidable uncertainties. Nevertheless, munitions procurement shortfalls (particularly for smart weapons) stemming from lower defense budgets could dilute the deterrent value of these new systems to NATO. Thus it is likely that the modern systems that concern the Soviets will be only partially deployed throughout NATO.

Soviet assessments of the nuclear balance indicate they have a healthy respect for NATO's nuclear capability, especially the Alliance's nuclear-capable aircraft. Despite significant conventional and theater-nuclear force advantages, it is unlikely that the Soviets feel any significant degree of confidence that they can achieve their politico-military objectives while keeping a conflict from escalating out of control. They remain concerned about any further modernization of NATO's land, air, and sea-launched theater-nuclear systems, and the combined strategic assets (now being modernized) of the United States, Britain, and France. The Soviets hope that NATO will not modernize its theater-nuclear forces, thereby weakening the links between the defense of Europe and the strategic nuclear forces of the United States, and allowing the USSR to prevail in a conflict with their numerically superior conventional and theater-nuclear forces. The Soviets also hope to reduce (possibly through negotiation) the increasingly formidable independent French and British nuclear forces.

Ally cohesion will remain a factor in calculating the credibility of both sides' warfighting capabilities. Both Moscow and Washington must be concerned that the other will attempt to undermine their warfighting coalition both during a crisis leading to conflict and during the conflict itself. There also is concern that Gorbachev's promises of reduced forces and a new Soviet defensive posture will tempt political elements in some Alliance countries to encourage their governments to forego the modernization and force improvements needed for NATO to deter war.

The Soviet leadership, however, also is concerned that reforms stemming from General Secretary Gorbachev's policy of *perestroika* may have the effect of encouraging demands from its allies for greater independence from Moscow's dictates. The loyalty of Warsaw Pact countries has yet to be tested in an atmosphere of relaxed political controls. Furthermore, the political effects of greater autonomy threaten to erode the Soviets' traditional ability to make the Pact's important political and military decisions, thereby increasing the uncertainties in Soviet correlation of forces computations.

In summary, each side's military capabilities are becoming increasingly difficult to assess due to the tremendous uncertainties associated with the deploy-

ment of highly sophisticated weaponry by both sides, the changing perception of the Soviet threat inspired by Gorbachev's initiatives, and the liberalization and economic restructuring programs currently in progress in Eastern Europe and the Soviet Union.

Defense Planning Assessments

When NATO implemented the flexible response strategic doctrine more than two decades ago, it enjoyed unquestioned theater-nuclear superiority in both quality and quantity of weapons. Since then the Soviets have achieved superiority in the quantity, flexibility, and survivability of theater-nuclear forces. This imbalance concerns NATO since it has traditionally viewed nuclear weapons (in the face of Soviet conventional superiority) as vital for deterrence.

Furthermore, the Soviets and their Pact allies are better equipped, structured, manned, and trained than NATO to conduct either offensive or defensive chemical operations. The Soviet Union has fielded the world's largest and most capable inventory of chemical weapons. In addition, the Soviet Union is known to possess the means to field biological weapons. This

TASS/SOVFOTO

The USSR and its Warsaw Pact allies possess the world's most formidable chemical warfare arsenal, which is enhanced by their ability to protect themselves in a contaminated environment using specially trained and equipped decontamination units.

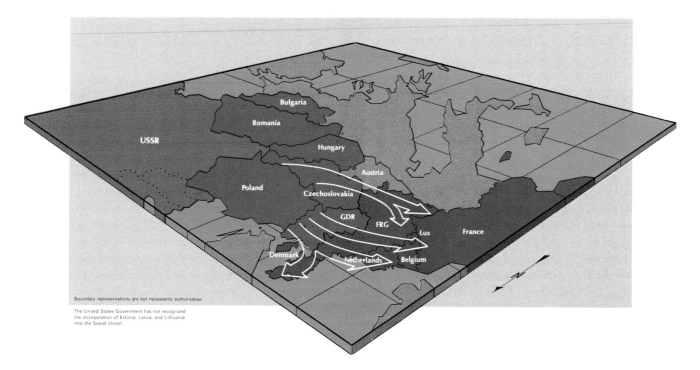

Boundary representations are not necessarily authoritative.

The United States Government has not recognized the incorporation of Estonia, Latvia, and Lithuania into the Soviet Union.

significant asymmetry raises uncertainties about the deterrent effect and operational effectiveness of NATO's chemical weapons. Given the present Pact perception that NATO is fielding systems designed to stalemate a conventional conflict with high-tech weaponry, the Pact may consider that it would be to its advantage to employ chemical-biological weapons against NATO forces. The Alliance has a limited ability to respond in kind to a chemical attack, and not all NATO nations have a credible defense for their forces against such an attack. The United States' ability to retaliate is significantly less than that of the Soviets. This asymmetry may force NATO to consider the use of nuclear weapons to counter the effects of a Pact chemical attack.

Despite their recent emphasis on defensive operations, largely stemming from significant advances in NATO's ability to strike deep into their rear areas with improved air forces, the Pact still pursues an offensive strategy for theater operations. They are still expected to attack perceived NATO weak spots with high-quality armored formations (called operational maneuver groups, or OMGs) whose objective will be to by-pass strong points, get into NATO's rear, and link up with other advancing Pact forces to encircle NATO forces. (Although the Soviets have mentioned OMGs as part of their current unilateral cuts, it must be noted that an OMG is a task force organized during wartime and is not a standing military unit.) Simultaneously, we can expect the Soviets to use their

offensive air forces along with Spetsnaz commandos, attack helicopters, artillery, and long-range missiles and rockets in an attempt to eliminate NATO's air forces and theater-nuclear capability.

Planning Scenarios

Analysts use numerous scenarios to evaluate a potential NATO/Warsaw Pact conflict. NATO planning assumes that the Pact will initiate aggression. Great uncertainty exists, however, over how much warning time NATO will have to mobilize for its defense. The Pact could minimize the preparation time available to NATO by attacking with only forward-based forces and minimal preparations. On the other hand, the Pact could fully mobilize and reinforce its forces, giving NATO more time for its own mobilization and reinforcement and to prepare its defenses.

The short-warning scenario is very worrisome because an adequate response depends on a prompt decision by NATO's political authorities to mobilize and reinforce. The Pact can mount a significant attack even with limited preparations, and initial reinforcements from the United States must arrive before the war starts to provide operational reserves to block breakthroughs.

Fortunately, the short-warning scenario also entails great risks for the Pact. With limited preparations, a much smaller number of divisions would be available and follow-on echelons would have had little time to prepare. These lesser forces would still have to deny NATO air superiority to allow successive Pact echelons to move forward. Additionally, they would have to disrupt NATO's command, control, and communications to slow NATO's response. They would try to degrade NATO nuclear forces and the independent nuclear forces of France and the United Kingdom to complicate NATO's moving to deliberate escalation. To the extent the Pact failed to accomplish these missions, NATO would be able to move forces forward to meet the enemy and, if successful in slowing the attack, to counterattack or, if necessary, move to deliberate escalation through the use of NATO's theater nuclear forces. In summary, the outcome for the Pact would be highly uncertain.

The extended mobilization scenario would allow the Pact to bring the full weight of its forces to bear on NATO. We can expect it to operate under a diplomatic and propaganda blitz, attempting to divide NATO and exploit genuine desires for peace and stability while they prepare for war. To defeat such an effort, NATO would have to recognize — and act upon — early warning indicators of Pact mobilization. This implies mobilizing reserves and lift assets (particularly sealift), moving forces forward, and preparing defensive positions. Forces from the continental United States, Canada, and Great Britain would need to move quickly to the Continent. If the Pact did attack, and the weight of its conventional superiority was insurmountable, the Alliance might have no other choice but to escalate, in a matter of weeks or even days, to a nuclear response.

NATO Central Region Army Groups' Operational Depth

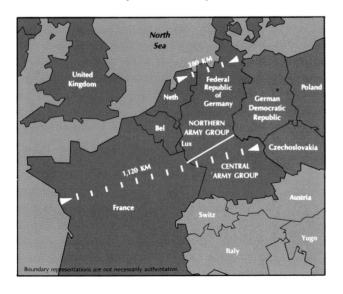

Boundary representations are not necessarily authoritative.

Rapid deployment of forces is a problem for both sides. In any scenario, NATO would be unable to deploy rapidly sufficient forces from overseas due to shortfalls in airlift and equipment prepositioning. This would place NATO at a serious disadvantage and force it to place greater emphasis on theater-nuclear forces. The Pact, however, also would have deployment problems, particularly in a short-warning scenario. Only the portion of Pact forces comprising the first operational echelon are in high-readiness formations. Eighty-five percent of the Soviet maneuver divisions in the Western Group of Forces fall into this category, as well as over 30 NSWP divisions. Most of the remaining Soviet divisions are in less ready or cadre formation status. While these divisions have most of their equipment on hand, it would take them from three days to several weeks to achieve full mobilization status. Furthermore, as second echelon forces move forward, they would be under intense attack from NATO air (and in the future, missile) systems as the FOFA doctrine was implemented.

An even more serious consideration, given its importance to the Soviets' military planning and command structure, is the questionable solidarity and cohesion of the NSWP countries in the event of war. Any long mobilization period may lead to the disaffection of some or all of these countries due to their concern over the political and economic effects of a war they may not want, but in which Moscow orders them to fight. Any such disruptions within the Pact would have extremely serious consequences for the Soviet war effort. Defection or slow action by a NSWP military force would hinder the Soviets and buy time for NATO to deploy and reinforce.

Defense Implications for NATO

The greatest military danger to NATO is the massing of forward-deployed Soviet tanks and tank divisions in East Germany opposite NATO's Northern Army Group (NORTHAG), where limited in-place forces, lack of operational depth, and relatively flat terrain make defense difficult. The 11 high-quality Soviet tank divisions (part of a total of 19 Soviet divisions in East Germany) remain a threat to NATO's rear.

The cuts promised by Gorbachev, especially from the Western Group of Forces (WGF), would significantly affect the Pact's capability to execute a successful short-warning attack. Of the six tank divisions Gorbachev has promised to withdraw, four are to come from the WGF's 3rd Shock Army or the 20th Guards Army — both high-quality, tank-heavy organizations especially geared for high-speed armored offensive operations.

Other reductions are to come from restructuring the remaining forces so that tank numbers are reduced in all units. Beyond this, NSWP countries have announced their own unilateral reductions. These reductions, however, will not erase the Pact's overall military superiority in the region.

Further south, NATO is in much better shape with its Central Army Group (CENTAG), where high-readiness US and West German divisions have greater operational depth and better defensive terrain than NORTHAG. Opposite CENTAG, Gorbachev is proposing to cut approximately 1,500 tanks stationed in Czechoslovakia and Hungary. Together with the cuts in East Germany, this will amount to a reduction of 5,300 Soviet tanks, approximately 50 percent of the estimated Soviet tank strength in Eastern Europe. Reductions of this magnitude of active Soviet tank strength in Central Europe, especially from areas of NATO's greatest concern, should greatly reduce the probability of a short-warning attack, especially if the Soviets also remove these forces' substantial reserve stockpiles of ammunition and fuel. The potential, however, for large-scale Pact offensive operations will remain, as it will still enjoy a significant edge in conventional forces over NATO.

Naval Force Capabilities

NATO's naval forces have an advantage over those of the Warsaw Pact. In the Northern Region NATO's navies will assist in countering Pact actions in northern Norway and the Baltic approaches. In Norway carrier-based aircraft and USMC land-based aircraft will defend NATO forces in the region, interdict Pact forces en route to attack, and provide offensive air support at and near the point of attack. In the Southern Region, NATO's navies will be the key to defeating the SOVMEDFLOT in the Mediterranean, and will assist other NATO forces in countering Pact attacks on the Turkish Straits. In the Central Region NATO's navies will support AFCENT with carrier-based aircraft, particularly if the Pact decides not to attack NATO simultaneously on all fronts.

NATO's Supreme Allied Commander, Atlantic (SACLANT) also is charged with protecting the sea lines of communication which will provide the flow of heavy reinforcement forces and supplies to sustain NATO's defense against a Warsaw Pact attack. NATO currently has the advantage, but Soviet attack submarine forces and long-range Soviet naval aviation could attempt to deny NATO freedom of the seas. These Soviet forces will also probably contest control of the Norwegian Sea. If the Warsaw Pact chooses not to attack the Northern and Southern regions in conjunction with an attack in the Central Region, SACLANT's naval forces can be used in AFCENT to increase the air power available for NATO's defense.

Major Weapon Systems Production for NATO and Warsaw Pact 1979–1988[1]

	US	NUSN[2]	NATO : PACT Ratio	NSWP[3]	USSR
Tanks	7,400	3,600	1 : 2.85	5,400	26,000
Other Armored Vehicles[4]	8,900	10,200	1 : 2.88	5,100	50,000
Artillery, Mortars, and MRLs (> 100-mm)	3,600	2,600	1 : 4.08	6,300	19,000
Long- and Intermediate-Range Bombers	103	0	1 : 3.88	0	400
Fighter/Attack Aircraft	3,600	2,300	1 : 1.20	900	6,200
Military Helicopters	2,200	1,700	1 : 1.28	800	4,200
Major Surface Warships (> 900 tons)	81	94	1 : 0.61	23	84
Submarines[5]	40	29	1 : 1.14	4	75
ICBMs and SLBMs	600	85	1 : 3.94	0	2,700
IRBMs and MRBMs	20	45	1 : 14.2	0	925
Surface-to-Air Missiles[6]	19,700	39,000	1 : 2.07	9,700	112,000

[1] That portion of military production for own armed forces to include imports, but excluding exports.
[2] Non-US NATO; includes France and Spain.
[3] Non-Soviet Warsaw Pact
[4] Excludes combat service support vehicles.
[5] Includes SSBNs, attack, and coastal submarines.
[6] Includes naval SAMs, excludes man-portable SAMs.

Long-Term Trends

Air Forces

Soviet air doctrine and exercises indicate that they plan to use the Pact's combined air forces against NATO's air defense forces, vital C³ links, and theater-nuclear forces at the outset of a conflict. Warsaw Pact objectives would be to provide freedom of action for its air and ground forces while restricting NATO's flexible response options — particularly the ability to escalate the conflict using theater-nuclear weapons. The Pact also hopes to limit NATO's ability to employ its tactical air forces to support ground force commanders facing numerically superior Pact ground forces at or near the point of attack.

In response, NATO air forces must survive Pact offensive air operations and then destroy or seriously damage sufficient Pact aircraft to establish air control over the battlefield. Once this occurs, the Pact would be limited in its ability to conduct reconnaissance or air support operations, airborne insertions of Spetsnaz troops, or airborne air defense activities. This would expose the Pact ground offensive to attack from NATO's combined air forces.

The Warsaw Pact has far more combat aircraft in Europe than does NATO. The Soviets, moreover, have made significant qualitative upgrades, as reflected in ground-attack-dedicated aircraft and variants such as the Fencer, Frogfoot, and Flogger. In many cases, these aircraft have doubled and even tripled the range and payload capability of comparable earlier-generation Soviet aircraft. Soviet deployment continues with even more advanced Soviet fighter/interceptors such as the Foxhound, Fulcrum, and Flanker. These aircraft represent new or upgraded designs with significantly improved airframes and avionics. The Soviets continue deploying the Mainstay AWACS and Midas air-refueling aircraft, although in significantly fewer numbers than their NATO counterparts. Trends for the non-Soviet Warsaw Pact countries, however, are much less impressive. These air forces contain mostly older-generation Soviet fighters that are inferior to both Soviet and NATO aircraft. Warsaw Pact writings indicate that the NSWP countries will employ their aircraft primarily for homeland defense and air support.

NATO air forces also are in the midst of a major equipment upgrade. The United States Air Forces in Europe have retired most of their older F-4 Phantoms and replaced them with newer, more capable F-15 Eagle and F-16 Fighting Falcon fighters. Similarly, the West German Air Force has replaced its F-104 fighter-bombers with the Tornado, and the Italians are in the process of doing the same. The Belgians, Danes, Norwegians, and the Dutch have nearly completed their upgrade to the F-16 as their primary aircraft, while the Canadians and Spanish are upgrading to the F-18. Furthermore, the British have replaced most of their older Jaguar GR-1s and Buccaneers with interdiction/strike Tornados. In addition, they have completed replacement of their Lightnings and are in the process

The MiG-29 Fulcrum, which incorporates sophisticated aerodynamic design concepts, entered serial production in the mid-1980s. The Fulcrum reflects the Soviet Union's determination to produce aircraft that are qualitatively equivalent to their NATO counterparts.

The F-15 Eagle is the United States Air Force's front-line air superiority fighter. This F-15C, shown carrying a full complement of AIM-9 Sparrow and AIM-7 Sidewinder air-to-air missiles while flying an alert mission over Northern Holland, is a symbol of the United States' commitment to the defense of Western Europe.

Production of Aircraft: Warsaw Pact and NATO[1]

Equipment Type	USSR	NSWP[2]	USSR	NSWP	USSR	NSWP	US	NUSN[3]	US	NUSN	US	NUSN
	1986		1987		1988		1986		1987		1988	
Bombers	50	0	45	0	45	0	26	0	52	0	22	0
Fighters/Fighter-Bombers	650	10	700	15	700	10	375	250	525	200	550	200
Fixed-Wing Antisubmarine Warfare	5	0	5	0	5	0	5	0	10	0	5	0
Helicopters	500	150	450	150	400	125	350	200	375	200	375	200
AWACS	5	0	5	0	5	0	10	0	10	0	5	0

[1] Revised to reflect current total production information, NATO figures include France and Spain.
[2] Non-Soviet Warsaw Pact
[3] Non-US NATO

of replacing most of their Phantom interceptors with the Tornado air-defense variant. Improved Harriers are supplanting older versions for ground support operations.

NATO also has considerably improved its support infrastructure. For example, while serious problems remain with providing support for aircraft deploying to Europe from the United States, NATO has made dramatic progress with the colocated operating bases (COBs) from which these aircraft must operate. However, initiatives must continue to correct lack of adequate facilities for US Air Force fighter squadrons at the COBs. The ability of NATO's main operating bases (MOBs) to operate in combat also has been improved by building more aircraft shelters, hardening critical facilities, and employing camouflage and other passive defensive measures. In active defense, the introduction of the Patriot surface-to-air (SAM) missile with US, West German, and Dutch forces significantly improves NATO's ability to counter Soviet air operations. From an assessment perspective, however, Soviet air defense fighter modernization and the density of Warsaw Pact SAMs and air defense artillery gives the Warsaw Pact a more robust, integrated air defense system.

In summary, the Warsaw Pact retains a large numerical superiority in combat aircraft in Europe, while NATO leads in numbers of modern aircraft and in the quality of its upgrades. Pact qualitative improvements are limited primarily to the Soviets, and contrast with NATO improvements, which are occurring across the board. The quality of NSWP fighter/interceptor and bomber aircraft in terms of range, payload, missile systems, and avionics is much lower on average than NATO aircraft. Both the Pact and NATO have about equal numbers of ground attack aircraft. The Pact, however, is decidedly superior in the total number of airframes dedicated to air defense and in bombers available for theater use.

Ground Forces

The problems facing NATO forces in Europe are the result of a steady Pact modernization effort over the last decade which has increased the Pact's superiority, especially in armor, antiarmor, and artillery systems. In the past, NATO depended upon the greater qualitative advantages of its ground forces to compensate for its numerical inferiority. During the last decade, however, Pact qualitative improvements have eroded much of NATO's advantage.

These modern Soviet main battle tanks deployed in Eastern Europe are equipped with reactive armor, which substantially reduces the effectiveness of NATO antitank missiles. Roughly 3,000 modern Soviet tanks are fitted with reactive armor mounting apparatuses.

The number of Warsaw Pact divisions equipped with the Soviet BMP-2 infantry fighting vehicle is steadily increasing. Unlike its Western counterparts, the BMP-2 can be made amphibious quickly, greatly enhancing the Warsaw Pact's ground forces' capability to negotiate water barriers.

The US Army's M1A1 main battle tank, along with the Challenger and Leopard II MBTs, constitute the cutting edge of NATO's armored forces. The ability of these forces to blunt the Warsaw Pact's first-echelon tank assault will be crucial to any successful defense of Western Europe.

The US Army Bradley Infantry Fighting Vehicle System, shown here firing a TOW 2 antitank missile, has improved significantly NATO's capability to defeat advanced enemy armor.

The Soviets are fielding newer tanks such as the T-64B, T-72M1, and the T-80 while retiring older model T-54/55 and T-62 tanks. The most serious threat to NATO ground forces, however, is the Pact response to the NATO antitank missile (ATM) capability. Over the last 15 years Soviet improvements to their latest model tanks have seriously diminished the threat from early model NATO ATMs. Recently the Soviets have fitted reactive armor in the form of applique boxes to the front and sides of most of their tanks facing NATO. The combination of reactive armor and previous armor improvements may negate much of NATO's modern antiarmor forces armed with present-generation ATMs. Furthermore, these improvements to the older-model tanks — such as T-54/55s and T-62s — fielded by the NSWP countries can significantly upgrade their combat potential against NATO armor and antiarmor teams.

Like the Soviets, NATO has been fielding modern main battle tanks (MBTs), but in much smaller numbers. The United States has made substantial progress in replacing many of its older M-60s with M1 and M1A1 MBTs. Likewise, the Germans and Dutch fielded the Leopard II, and the British are fielding the Challenger. However, the trends in armor improvements over the last decade decidedly favor the Soviets.

The Soviets have improved their infantry fighting vehicle (IFV) forces as well. These vehicles are extremely versatile and offer the Soviets and their allies the mobility and fire support needed to protect their modern

Production of Ground Forces Materiel: Warsaw Pact and NATO[1]

Equipment Type	USSR	NSWP[2]	USSR	NSWP	USSR	NSWP	US	NUSN[3]	US	NUSN	US	NUSN
	1986		1987		1988		1986		1987		1988	
Tanks	3,300	700	3,500	750	3,500	700	750	400	950	150	775	150
Other Armored Fighting Vehicles	4,200	1,250	4,450	1,075	5,250	600	1,050	1,360	800	1,300	1,000	950
Towed Field Artillery	1,100	75	900	75	1,100	50	200	50	25	50	50	25
Self-Propelled Field Artillery	900	600	900	600	900	650	75	50	200	50	175	25
MRLs	500	100	450	100	500	50	60	5	48	5	48	5
Self-Propelled Antiaircraft Artillery	100	50	100	75	100	75	0	0	0	0	0	120
Towed Antiaircraft Artillery	0	200	0	100	0	75	0	75	0	0	0	50

[1] Revised to reflect current total production information, NATO figures include France and Spain.
[2] Non-Soviet Warsaw Pact
[3] Non-US NATO

armor formations. They are fielding larger numbers of the BMP-2, one of the world's finest IFVs. They also have made significant improvements to their more numerous stocks of older BMP-1s. While the Soviets and all Pact allies have large stocks of these IFVs, in NATO only the United States, Germany, and France possess IFVs in large quantities. Thus the Soviets and their Pact allies are not only out-producing NATO, they currently field over 17,000 more IFVs than NATO.

The Pact also has upgraded its artillery forces considerably over the last decade. In the early 1970s it fielded World War II vintage towed artillery in most of its combat divisions. However, it now has significant numbers of self-propelled systems such as the 2S1 and 2S3 that have superior rates of fire and longer ranges than NATO artillery. The ability of this self-propelled artillery to keep up with high-speed armor offensives in Soviet-style combined-arms operations has greatly increased the combined-arms combat potential of Pact forces facing NATO. Indeed, the qualitative edge in artillery that NATO once enjoyed no longer exists.

Until the Soviets field new Havoc and Hokum attack helicopters (estimated to be operational within the near future), NATO will have a qualitative advantage in attack helicopters. The fielding of the United States' new AH-64 Apache attack helicopter significantly improves the range, payload, and firepower of the NATO attack helicopter fleet. In addition to modernization efforts, the US Army is modifying its aviation force structure to form combat aviation brigades that will provide a highly flexible aviation attack force for the operational and tactical level commander. Other allied attack helicopter

forces supplement this significant NATO capability. Within the last five years, however, the Pact has increased its helicopter fleet and established numerical equality with NATO. Current Pact attack helicopters are the multi-role Hip and Hind. They provide both troop/cargo carriage and fire support in the Soviet combined-arms operation.

Naval Forces

Trends for the last five years have favored NATO's naval forces. The Pact navies have been growing smaller,

Operating in NATO's Northern and Southern regions, carrier-based aircraft like the US Navy F/A-18 shown here will help defend NATO forces through interdiction and close air support operations.

as fewer but more capable ships replace older models. NATO naval forces, however, have maintained their size. They also have been upgraded significantly in antisubmarine warfare, antisurface warfare, and air defense capability. The German Navy has replaced its F-104s with the Tornado, significantly upgrading NATO's defense of the Baltic approaches from Warsaw Pact attack. US Navy and Marine aircraft upgrades include the F/A-18, F-14D, and AV-8B, providing SACLANT more offensive and defensive capability in the Norwegian and Mediterranean Seas to defend NATO forces or project power ashore. NATO navies also have engaged in integrated training exercises to improve their ability to conduct combined operations. The trend for the next five years will likely see NATO maintain its quantitative and qualitative edge in naval forces. The Pact's only edge will be in attack submarines and long-range naval aviation forces.

Conclusion

Today the Soviets and their allies have a significant numerical advantage in both conventional forces and theater-nuclear forces over the NATO Alliance. In addition, fielding of modern equipment like the T-80 MBT with reactive armor, and the MiG-29 Fulcrum and Su-27 Flanker fighters narrows the qualitative lead NATO enjoys. NATO's advantages include technological and qualitative leads in equipment and training, and superior air and naval forces. NATO's capability to execute its strategic doctrine of flexible response remains the vital ingredient of deterrence. The peace Europe has enjoyed for over forty years is largely because NATO's triad of forces — conventional, non-strategic nuclear, and strategic nuclear — has deterred aggression. Should deterrence fail, however, given the current asymmetries favoring the Pact in conventional, chemical, and theater-nuclear forces, there is a danger that NATO will be unable to terminate a conflict on terms favorable to the Alliance solely with conventional weapons. Nevertheless, the Soviets and their Pact allies realize that should they attack NATO, they have no guarantee of success due to the tremendous uncertainties inherent in such a decision. Indeed, Pact writings indicate that they believe the long-term trends favor NATO due to what they see as its ability to field increasingly sophisticated high-technology weaponry. Finally, current arms control efforts designed to decrease conventional forces asymmetries favoring the Pact, if successful, may increase stability in Europe.

THE EAST ASIA/PACIFIC MILITARY BALANCE

The East Asia/Pacific military balance has two components. The first concerns the military balance as it pertains to superpower competition and a potential global war involving the United States and the Soviet Union, their respective allies, and nonaligned nations in the region. The second component concerns regional sub-balances, to include the Sino-Soviet, the Korean Peninsula, and the Southeast Asian balances. These sub-balances are important because regional military powers help provide stability for growth and prosperity in the region, and because of their potential influence on both regional and global geopolitics.

Strategic Objectives

The first component, the military balance of the United States and the Soviet Union, must be assessed in relation to the opposing sides' strategic objectives and their capability to achieve those objectives in wartime. This assessment takes into account trends in military force developments, existing force structure, and projections of near-term force levels and equipment upgrades.

The underlying United States strategic objective in the East Asia/Pacific theater is to deter war. The United States' strategic strike capability, Pacific Command (PACOM) forces, bilateral defense treaties with regional nations, forward deployment and basing, and the application of weapons technology all contribute to deterrence. PACOM forces deter aggression both in the theater and on a global scale. If deterrence fails, these forces are prepared to achieve the US wartime strategic objectives of providing for forward defense of the United States, protecting US allies and US interests throughout the Pacific basin, protecting sea lines of communication (SLOCs), countering Soviet strike capabilities, and placing at risk Soviet Far East military forces.

Soviet military plans in this theater call for a defensive force posture designed to defend the Soviet Union against an attack in the East. Such a force posture would allow the Soviets to concentrate forces in other regions for offensive operations. Although defense is foremost in Soviet military planning in the Pacific region, offensive elements are present in each of the strategic military objectives supporting this primary objective. Secondary strategic military objectives, although far ranging due to the scope and geopolitical complexity of the Far East and Pacific Ocean TVDs, include: protecting Soviet strategic strike capabilities (specifically their ballistic missile submarine force), conducting strategic and theater-nuclear strikes when ordered, keeping the People's Republic of China out of any war, and neutralizing Japan and South Korea by military or political means to prevent them from supporting the United States. These Soviet strategic military objectives, as is true of US objectives, shape the Soviet military force structure in the Pacific theater.

Uniqueness of the East Asia/Pacific Assessment

Certain geopolitical and military characteristics of the East Asia/Pacific region make assessing the military balance there different from the balance assessment in Europe. Unlike Europe, there is no cohesive superpower-led alliance system in the Pacific region similar to NATO. There are instead a variety of bilateral and regional ties, some involving the United States and some the Soviet Union. The region's immense geographic size contrasts sharply with the geography of the Atlantic and Europe. This also is true from the Soviet perspective when one considers the isolation of the Soviet Far East from the main industrial centers in central and European Russia. These distances affect both sides' ability to deploy and employ men and equipment, provide reinforcements, and conduct resupply operations.

The Global War Perspective

The major threat to the United States and its allies in the region is Soviet naval and air power. The United States does not possess, nor does its national military strategy demand, predominance in ground forces in the region, and this will remain the case.

The improved weapon systems the Soviets are introducing into the Far East theater are narrowing many military advantages long enjoyed by the United States and its allies. Thus, although the impact of the announced Soviet cutback in the Far East is unknown, we do not expect Gorbachev's announced force cuts to alter significantly the military balance in the region.

Soviet General Secretary Gorbachev's announced reductions in Soviet forces reportedly allocate 200,000 of the 500,000 troop cuts to Moscow's forces in the Far East. Gorbachev stated in Beijing that 50,000 troops — including three divisions of ground forces and all aviation units in Mongolia — will return to the USSR. Additional Soviet force reductions in the Far East will likely come primarily from ground forces along the Sino-Soviet border, rather than from air defense forces. There are currently some 600,000 troops in the Far East TVD ground and air forces comprising 59 divisions and nearly 1,700 aircraft.

Recent reports also suggest that the Soviet Pacific Ocean Fleet (POF) will incur manpower and ship reductions. The Soviets apparently will scrap some POF units as part of a navy-wide program to eliminate inactive and reserve ships from the Soviet fleets, thereby reducing manning requirements and operating costs. The POF is currently the largest of the four Soviet fleets with 260 ships and submarines, and 480 aircraft. Although impressive in numbers, the POF has numerous aging submarines and destroyers, most of which are of little utility in modern warfare. The POF is, however, acquiring more modern and sophisticated surface warships, submarines, and aircraft at a pace comparable to the Northern Fleet. Consequently, the POF's overall combat effectiveness is not expected to diminish significantly with the retirement of older and less capable ships. Indeed, the Fleet's combat potential may actually increase with the addition of fewer, but more capable ships into service.

In a global war, specific Soviet objectives in the Pacific would likely include the following:

- Controlling the ocean areas contiguous to the Soviet Union, including the Sea of Japan and Sea of Okhotsk;
- Preventing strikes by US naval forces against the Soviet Union by seeking out and destroying those forces at sea;
- Maintaining the ability to conduct nuclear strikes against the United States, its forces, or regional targets;
- Containing China and keeping it out of the conflict;
- Controlling key straits in the region;
- Isolating the United States from its allies, either diplomatically or militarily;
- Neutralizing either diplomatically or through military means, US bases throughout the Pacific region and Alaska; and
- Attacking allied sea lines of communication (SLOCs) throughout the region.

Comparison of European and Pacific Theaters of Operation

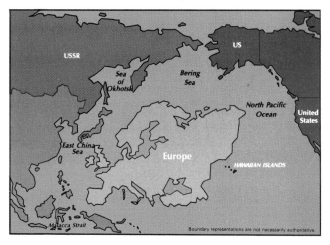

These missions highlight the strategic importance of the Soviet and Japanese islands that guard the entrances to the Sea of Japan and the Sea of Okhotsk. These islands and straits form a natural barrier for the defense of the Soviet Union and the protection of its SSBNs within "bastions" close to the USSR. It is therefore not surprising that Japan and the key straits formed by the Japanese islands fall within the Soviet "sea control"

zone — an area which the Soviets would attempt to dominate militarily during wartime. This represents the Soviets' highest priority regional objective.

Control of the key straits and adjacent bodies of water in the region is vital to Soviet war plans in the Pacific theater. Aside from defensive concerns, such control provides the Soviets access to the open waters

Soviet Perspective of Northwest Pacific and Deployment Routes

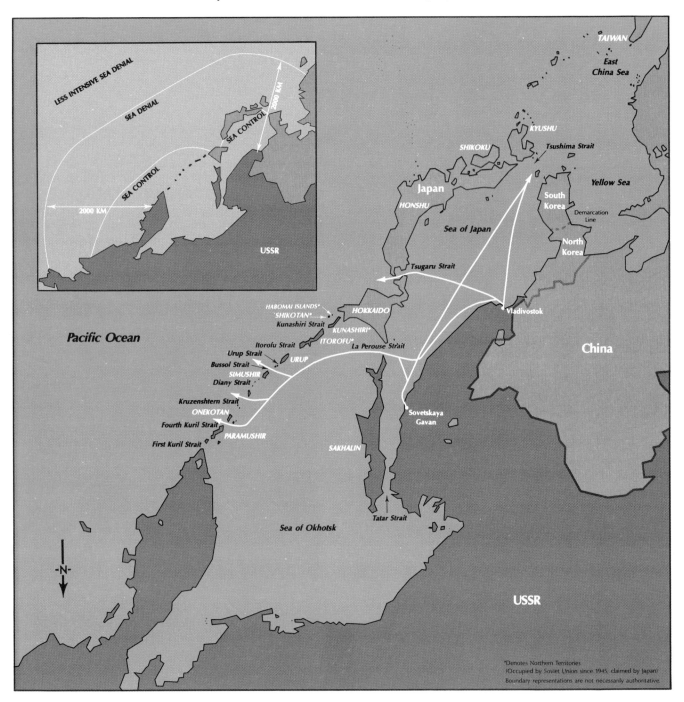

114

of the Pacific, where their forces can position themselves for attacks against US and allied naval forces far from Soviet territory. Control also facilitates the movement of Soviet naval forces between the Sea of Okhotsk and Sea of Japan, and resupply of the isolated Kamchatka Peninsula. The allies also hope to control the straits in order to defend Japan, block Soviet access to the Pacific, and facilitate attacks on Soviet naval forces in the Sea of Japan and the Sea of Okhotsk.

Control of the straits will be hotly contested by both sides. The Soviets occupy or could provide a credible naval (surface and submarine) and air defense of the Kurile Islands, the Japanese Northern Territories, and the Pacific Ocean bordering the Asian rim. The newer and more capable antiair warfare (AAW) surface ships

Soviet Operations in the Sea of Japan

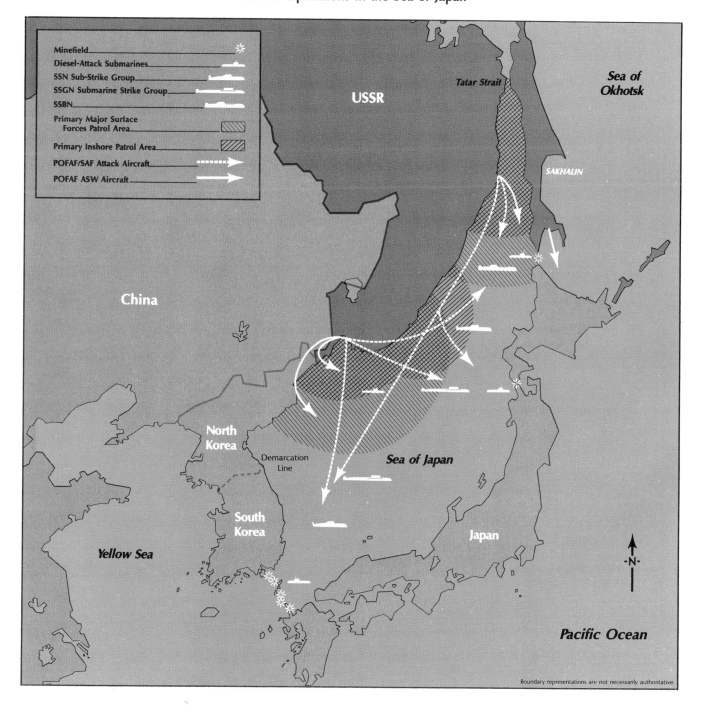

and naval aircraft entering the POF will allow the Soviets to extend their air defense umbrella over this "sea control" zone. The escorting of Soviet bombers by long-range fighter aircraft also represents a new threat to allied naval operations in the northwest Pacific. This practice will make it more difficult for the allies to secure air superiority over the area, and may require US carriers to move forward early in the war to integrate

fully US and allied sea- and land-based air power in confronting massed Soviet air power.

Allied control of the straits is important to block Soviet surface ships and submarines from deploying to their defense and attack positions along the Kuriles, Japan's Northern Territories, and in the Pacific Ocean. Since Soviet deployment prior to hostilities would cir-

Soviet Operations in the Sea of Okhotsk/Northwest Pacific

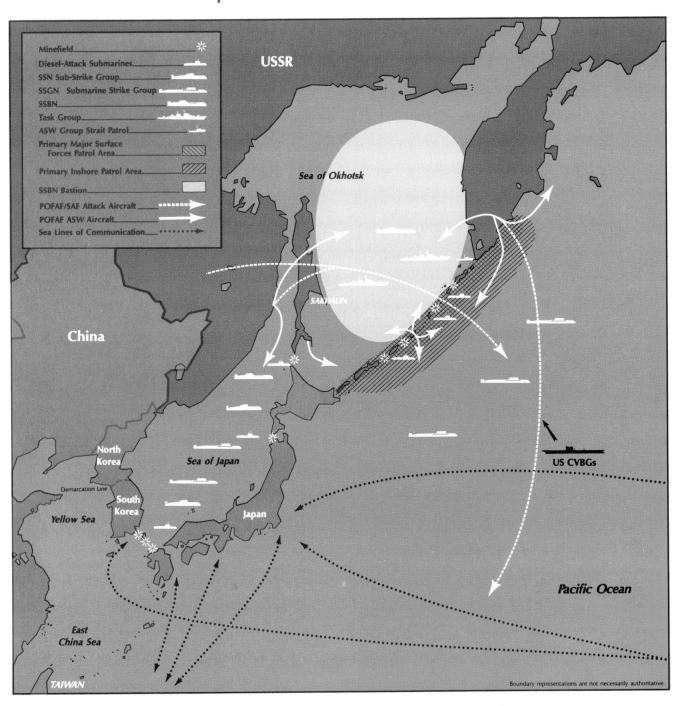

cumvent this blocking action, it then becomes important for the allies to block the reentry of Soviet ships to their ports for repair and resupply. Since the United States and its allies are capable of effecting high attrition on Soviet surface ships and submarines exiting or entering confined waters, Soviet submarines and strike bombers (some with fighter escort) will attack US and allied naval and air forces that could prevent the Soviets from transiting the strategic straits. The attacks would be conducted against any US or allied forces located within strike range as well as such forces in the Pacific at the extreme ranges of the Soviet defense line (out to about 2,000 kilometers). In particular, the Soviets hope to destroy the US carrier battle groups (CVBGs) before they get within strike range of the Soviet Union and before they can contribute to the air battle over the Kuriles and northern Japan.

Both the Soviets and the United States are constrained in their ability to conduct amphibious operations to seize and control areas near the key straits. On the other hand, both sides will use mine warfare extensively in attempting to control these straits.

Soviet submarines will play a key role in defending the "bastions," and in attacking US CVBGs and cruise-missile-capable ships. The Soviets are continuing to improve the size and quality of the POF submarine force, most notably with the addition of Delta-class ballistic missile submarines (SSBNs), Akula-class nuclear attack submarines (SSNs), and modern diesel submarines (SSs) of the Kilo class. United States superiority in ASW will continue, although it will be eroded somewhat by Soviet improvements in submarine quieting and weapons capabilities. The US lead will be derived primarily from technological advantages in submarine quieting, acoustic detection capability, and superior ASW training.

United States fleet air defense capabilities, designed to combat the Soviet bomber and cruise-missile force, remain formidable. These AAW defenses center on Aegis-class antiair warfare cruisers, E-2C airborne early warning and control aircraft, F-14 aircraft with improved Phoenix missiles, F/A-18 fighter/attack aircraft, and shipboard missile and gun defenses.

To penetrate this layered fleet air defense and attack the US CVBGs in the Pacific at ranges deemed necessary to protect the Soviet homeland, the Soviets plan to conduct mass coordinated attacks with long-range, land-based, air-to-surface missile-capable bombers and submarine-launched cruise missiles (SLCMs). Meanwhile, long-range fighters will protect the homeland from attack. Modern Su-27 Flanker and MiG-31 Fox-hound fighters deployed in the Far East have significantly enhanced Soviet regional air defense capabilities.

Although the United States and allied submarine, surface, amphibious, mine warfare, and ASW capabilities constitute a formidable threat, the great number of cruise missiles that the Soviets will launch from air and undersea platforms will pose a grave test of US defense capabilities. This requires the United States to emphasize attacking Soviet bombers on the ground early in a conflict, or employing land- and sea-based AAW forces to destroy Soviet bombers before they reach their cruise-missile-launch points (about 200 miles from their targets). Geography and the range limitations of US strike aircraft combine to limit the US capability to conduct deep strikes against some Soviet air bases where the cruise-missile-launch platforms are deployed. This highlights the importance of establishing air superiority over the eastern Sea of Japan, the southern Sea of Okhotsk, Japan's Northern Territories, and the Kurile Islands.

In this type of conflict, where operations will be conducted far from the continental United States, bilateral defense ties, important for the defense of US allies, are also important for the essential infrastructure support they offer US forward-deployed forces. America's friends and allies in the region boast some of the world's strongest and fastest-growing economies, which add to the vitality of defense arrangements. This contrasts to Soviet allies like Vietnam and North Korea, who are facing severe economic problems.

Japan occupies a strategic position in the northern Pacific and has assumed significant self-defense responsibilities for its lines of communication (LOCs) to the south and southwest. Japanese Self-Defense Forces and US aircraft and naval support facilities located in Japan will play crucial roles in defending against the Soviet air and naval threat to Japan and the western Pacific. South Korea and the Philippines, in turn, provide forward staging, repair, and resupply facilities critical to both peacetime and wartime operations, although other facilities also are available. American forces in South Korea will deter attacks from the North and assist in defending South Korea if deterrence fails.

Global Perspective: Summary

The Soviets possess superior ground combat power on the Asian mainland, oriented primarily against China, and are challenging the United States in many areas of air and naval warfare. Nevertheless, US and allied forces in the region will be capable of responding effectively in global and regional conflicts for the foreseeable

Ticonderoga-class guided-missile cruisers, like the *USS Valley Forge* shown here, are bolstering the warfighting capabilities of US naval battle groups, particularly in the area of antiair warfare.

future. Indeed, the United States and its allies hold an edge in the military balance in the East Asia/Pacific region in antisubmarine warfare, antiair warfare, naval long-range strike systems, amphibious warfare, and overall maritime capabilities. The margin of superiority is narrowing, however, as the Soviets deploy larger numbers of newer and more capable systems. Announced Soviet force reductions, although welcome, must not be allowed to cloud the fact that more sophisticated and powerful forces are, in many instances, replacing retired systems.

Sino-Soviet Military Balance

The majority of Soviet ground troops (over 50 of 58 divisions) and tactical aviation in Asia is positioned opposite China. The Soviet strategic objective of encircling China and avoiding a major two-front ground war during a global confrontation requires the stationing of these forces along the Sino-Soviet border. As both sides have come to view a major confrontation as unlikely in the near future, each has recently deemphasized military confrontation in favor of a more balanced policy involving diplomatic and economic initiatives.

The Soviet approach is clearly one of accommodation with the Chinese. It began with the withdrawal of one motorized rifle division and one tank regiment from Mongolia in mid-1987; at the same time, however, the Soviets replaced antiquated equipment in the hands of indigenous forces with newer, more combat-capable hardware, and the enhancement of Soviet ground forces remaining in the region continued apace. Nevertheless, if Moscow carries out its announced reductions, Soviet forces in Asia, which comprise approximately 25 percent of Soviet forces worldwide, will absorb nearly 40 percent of the total manpower cuts. The Soviets probably believe that their mobilization base and the more capable units remaining after reductions can respond effectively to the limited scenarios envisioned in the near future. These force reductions will be watched closely to determine whether there is a significant cut in actual Soviet combat potential relative to China. In any event, the force reductions by Moscow are a welcome movement toward reducing tensions in the region.

The Chinese have over one million troops positioned opposite Soviet forces along their common border and outnumber Soviet forces by a ratio of nearly 3:1. Chinese forces are not positioned for an offensive thrust into Soviet territory, and they do not possess the logistics, mobility, or firepower of Soviet forces. Moreover, the Chinese are seeking to reduce tensions with adversaries in order to reallocate resources devoted to defense for internal modernization. The Chinese look to a period of peace to pursue military reforms aimed at modernizing their armed forces.

North/South Korean Military Balance

The continuing threat posed to South Korea by the North Korean Army (NKA) is significant, and is of particular concern to the United States because of the aggressive and unpredictable nature of the government in Pyongyang. For nearly 40 years the United States' support for the Republic of Korea (ROK) has provided a counter to North Korean ambitions to reunify the peninsula by force of arms.

North Korea continues inexorably to modernize its large military forces through reorganization and the addition of more modern equipment. The current overall balance of military forces on the peninsula continues to favor the North. The recent apparent increase in military cooperation between the Soviet Union and North Korea — including Soviet shipment of modern fighter aircraft and air defense systems — is thus of special concern. Although Pyongyang faces severe economic constraints, it is difficult to forecast the extent to which economic factors will constrain the pace of military modernization. It appears that North Korean forces will likely continue to improve their firepower capabilities, as well as their mobility and logistics support.

The Republic of Korea is also modernizing its forces with the objective of establishing a technological lead over the North in key areas of weaponry, thereby compensating for the North's considerable numerical superiority. The foundation of Seoul's military modernization rests on its dynamic and expanding economy, which is over four times the size of North Korea's and growing over three times as rapidly.

Analysis indicates that US and ROK forces are capable of blunting a North Korean attack and restoring the Republic of Korea's territorial integrity. Superior US and South Korean air power, in conjunction with US Army forces, would play key roles in turning back such an attack.

The outlook for reducing tensions on the peninsula remains uncertain, although recent moves toward harmonizing contacts between the ROK and both the USSR and China, as well as other communist countries, are encouraging. In the long run, the strong economy of the South contrasted to the weak economy of the North, and the trends toward democracy in the South contrasted to totalitarianism and patriarchal succession in the North are encouraging.

Southeast Asia

Vietnam is the centerpiece of the military regional balance in Southeast Asia. Conditions are improving in this region as Hanoi has committed itself to withdrawing its troops from Cambodia by 30 September 1989, although Cambodia could become another potential crisis spot after the Vietnamese pullback. The United States is working with the USSR, PRC, and other parties to resolve the Cambodian issue peacefully, while seeking to ensure that the Khmer Rouge do not return to power. Vietnam, much like its communist ally the Soviet Union, also is beginning to look at restructuring its economy and relying less on military force for regional influence. The Vietnamese are even discussing large cuts in their military forces. However, since Vietnam currently fields the fourth largest army in the world, even major force reductions would not eliminate Hanoi's ability to threaten its neighbors. Major cuts would, however, be a significant step toward reducing tensions and promoting a regional dialogue for the peaceful resolution of disputes.

THE MIDDLE EAST/SOUTHWEST ASIA MILITARY BALANCE

The Middle East/Southwest Asia (ME/SWA) region is bounded in the west by NATO's Southern Region and in the east by Southeast Asia. The Soviets refer to roughly the same region as the Southern Theater of Military Operations (STVD). The US Central Command's area of responsibility is somewhat smaller. The region is a study in extremes. The topography varies from mountains higher than 24,000 feet to desert floors below sea level; temperatures range from more than 130 degrees to below freezing. There are numerous ethnic groups, cultures, and religions which go back over 15 centuries, yet some of the national boundaries have been in place for little more than 15 years. To further complicate matters, there are at least six major languages, and hundreds of minor ones.

Strategic Importance of the Middle East/Southwest Asia

The region is of immense strategic importance to the industrial world, dependent as it is on the area's principal resource, oil. Fifty-five percent of the world's proven oil reserves are located in the Gulf region. As world demand for oil continues to grow and as reserves elsewhere dwindle, Gulf oil will undoubtedly become even more important to the world economy. The region also includes potential choke points along important international waterways, such as the Suez Canal and the Bab el Mandeb Strait, which are located at opposite ends of the Red Sea, and the Strait of Hormuz, located at the mouth of the Persian Gulf. Roughly 10 percent of the world's seaborne commerce passes through the Bab el Mandeb-Suez Canal route. Much of the Persian Gulf's oil currently passes through the Strait of Hormuz. Western dependence on this route, however, is being steadily reduced by an expanding overland oil pipeline system that connects to termini outside the Persian Gulf.

Soviet Regional Objectives and Strategy

Many Soviet interests converge in this region. From a historical perspective, they have long viewed it as a potential threat to Russian security, emanating from British military power in the 19th and early 20th century and, more recently, from the power of Islamic fundamentalism. Moscow also is aware of the importance of oil to Western economies and the strategic benefits that would accrue should they gain control of a significant portion of regional oil reserves. This undoubtedly plays a role in Soviet regional calculations. A historical interest in obtaining access to a warm water port in the Persian Gulf also is mentioned frequently as a regional Soviet objective. However, because of poor rail and road networks, both in Iran and in regions adjacent to the Soviet Union, the economic benefits of a Persian Gulf port would be marginal. While a permanent regional naval base would be of use to the Soviet Union, it would have to transfer much of its Pacific Fleet to the Persian Gulf in order to directly challenge the US naval presence. This would require a long-term commitment to a naval power-projection strategy that is not now evident. It is, therefore, unlikely that this objective has sufficient priority to motivate current policy decisions.

Middle East/Southwest Asia Area of Operation

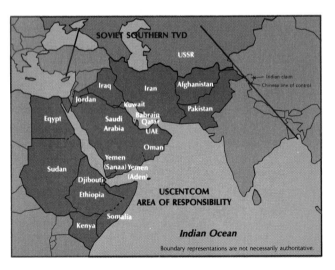

SOVIET SOUTHERN TVD
USSR
Iraq
Iran
Afghanistan
Indian claim
Chinese line of control
Jordan
Kuwait
Pakistan
Egypt
Saudi Arabia
Bahrain
Qatar
UAE
Oman
Yemen (Sanaa)
Yemen (Aden)
Sudan
Djibouti
Ethiopia
Somalia
Kenya
USCENTCOM AREA OF RESPONSIBILITY
Indian Ocean
Boundary representations are not necessarily authoritative.

Soviet regional strategy in the past has focused on undermining the stability of regional states friendly to the United States. This policy has had the effect, at least in North Africa and the Middle East, of linking the Soviet Union to the more radical Arab states (i.e., Libya, Syria, Ethiopia, and South Yemen) and limiting its influence with many moderate states. Although there is some disagreement concerning Soviet motives for the invasion of Afghanistan, clearly their policy was a failure there as well. Until recently their close relations with India represented the major exception to a general lack of success in extending their regional influence with moderate states.

Soviet regional strategy also has focused on building influence through the sale of military arms and equipment. Recent deliveries of MiG-29 Fulcrums to Syria and Su-24 Fencers to Libya, and possible future arms sales to Iran indicate that such sales will remain an important element of regional policies. Nevertheless, over the past year there have been several indications that the Soviets are attempting to reorient significantly their regional policies. They now appear to be engaged in a concerted effort to improve diplomatic ties with moderate regional states. Moscow argues that its withdrawal from Afghanistan provides proof of its new moderation.

US Regional Objectives

United States interest in the region is a relatively recent phenomenon. Up until World War II, Britain and France were the predominant powers in the region. Much of France's influence ended following World War II with the termination of direct ties with Syria and Lebanon. When the British withdrew from the Persian Gulf in 1971, the United States filled the resultant vacuum. Today, a major US goal is to ensure Western access to regional oil supplies. The potential Soviet threat to free access is a primary influence on US regional policies. The United States also has a considerable interest in promoting the security and stability of regional states, to include a strong and independent Israel.

Soviet Forces

The Soviet invasion of Afghanistan in 1979 marked a dramatic shift in Moscow's military focus on Southwest Asia. The Soviet withdrawal marks an equally dramatic reversal. Nevertheless, at least 25 active ground divisions and one airborne division will remain stationed in the Soviet Union's North Caucasus, Transcaucasus, and Turkestan Military Districts (MDs). Eighteen fighter and fighter-bomber regiments, with over 700 tactical

aircraft, are available to support ground operations. It is not yet clear what will happen to the three motorized rifle divisions and one airborne division that left Afghanistan, although Gorbachev has publicly claimed that there will be reductions in the military forces of the "southern region."

The Soviets first deployed their naval forces to the Mediterranean on a continuous basis in 1964. During regional conflicts, particularly the Arab-Israeli wars, the Soviets have always reinforced their Mediterranean Flotilla, but it has not played a combat role. For example, during the 1973 Arab-Israeli War the squadron expanded to some 100 ships, almost one-third more than the number of US 6th Fleet ships in the area at the time. During the Israeli invasion of Lebanon in 1982, however, the flotilla was augmented with only a handful of combatants. Today the average Mediterranean Flotilla strength is 31–42 ships and comprises cruisers, destroyers, frigates, auxiliaries, and submarines. Additionally, Soviet Naval Aviation aircraft make periodic deployments to Syria and Libya. Although the Soviets have limited access to naval facilities in Syria, Libya, Tunisia, Algeria, and Yugoslavia, they have relied primarily on open-ocean anchorages in shallow international waters since their loss of access to Egyptian bases in 1976. These anchorages include sites northwest of Egypt, off Cape Andreas in northeast Cyprus, and west of Crete. Additionally, the flotilla has been making increased use of port facilities in Tartus, Syria.

Soviet Indian Ocean Squadron forces average 14–18 ships and include the same types of ships found in the Mediterranean Flotilla, as well as minesweepers and an amphibious ship. Soviet access to facilities in this region includes anchorages off the island of Socotra, the use of port facilities in South Yemen, and a small facility on the Dahlak Archipelago of Ethiopia. The squadron suffers from the same shortfalls endemic to other Soviet naval forces deployed to distant areas: a lack of adequate air defense, limited logistic support, and a poor antisubmarine warfare capability.

US Forces

The US military presence in the region comprises the 6th Fleet in the Mediterranean Sea, naval units in the Indian Ocean and Persian Gulf, and US Central Command (CENTCOM) forces. United States 6th Fleet units in the Mediterranean comprise one or two aircraft carriers, with roughly 100 aircraft per carrier; supporting cruisers, destroyers, and frigates; amphibious ships; supply, fuel, and service ships; and nuclear submarines. The fleet also includes a 2,000-man Marine Expeditionary Unit (Special Operations Capable). CENTCOM forces on station in the Middle East/Southwest Asia region routinely include a command ship and four combatants. The United States substantially expanded this force in 1987 with the deployment of the Joint Task Force Middle East (JTFME). As the situation in the Gulf stabilizes, this force is being gradually reduced. Total forces available to CENTCOM on a priority basis include five Army divisions and two separate brigades; one Marine Expeditionary Force (comprising a division and an air wing); 21 Air Force tactical fighter squadrons; strategic power-projection forces, including B-52 bombers; three carrier battle groups; one battleship surface action group; and five maritime patrol aircraft squadrons. The availability of these units, however, depends upon the absence of competing crises, since most of these forces have dual or even triple regional planning commitments. CENTCOM's force posture is enhanced by regular bilateral exercises in the region that include the exercise and evaluation of capabilities to deploy military forces from the United States.

Soviet Invasion of Iran Contingency

Given the current Soviet focus on internal economic and political reform, a Soviet invasion of Iran is, at present, difficult to imagine. Even if Gorbachev were to be replaced, there would be significant pressures to continue many of his economic reform initiatives. Nevertheless, a return to a much more conservative, and possibly militarily aggressive Soviet Union remains a concern. Should such a change take place, particularly if it should coincide with a period of significant internal instability in Iran, the threat of a Soviet use of military force could not be ruled out.

Notwithstanding the discussion above, the Soviets would encounter numerous obstacles in an invasion of Iran. For example, north-south lines of communication cross extremely difficult terrain that restricts movement largely to major arteries and makes it extremely vulnerable to interdiction from both air and/or special operations forces. Soviet operations would be further hampered by a shortage of easily accessible water and by temperature extremes. In addition to these obstacles, the Soviets' bitter experience in Afghanistan provides a compelling reason for Moscow to weigh carefully any decision to invade Iran, which has twice the area, three times the population, and equally difficult terrain. Another disincentive would be the damage that would occur to Soviet political objectives in Western Europe, Japan, and the Middle East region. In the highly unlikely event a Soviet invasion does occur, however, Iran would require substantial outside support to resist successfully a major Soviet operation.

Regional Intervention

Although both superpowers are cautious about situations which might lead to a direct US-Soviet confrontation, local interests have led both sides to intervene directly in the region. Intervention has ranged from providing equipment and supplies, to the direct employment of military force. For example, major Soviet resupply operations occurred during the Arab-Israeli wars of 1967 and 1973. In addition, the Soviets conducted significant airlift operations in 1967–68 in support of a republican faction in North Yemen, and in 1977–78 in support of Ethiopia in its clash with Somalia. The Soviets also conducted a substantial airlift resupply of Syria in 1982–83, following Syrian military losses in their clash with Israeli forces in Lebanon. Soviet air defense forces fought in combat with Egyptian forces against Israeli forces in 1969–70. However, proxies like Cuba have conducted most of the ground fighting in the region. Cuban forces played a critical role in the Ethiopia-Somali war in the Ogaden in 1977–78.

The United States, on the other hand, conducted a major resupply of Israel in 1973, and deployed combat forces to Lebanon in 1956, 1968, and 1983 (in the latter case as part of a multinational peacekeeping force). In addition to several direct clashes with Libyan military forces, the United States also deployed major naval forces to the Persian Gulf in 1987-88 to protect freedom of navigation.

In unopposed operations, both superpowers have adequate airlift and sealift capabilities to support a high level of resupply to friendly states in both the Middle East and Asia. In a time of crisis short of general war, the United States could easily marshal sufficient naval forces to operate freely throughout the region, to include providing military escort for resupply operations. In contrast, Soviet options, particularly in the Mediterranean, are more constrained. If contested, Moscow would be unable to maintain either air or sea lines of communication into the region. For example, massive air strikes on regional airfields and ports could totally disrupt a Soviet airlift or sealift operation to resupply Syria.

Sending a Soviet airborne division to the Middle East would take several days, assuming that flights could proceed undisturbed and that airports of debarkation were serviceable. This would be an effective military option if the objective was to provide support to a friendly regime in the suppression of internal opposition. In a major Arab-Israeli war, however, the deployment of an airborne division would have a marginal impact on the outcome, except to the extent that its presence deterred the Israelis from pursuing objectives that would inevitably involve them in combat with Soviet forces. Should deterrence fail, the Soviets would be forced to decide between accepting a damaging loss of prestige or a major escalation of the conflict. Yet even a major Soviet conventional escalation would not assure success. It would take at least two weeks or more to deploy a motorized rifle or tank division from the Black Sea region to the Middle East or North Africa, assuming no interdiction occurred. The Soviets would require several more days to deploy this force to its combat location. If history is any guide, the war might well be over by this time. Even if it were not, a single tank division is insufficient to exert a compelling influence on armies as large as those found in the Middle East. A significantly larger force would take much longer to deploy and would represent a totally unprecedented Soviet effort. In addition, it is questionable whether Moscow could adequately supply such a large force, particularly if a maintenance and supply infrastructure did not exist.

In contrast, American forces are capable of intervening to strengthen the position of a friendly regime against internal challenges (e.g., mass riots or civil war), or against pressure and subversion by a neighboring state. Rapidly deployable US forces supported by carrier air forces would probably have the advantage if faced by Soviet forces not operating in areas directly contiguous to Soviet borders. However, the United States would also find it very difficult to employ significant ground forces to oppose directly a major regional power.

The Threat to Israel

Over the past 40 years Israel has defeated the forces of Egypt, Jordan, and Syria, as well as token forces from other Arab states. Unless Egypt were to reoccupy the Sinai with significant ground forces, even it would not constitute an immediate military threat to Israeli security. The requirement for Egypt to first move large forces across the Sinai would make its participation in a coordinated Arab attack impossible. Iraq also is unlikely to pose a near-term threat to Israel. Although the near collapse of the Iranian military makes a full-scale resumption of the Iran-Iraq War unlikely in the near future, Iraq is likely to remain preoccupied with Iran for some time to come. In addition, the strong personal animosity between Presidents Hussein and Assad makes military cooperation between Iraq and Syria against Israel unlikely until at least one of these men departs from the scene. Although Syria continues purchasing massive quantities of military equipment, her goal of strategic parity with Israel appears little closer to realization. A major Syrian attack on Israel with limited

political goals is always a possibility, but Israel retains a strong deterrent to such an attack.

Although Israel retains strategic superiority over any likely combination of Arab adversaries, it faces numerous problems that may eventually undermine its stability. The most contentious of these is the Palestinian question. Full resolution of the problems associated with the uprising in the West Bank and Gaza Strip may not bring peace to the Middle East. Still, failure to accommodate Palestinian aspirations in some manner will likely undermine long-range Israeli, and US, regional objectives.

Iran-Iraq Conflict

The Iran-Iraq War proved a disaster for both sides and posed special problems for both the United States and the Soviet Union. Despite an overwhelming advantage in trained military manpower, tanks, artillery, and aircraft, the Iraqi invasion of Iran in September 1980 failed. After nearly eight years of bloody struggle, during which time Iran gained but then lost the strategic initiative, Iranian resolve began to dissipate. Tehran's resistance crumbled in the face of Iraqi offensives, which included the apparently effective use of chemical weapons. Low civilian morale, increasing opposition to the war, and intense competition for control among leadership factions undoubtedly contributed to Iran's willingness to stop fighting. Given the limited capability of either superpower to influence Iranian behavior, and the visceral opposition of Islamic fundamentalists to US and Soviet regional influence, neither US nor Soviet regional goals would have been well-served by an Iranian victory in its war with Iraq.

Both superpowers recognize the potential long-range significance of Iran's geostrategic position, large population, and significant oil reserves. While Moscow is restrained by commitments to Iraq, which the Soviets are not ready to abandon, by the gulf between Muslim fundamentalism and communist atheism, and by a desire to improve relations with other moderate Arab states, it has moved ahead on improving ties to Iran. Washington is restrained by the current Iranian leadership's intense anti-Americanism, in addition to its anti-Western, xenophobic fundamentalism.

The Subcontinent

Following its rift with China in the early 1960s, the Soviet Union sought to promote a special relationship with India in order to expand its own regional influence and limit that of China, and to a lesser extent, the United States. The Soviets played a major role in

These Iraqi-modified Scud B ballistic missiles offer tangible evidence of the diffusion of sophisticated weaponry and weapons technology to Third World nations.

Furthermore, by the late 1990s India may have medium- and even intercontinental-range ballistic missiles with nuclear warheads.

Although India will play an increasingly assertive role throughout the Indian Ocean region, economic factors, dominated by India's lack of competitiveness with the West and Japan, will tend to constrain the scope of Indian influence in Southeast Asia in the near term. Friendship with Vietnam will also limit India's appeal to ASEAN countries. Militarily, India is unlikely to risk a serious confrontation with the Chinese. Beyond the next decade, however, as India develops its economic and military potential, it is likely that New Delhi will become an even more influential regional player. There is nothing to indicate that India will make serious efforts to exercise its military power outside the Indian Ocean, even in areas with large overseas Indian communities. Troubled relations with her neighbors, especially Pakistan, will tend to preoccupy Indian attention, as will domestic sectarian strife in the Punjab and elsewhere.

Future Trends

The Middle East and Southwest Asia region is steadily becoming a more lethal operational environment. Over the last 10-15 years, countries in the area have amassed advanced, highly destructive military capabilities. Along with an increase in the numbers of weapons deployed, we also are seeing the spread of high-technology weapons as well. The Saudi acquisition of the Chinese CSS-2 MRBM is only the most recent and highly visible example of regional missile proliferation. Furthermore, widespread Iraqi use of chemical weapons and the Iranian retaliation in kind may have lowered the threshold for chemical weapons use throughout the region. Since nuclear weapons represent the ultimate threat, Israel, India, Pakistan, and other regional states are working hard to develop them. In light of the intricate and unstable nature of local political relationships, nuclear proliferation increases the odds of a miscalculation that could produce a disaster not limited to the region.

CENTRAL AMERICA

Soviet Regional Objectives and Strategy

Political and economic problems in Central America threaten American interests in the region. The Soviets desire to undermine US influence in the region, promote Marxist-Leninist regimes, and expand their political and economic ties. Two Soviet clients, Cuba and Nicaragua, support Soviet objectives and provide them access to the area.

mediating an end to the 1965 Indo-Pakistan conflict, and provided strong diplomatic support to India in its 1971 war with Pakistan. In 1971 the Indians signed a friendship treaty with Moscow, probably motivated, in part, by concern over improving Chinese nuclear and nuclear-delivery capabilities. Over the past eight years, India has expanded its ties with the West and appears to be interested in a more balanced relationship with the superpowers. In opposition to this trend, Moscow continues to cultivate close ties with New Delhi.

India sees itself as an emerging great power and is determined to achieve a dominant position in South Asia commensurate with its overwhelming preponderance in population, resources, and economic strength. Over the next ten years, we expect Indian power-projection capabilities to improve substantially in the areas of maritime strike, amphibious assault, carrier air, heavy airlift, and naval and forward air base construction.

To accomplish their objectives, the Soviets have pursued a multifaceted policy. They support communist and socialist political and military factions in the region by providing military and economic assistance, including $5 billion a year in aid to Cuba and over $800 million annually to Nicaragua. Soviet and East bloc ships deliver military equipment to Cuba and Nicaragua, some of which is rerouted to Soviet-backed insurgencies, including Farabundo Marti National Liberation Front (FMLN) forces in El Salvador. The Soviets also are aggressively seeking new clients for military arms sales to gain greater regional access, influence, and hard currency. Finally, Moscow also seeks, through political and propaganda means, to identify the United States as the source of regional problems.

Capabilities

Although the Soviets' capability to give away modern military equipment is diminishing due to economic problems at home, they will, for the foreseeable future, continue providing Cuba with extensive military support, as Gorbachev promised during his April 1989 visit to Havana. Economic support also will continue, although such assistance will probably decrease as Soviet domestic economic demands place increasing restraints on Moscow's ability to support overseas clients. (Cuba itself has come under growing Soviet criticism for failure to reform and make more efficient use of Soviet aid.) Total Soviet bloc military deliveries to Nicaragua will probably not diminish through 1990, although no major force improvement to the Sandinista military is expected before 1991. Meanwhile, most Soviet-backed insurgencies will continue receiving Cuban and Soviet-bloc support for their campaigns against the elected governments of the region.

Soviet Regional Clients: Objectives and Strategies

Cuban and Nicaraguan support for Soviet regional objectives is a means to an end. Castro continues

These weapons were among the more than 300 AK-47 rifles and other Soviet-bloc arms, such as RPG-7 and RPG-18 rocket-propelled grenade launchers, uncovered by the Salvadoran Government on 30 May 1989. This insurgent weapons cache — the largest yet discovered by government forces — underscores the continuing commitment of Cuba and Nicaragua to support the marxist guerrilla forces in El Salvador.

to assist the Soviets because of the economic lifeline they provide and because it coincides with his goal to establish Cuba as the primary military and political power in Latin America. He seeks to establish himself as the leader of a new Latin American socialist order and hopes to gain recognition as an alternative to American power and influence in the region. To achieve this goal, Cuba continues to channel arms and limited funds to Nicaragua and other Marxist-Leninist movements in the region. Indeed, Castro has shunned Soviet-style political changes, and insists on employing more traditional communist methods. He has developed a close relationship with the Sandinista regime in Nicaragua and increased his influence with the military in Panama after Washington opposed the continuation of military control over the elected Panamanian government.

In Nicaragua, the Sandinistas are attempting to consolidate a Marxist-Leninist government under their control. They are using their excessively large armed forces to intimidate their neighbors concerning regional and bilateral issues, including the demobilization and resettlement of the Nicaraguan Resistance. The Sandinistas also will likely attempt to spread Marxist-Leninist revolution via political and covert military efforts. The Sandinista regime needs Cuban and Soviet assistance and will support Soviet objectives in exchange for economic and military support. During the first eight months of 1988, the Soviets provided Nicaragua with over twice the amount of economic and military assistance provided by the United States (the former greatly exceeding the latter) to all of Central America.

Nicaraguan Military Capabilities

With Cuban and Soviet assistance Nicaragua has become the region's strongest military power, with a military force outnumbering the forces of all other Central American states combined. There are over 80,000 troops in the active duty military force, which comprises 10 regular motorized/mechanized infantry battalions and 12 counterinsurgency infantry battalions, and they are supported by some 240 reserve and militia battalions. The army has 150 tanks, 250 armored vehicles, over 600 pieces of heavy artillery, nearly 400 antitank guns, and hundreds of mortars. The air and air defense forces comprise 3,000 men and they have received over 60 armed-transport Hip and 13 Mi-25 Hind-D attack helicopters. The 3,500-man navy now has 30 patrol boats and minesweepers.

To help the Sandinistas field this impressive force, 1,000-1,500 Cuban military and security advisers, and 200-300 advisers from the Soviet Union, East bloc, and Soviet client states are in Nicaragua. Total Soviet military deliveries to Nicaragua are approaching $3 billion since the shipments began in 1980.

US Interests and Objectives

Latin America is of vital strategic importance to the United States. Critical air and sea lines of communication linking the United States to trading partners worldwide crisscross the region. The United States intends to preserve these lines of communication by ensuring regional stability. To accomplish this, United States regional objectives remain founded on a desire for democracy and freedom, peace, and economic progress. To this end, the United States continues to encourage and assist its allies in the region in defending themselves, particularly against the huge Sandinista military build-up in Nicaragua.

US Strategy

The United States seeks to avoid a major military presence in the region. There is a limited US force in Panama whose purpose has been to defend the US-operated Panama Canal and protect other American interests in the region. US strategy is based on security assistance programs for the region's democracies that link foreign policy and security policy. These programs are designed to deter aggression and subversion, while supporting democracy, stability, and economic growth, and are based almost exclusively on economic assistance.

The United States hopes to isolate the two Soviet clients in the region, Cuba and Nicaragua, until their behavior changes. To this end, it has cut off Cuba both diplomatically (although there is a small "interests section" in Havana) and economically, while also maintaining sufficient US-based forces to counter any regional military actions by the Cubans or the Soviets. Furthermore, the United States imposed economic sanctions on Nicaragua in 1981, and has continued providing humanitarian assistance to the Nicaraguan Resistance while supporting the peace process sponsored by the nations of the region.

In El Salvador, US efforts have centered around providing military and economic assistance to counter Soviet-supported and Cuban/Nicaraguan-sponsored insurgent actions aimed at overthrowing the democratically elected government.

US Capabilities

Regional developments have allowed the United States to shift the emphasis of its policy from military pressure on Nicaragua, via the Nicaraguan Resistance, to diplomatic support of the Central American Peace Accords. In addition, since early 1988 Congress has restricted support for the Nicaraguan Resistance to humanitarian assistance, and congressional limitations on security assistance have limited the effectiveness of US programs designed to promote regional stability. The bipartisan accord between the Bush Administration and the Congress renewed humanitarian assistance to the Nicaraguan Resistance, affirmed the need for democracy in Nicaragua, and asked the Soviet Union and Cuba to stop supporting the Sandinistas. Meanwhile, the Sandinistas are continuing to consolidate their political power in the country, making a future pluralistic and democratic government unlikely.

Other Nations in the Region

The region's four democracies seek self-determination, sovereignty, pluralism, support for democratic institutions, and economic growth and prosperity. The strategy of the democracies, led by Costa Rican President Oscar Arias, has been to negotiate a regional peace plan based on diplomatic initiatives that put pressure on the Sandinistas. The peace plan calls for negotiations between insurgents and governments in Central America, an end to arms shipments to rebel groups and the use of sanctuaries in neighboring countries by these groups, international verification and follow-up, and the implementation of democracy. While the Sandinistas have been willing to agree to the broad terms of the regional agreements, they have been unwilling to take internal actions to comply fully with these terms. The reduced pressure on the Sandinistas, caused by the end of US military support for the Nicaraguan Resistance, has removed the major incentive for them to make genuine democratic reforms. It also remains to be seen if the Soviets will modify their military support for the Sandinistas and remove this obstacle to successful implementation of the peace accords.

Each of Nicaragua's neighbors is threatened by its large armed forces. Costa Rica, Nicaragua's southern neighbor, has no army and relies on an 8,000-man paramilitary Civil Guard and Rural Guard. These forces are, in fact, constabulary units and have no heavy military equipment to oppose the modernized Sandinista Army. Honduras, on the northern border, has an army of 16,000 troops organized into 20 battalions. They have no tanks, but they do have a regionally significant air force with more than 20 F-5, A-37, and Super Mystere jet-fighter and attack aircraft.

The Cubans and Sandinistas have not become di-

rectly involved in military action against Costa Rica and Honduras, but they are supporting military operations against both Guatemala and El Salvador. Guatemala's 36,000-man military is facing a persistent leftist insurgency, and the 44,000-man Salvadoran Armed Forces are fully committed to a war against the FMLN guerrillas.

Anticipated Trends

The growing tend toward stable democracies in Central America and South America (with the notable exceptions of Nicaragua and Panama) both supports US regional goals and provides the Soviets with increased access. Expanded economic and diplomatic activities, as well as increased activities by leftist political parties, have given the Soviets a greater role in the region. For the foreseeable future the United States will continue to restrict its support for the Nicaraguan Resistance to humanitarian aid, while allowing the peace process to produce a resolution to the conflict. The Sandinistas claim they support the peace process, yet they continue to consolidate their control over an increasingly totalitarian state, while actively promoting subversion in other regional states. Soviet and Cuban support of the Sandinistas will continue, along with Soviet-Cuban-Nicaraguan interference in regional affairs. In the near

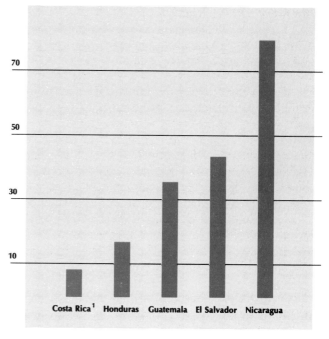

**Central America
Active Duty Armed Forces 1989**

Thousands

Costa Rica[1]   Honduras   Guatemala   El Salvador   Nicaragua

[1] Civil and Rural Guard

term, however, the Soviets will probably downplay their support for leftist political groups in the region's democratic countries while encouraging Cuba and Nicaragua to support them.

Conclusion

From a security perspective, Central American problems do not have the high visibility of a potential European conflict. However, the Soviet-sponsored actions of Cuba and Nicaragua threaten the United States' vital interests. Instability, both economic and political, affects US access to the regions' markets and lines of communication. Militarily, the United States has the capability to take action to resolve problems in the region, but at great cost.

THE MARITIME BALANCE

The maintenance of maritime superiority is essential to the security of the United States and to the preservation of its economic and security ties to nations across two oceans. Worldwide seaborne trade is vital to US economic well-being in peacetime, and the United States, in coordination with its allies, must have the capability to secure critical sea lines of communication (SLOCs) during crises and in wartime.

The Soviet Navy has the potential to threaten US freedom of movement on the seas. Additionally, the proliferation of modern naval weapons systems, and long-range air- and ground-based missile systems, provide many regional powers with the capability to challenge US free movement on and above international seas. To prevail in a global conflict, the United States and its allies must retain a margin of superiority against these global threats.

Although the US Navy alone has fewer ships and submarines than the Soviet Navy, there are many other measures of the maritime balance that, taken together, provide a clearer picture of true maritime power. We must view each side's objectives and missions in relation to their respective capabilities to execute those missions successfully and accomplish their objectives when challenged by an opponent. Furthermore, the allied contribution — both in number of ships and basing support — is significant, especially for the United States. Important also are several factors which relate directly to naval combat potential. They include the level of expertise in ASW, power-projection capability, quality of sea-based air power and antiair warfare (AAW) defenses, logistics capability (including sustainability while at sea), and application of modern technology to all aspects of naval warfare. Geography also plays a

role, as do friendly nations not formally allied to either side but potentially capable of favoring one or the other in crises or conflict.

Comparative Maritime Missions

The primary strategic wartime mission of the Soviet Navy is to be prepared to conduct strategic or theater-nuclear strikes from ballistic missile submarines (SSBNs) operating in protected waters near the Soviet Union. The strategic defense of the seaward approaches to the Soviet homeland is crucial for the Soviets' ability to carry out this mission. The Soviet Navy, in coordination with the combined arms of Soviet military forces, will attempt to control the peripheral seas and key approaches to the Soviet landmass to deny Western navies the access needed to threaten Soviet SSBNs or attack the homeland. These areas are defined as "sea control" zones. From these zones the Soviets would oppose US and allied naval nuclear- and conventional-capable long-range strike forces by denying them access to areas from which nuclear or conventional strikes could be launched against the Soviet homeland. These zones could range out to 2,000 kilometers from the Soviet coastline. Targets for Soviet conventional and nuclear attacks in the "sea denial" zones include sea-launched cruise missile (SLCM)-equipped submarines and surface ships, and aircraft carriers. The Soviets also will attempt to locate and destroy US SSBNs in their forward patrol areas. Furthermore, the Soviet Navy will contribute to combined-arms warfare by defending the seaward flanks of the army, assisting the army's advance by amphibious assaults, seizing and controlling key straits and choke points, and defending against amphibious assaults that threaten land operations.

Disruption of US reinforcement and resupply operations to Europe and Asia is another Soviet objective, although SLOC interdiction and sea denial are lower priority missions for the Soviet Navy. Nevertheless, we can anticipate Soviet attacks on the critical SLOCs linking the United States to its allies.

In contrast, deterrence, forward defense, and collective security are the cornerstones of United States national security strategy. Forward-deployed combat-ready naval forces of the United States and its friends and allies provide a visible form of deterrence on the oceans and seas and in ports around the globe. United States naval forces, operating globally in support of bilateral and multilateral security commitments, provide a mobile and highly combat-capable force that can project military power nearly anywhere in the world that borders oceans or seas. American naval forces have four primary peacetime objectives: defending the continental

United States from attack; assuring freedom of the seas and protecting important sea lines of communication from any adversary; promoting regional stability by supporting friends and deterring aggression; and functioning as a visible sign of America's capability to deal with crises and low-intensity conflicts on short notice nearly any place in the world.

Should deterrence fail, US strategy and navy missions call for a forward defense of the United States and its allies. The intent is to protect the key SLOCs from America to Europe and Asia for the movement of both commerce and war materials. To accomplish this, US and allied navies expect to conduct an early campaign against Soviet Navy forces in Soviet "sea control" and "sea denial" zones. The objective will be to eliminate Soviet offensive and defensive capability, thereby assuring freedom of the seas for US and allied military operations while deterring Soviet use of nuclear weapons at sea.

The battleship *USS Missouri* and the carrier *USS Kitty Hawk* shown here are centerpieces of the US Navy's principal power-projection forces — the surface action group and the carrier battle group.

The Maritime Balance — Trends and Asymmetries

The submarine is the Soviet Navy's principal platform for the conduct of both offensive and defensive naval warfare. Although submarines also play key roles in US offensive naval warfare, it is the carrier (CV) and its supporting ships and submarines comprising a carrier battle group that constitute the principal naval peacetime deterrent, presence, and power-projection force.

The SSBN serves as the strategic offensive arm of the Soviet Navy, while attack (SS and SSN) and cruise-missile (SSGN) submarines are the principal weapons to counter the allied submarine and surface ship threat, and constitute the primary threat to allied SLOCs. The Soviet general purpose submarine force is the world's largest, numbering nearly 300 active units. We expect this force to shrink in size as Moscow scraps older 1950s technology diesel boats, and 1960s and early 1970s nuclear boats, as part of Soviet force reductions. These submarines, however, are only of marginal ASW value, many being useful only for coastal defense. Furthermore, the newer diesel and nuclear submarines entering the Soviet fleets today are far superior in design, stealth, and combat capability to those they replace, and they represent a significant challenge to US ASW superiority. Finally, the newer submarines will comprise a growing percentage of the active submarine force, raising its overall combat potential. Even after the Soviets effect their anticipated reductions, the total submarine force will still be over twice as large as the US force.

Despite measurable improvements in the Soviet submarine force, however, the United States maintains an overall lead in submarine quieting, combat systems, and ASW open-ocean acoustic surveillance and detection systems. The US complement of sea- and land-based ASW forces — comprised of fixed-wing aircraft (P-3C,

The US Navy emphasizes the use of highly flexible carrier battle groups, centered on large-deck aircraft carriers such as the _USS America,_ to accomplish presence, power projection, sea control, and nuclear weapon strike missions.

Naval Ship Construction: Warsaw Pact and NATO[1]

Equipment Type	USSR 1986	NSWP[2] 1986	USSR 1987	NSWP 1987	USSR 1988	NSWP 1988	US 1986	NUSN[3] 1986	US 1987	NUSN 1987	US 1988	NUSN 1988
Submarines	8	0	9	0	9	0	3	3	2	4	5	6
Major Surface Warships	9	2	8	4	9	3	5	7	6	8	3	10

[1] Revised to reflect current total production information, NATO figures include France and Spain.
[2] Non-Soviet Warsaw Pact
[3] Non-US NATO

S-3A), helicopters (SH-2, SH-3, and SH-60), and surface ships and submarines — provides a broad open-ocean offensive and defensive ASW capability unmatched by the Soviets. Furthermore, the combined total of US and allied submarines is greater than what the Soviets and their allies possess.

Although a modern surface fleet supports the Soviet submarine force, developments in the surface fleet are not as dramatic as those in the submarine force. The Soviets have centered surface fleet improvements on building larger, more capable ships for conducting sustained operations on the open seas close to the USSR. Soviet design also tends to maximize the firepower of each ship so that it is heavily armed with multiple weapon systems, and contains increased magazine capacity over previous ships. These new ships continue to enter the fleet in sizeable numbers. Much as with the Soviet submarine force, as the Soviet Navy scraps older surface ships, the newer ships will comprise a larger percentage of the overall force. A smaller, more capable naval surface force will likely result.

Nevertheless, even the new ships entering Soviet naval service do not possess the surface fleet combat reach and power-projection capability provided by US CVBGs. Soviet carriers currently fitting out and under construction probably will extend the Soviet land-based air defense umbrella, and will not conduct long-range power-projection operations. Likewise, the Soviet surface fleet of today will function increasingly as an extension of the Soviet ground-based air-defense system, and thus provide greater defense in-depth from attacking US manned aircraft and cruise missiles.

This extension of the Soviet offensive reach and expansion of their defensive perimeter will test the US ability to defend the sea lanes. But it also complicates Soviet reconnaissance and surveillance capabilities and command, control, and communications (C^3). Never-

theless, the US Navy's antiair warfare systems combined with innovative antiair tactics, advanced missiles, and coordinated land- and sea-based air defenses would exact a high rate of attrition on attacking Soviet forces.

Future Trends in the Maritime Balance

The United States and its allies currently maintain an advantage over the Soviet Union and its allies in nearly all important areas comprising the conventional maritime balance. However, the Soviets may erode some of these advantages, most notably in ASW, as they continue upgrading their naval forces. The Soviets will likely continue to outnumber the United States in their total number of ships and submarines, but the combined fleets of the United States and its NATO and other allies far exceed the Soviet, non-Soviet Warsaw Pact and other Soviet allies in both the number and quality of major surface combatants.

The US Navy's fleet air defense capability is capable of exacting a high rate of attrition against attacking Soviet bombers and cruise missiles. More worrisome are the extended ranges at which Soviet systems can attack, their growing long-range fighter escort capability, and the large volume of Soviet launch platforms and cruise missiles that they can mass for conventional and nuclear attacks on US and allied naval forces. It is therefore essential that the United States continue to develop and eventually deploy submarine- and surface-launched systems to deter a Soviet attack.

The United States and its allies will continue to maintain significant advantages over the Soviet Navy in tactical sea-based air power, surveillance and reconnaissance, sustainability at sea, overall ASW capability, power projection ashore, and in the ability to move significant naval forces to trouble spots throughout the globe.

CHAPTER VII

Research and Development: The Technological Competition

High-priority Soviet research and development, coupled with technology transfer, have contributed to the initial success of its space shuttle orbiter program. The shuttle *Buran*, shown here, made its first unmanned orbital flight in November 1988.

INTRODUCTION

General Secretary Gorbachev has made clear his belief that economic revitalization brought about by the infusion of new and advanced technology will determine the "historic fate of the country and the position of socialism." Furthermore, Soviet writings have likened the coming era to previous "revolutions in military affairs," as significant as the introduction of nuclear weapons in the 1940s or the maturing of technologies for mechanized warfare in the 1920s and 1930s. Such statements indicate the Soviets recognize the critical

importance that research and development (R&D) and advanced technologies will play in sustaining their military power into the future.

This Soviet viewpoint is supported by recent advances in technology and the promise they offer for the future. Indeed, the United States has maintained its position of strength largely because it has remained competitive in advanced technologies. It has led the world in the number of patents, Nobel prizes for innovative R&D,

and research grants at prestigious universities. It has applied this research to its defense needs to produce weapon systems universally acknowledged to be of the finest quality. This US lead has been based not only on an ability to apply technology to defense needs and to move that technology to serial production, but also upon a solid basic research program.

But the nature of the threat facing the United States is changing largely due to developments that threaten to erode substantially the US advantage in many high-technology weapon systems. This phenomenon is evident in five developments:

- The United States no longer enjoys a monopoly on certain key defense-related technologies, and the current constrained budget environment threatens essential new research;
- The Soviet Union has outspent the United States in R&D for the last 20 years and is reducing the US technological lead in a number of important areas;
- The Soviet Union is continuing its efforts to acquire advanced Western technology by legal and illegal means;
- US allies are developing, fielding, and selling advanced technologies of their own, thereby contributing to the problem of weapons proliferation, and;
- The Third World is gaining access to technologies that can threaten regional stability.

These developments have the potential to disrupt regional and even global power balances. It is within this context that this chapter will review the significance of R&D and the implications for US security.

THE TECHNOLOGICAL COMPETITION

The overall US lead in technology relative to the rest of the world has eroded over the last 20 years, and the outlook is for even greater technological competition in the future. In the years ahead, the United States will confront new challenges, perhaps from a revitalized and restructured Soviet economy, but almost certainly from a unified and competitive Europe, a dynamic Japanese economy, rapidly developing countries like South Korea and Singapore, and an unstable Third World armed with increasingly sophisticated weapons. The sections that follow briefly address the nature of these challenges,

their implication for the US techno-industrial base and, by extension, the military balance.

The Soviet Union

Perestroika and *glasnost* are changing the way in which the Soviet Union's scientific research is conducted. The Soviets are exploiting improved relations with the West to implement cooperative science and technology (S&T) programs and exchanges. The resulting technology transfer from these activities provides significant benefits to the Soviet defense industry. Interaction with Western scientists and industry also will help the Soviets gain knowledge necessary to compete more effectively in the worldwide military technology arena.

Moscow's willingness to invest in R&D has gained the Soviet Union technological advantages in certain key areas, including pulsed-laser power and high-power microwave systems. Furthermore, Soviet work in hypervelocity projectiles and biotechnology is on a par with work being done in the United States. Production problems, however, could prevent extensive deployment of weapons with these technologies.

The Soviets also have invested heavily in five high-technology fields, and are actively pursuing military applications of these technologies. For example, work is under way on optical computing for high-speed information processing, microwave weapons that can destroy electronics components, lasers and particle beams for directed-energy weapons, electromagnetic rail guns for antiarmor systems, and biosensors for real-time detection of chemical and biological agents.

The Soviet Union also emphasizes the military uses of outer space. They routinely demonstrate the ability to place satellites in orbit on very short notice using expendable launch vehicles. Their *Energiya* is the world's largest heavy-lift booster. The Soviets also possess the only operational antisatellite capability. These developments threaten to put US space assets in near-earth orbit at risk. Finally, Soviet cosmonauts have spent much more time in space than US astronauts, providing a wealth of information on the effects of space travel on humans, and the military utility of men in orbit. As the Soviets' militarization of space continues, the United States will need to develop a more responsive

Relative USSR/US Technology Level in Deployed Military Systems[1]

DEPLOYED SYSTEMS	US SUPERIOR	US/USSR EQUAL	USSR SUPERIOR
STRATEGIC			
ICBMs		■	
SSBNs	■		
SLBMs	■►		
Bombers	■		
SAMs			■
Ballistic Missile Defense			■
Antisatellite			■
Cruise Missiles		◄■	
TACTICAL			
Land Forces			
SAMs (Including Naval)		■►	
Tanks		■►	
Artillery		■	
Infantry Combat Vehicles		■	
Antitank Guided Missiles		■►	
Attack Helicopters	■►		
Chemical Warfare			■
Biological Warfare[2]			■
Air Forces			
Fighter/Attack and Interceptor Aircraft	■►		
Air-to-Air Missiles	■►		

DEPLOYED SYSTEMS	US SUPERIOR	US/USSR EQUAL	USSR SUPERIOR
Air-to-Surface Munitions	■►		
Airlift Aircraft	■►		
Naval Forces			
SSNs	■►		
Torpedoes		■	
Sea-Based Aircraft	■		
Surface Combatants	■►		
Naval Cruise Missiles		■►	
Mines			■
C³I			
Communications		■	
ECM/ECCM	■►		
Early Warning	■		
Surveillance and Reconnaissance	■►		
Training Simulators	■		

[1] These are comparisons of system technology levels only, and are not necessarily a measure of effectiveness. The comparisons are not dependent on scenario, tactics, quantity, training or other operational factors. Systems farther than one year from IOC are not considered.

[2] The United States has no deployed biological warfare systems.

The arrows denote that the relative technology level is changing significantly in the direction indicated.

Relative comparisons of deployed technology levels shown depict overall average standing; countries may be superior, equal or inferior in subsystems of a specific technology in a deployed military system.

launch capability, and an ability to put Soviet space resources at risk, in order to maintain a military balance in space.

The long-running Soviet program of legal and illegal acquisition of foreign technology has not diminished. This program, coupled with the pursuit of technology through joint ventures and exchanges, is vital to the Soviets' strategy of upgrading their competitiveness in military technology. This approach reflects a continuation of the Soviets' historic propensity to adapt or exploit Western technologies for their own purposes. While the Soviets do not depend exclusively on Western technology to upgrade their military systems, they do derive major benefits from applying it. For example, the Soviets spent $25 million in their illegal acquisition of sophisticated machinery for producing quiet-running submarine propellers; however, it will cost the United States many times that amount to regain its previous

capability to detect Soviet submarines equipped with these propellers.

Progress in many key areas of warfighting capability will require advanced microelectronic and computer technology. Consequently, the Soviets have made acquiring this technology a high priority. As the US lead in semiconductor technology is reduced by formidable competition from Japan, the Soviets are increasing their technology acquisition efforts in Japanese laboratories and industries.

In some areas the technology gap between US and Soviet systems has diminished significantly over the last 20 years. Where traditionally the Soviets countered Western high-technology weapons by producing huge quantities of low-technology — but durable — weapons they are now, in some cases, fielding more technologically advanced systems than those of the United States.

The SA-X-12B Giant surface-to-air missile's long range and accuracy give it a flexible capability for use against a range of potential targets including tactical aircraft, stand-off command and control platforms, and possibly some types of cruise missiles and ballistic missiles.

Soviet scientists and engineers engaged in advanced Soviet research and development efforts receive high priority in the allocation of resources as the USSR strives to maintain technological competitiveness with the West.

The titanium hull on certain Soviet submarines is an example of this phenomenon. Overall, however, the Soviets have been hampered in narrowing the technology gap by their weakness in technological innovation and their limitations in areas such as microelectronics, computers, telecommunications, computer-numerically controlled machine tools and advanced composition — areas key to the production of high-technology weapons.

Europe

The highly industrialized nations of Western Europe have become increasingly competitive in advanced technologies over the last 30 years. Their already formidable science and technology base will very likely expand and become even more productive as the region moves toward economic integration in 1992. While in many ways these are positive developments for US security, they also represent a strong challenge to the United States' technology base.

Interestingly, many US allies in Europe make a concerted effort to tie their nation's technology policy to their national security goals — to include the political and economic dimensions, as well as the military dimension. Many provide direct aid to their defense industries, while others provide financial support through their economic policies.

The Pacific Rim

The Pacific Rim presents unique dilemmas for the United States. Japan is both a very important ally of the United States and its most formidable economic competitor. The Republic of Korea is important to US defense strategy in East Asia and the Pacific. Yet as the ROK increases its economic power it is seeking greater independence from US influence. Taiwan, Hong Kong, and Singapore also are increasingly important economic competitors. China has immense political and economic power potential, and can become a regional influence of the first order if it can stabilize its internal situation.

Many of these nations are already strong competitors with the United States in developing and marketing advanced technologies. To the extent that this competition

Comparison of Technology Programs With Military Applications

	WARSAW PACT	NON-US NATO	JAPAN	OTHERS
Microelectronic Circuits and Their Fabrication	■	■	■	Israel, Switzerland / South Korea
Preparation of Gases and Other Compound Semiconductors	■	■	■	
Software Producibility	■	■	■	Many Nations
Parallel Computer Architectures	■	■	■	
Machine Intelligence/Robotics	■	■	■	Finland, Sweden
Simulation and Modeling	■	■	■	
Integrated Optics	■	■	■	China, Israel, South Korea
Fiber Optics	■	■	■	Various Sources
Sensitive Radars	■	■	■	Sweden
Passive Sensors	■	■	■	Israel
Automatic Target Recognition	■	■	■	Israel, Sweden
Phased Arrays	■	■	■	Israel
Data Fusion	■	■	■	
Signature Control	■	■		
Computational Fluid Dynamics	■	■	■	Sweden
Air-Breathing Propulsion	■	■	■	
High-Power Microwaves	■	■		
Pulsed Power	■	■	■	
Hypervelocity Projectiles	■	■	■	Australia, Israel
Advanced Structural Composites	■	■	■	
Superconductivity	■	■	■	
Biotechnology	■	■	■	Many Nations

Legend:

■ National program is clearly ahead of the US in advancing the state of the art in technology.

■ Major national program overall on par with the US with significant leads over the US in specific important aspects of the technology.

■ Major-national program on par with the US overall and capable of making significant contributions to the state of the art.

■ Significant national effort generally lagging the state of the art except in certain niches wherein the country enjoys a significant world-wide lead.

■ Significant national effort generally lagging the state of the art except in certain niches wherein the nation is capable of contributing to advances.

■ Significant national effort generally trailing the world in all important aspects of the technology.

affects US trade and commerce, it affects the health of the US economy and, ultimately, its industrial base as well. Should the United States lose its competitive R&D edge, its ability to sustain those industries critical to defense would be diminished. A corollary issue is the increasing US dependency on foreign sources. The United States already is dependent on Japan for numerous critical weapon systems components that would be essential in the prosecution of any prolonged conflict. There is great concern that this dependence could, in the future, extend to other technologies as well.

The Third World

Despite US attempts to control the high-technology weapons trade, relatively sophisticated weapons are now available on the open market to those Third World nations that desire and can afford to purchase them. For example, the Saudis recently acquired ballistic missiles from the Chinese, while both the Iranians and Iraqis were able to develop crude but effective short-range missiles despite a US embargo of this technology. The United States also has been unable to control the spread

of nuclear and chemical weapons technology. By the year 2000 it is anticipated that over a dozen countries will be able to deploy nuclear weapons. Many more nations will have chemical weapons like those used in the Iran-Iraq War.

Even some of the lesser-developed Third World states have been able to acquire and use effectively weapons incorporating advanced military technology. For example, Afghan resistance fighters employed US Stinger antiaircraft missiles to great effect during the latter period of Soviet intervention in Afghanistan. Indeed, some of the most advanced technology weapons now under development actually compensate for the user's lack of competence through their simple operating procedures and low levels of required maintenance. Consequently, the risk will increase significantly that future low-intensity conflicts in the Third World will be highly lethal in nature.

The United States

Over the last 20 years the United States has lost

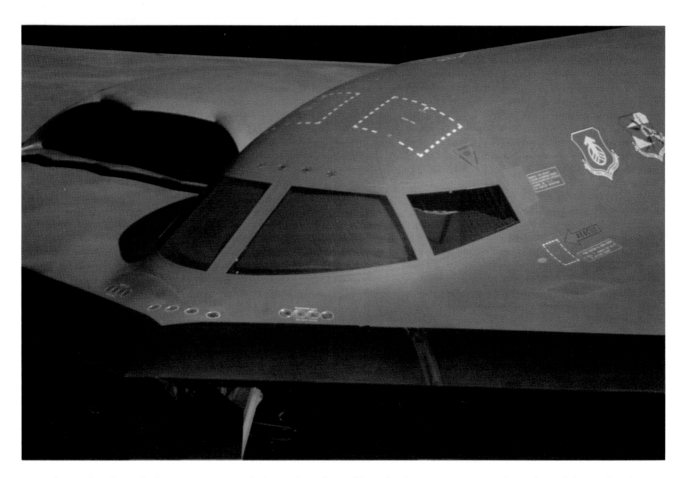

The B-2 bomber, which incorporates revolutionary low-observable technology to counter continuously evolving Soviet air defense systems, is designed to be the mainstay of the US strategic bomber force into the 21st century.

138

much of its lead in many important technology fields. This trend is, in part, a natural phenomenon that stems from the unique conditions that spawned an era of US dominance following World War II. The trend is also the product of a lag in funding for research and development. Furthermore, other factors — such as concentrating on short-term gains and adhering to out-dated management techniques — also have contributed to the erosion of the American R&D base. At the same time, other Western advanced industrial states have realized substantial benefits from investing in and developing a strong technology base. For example, in 1970 the United States, Germany, and Japan each invested about 1 percent of their gross national product in R&D. Yet by 1989 the Japanese and the Germans had increased this rate by 50 percent or more, while US investment remained stagnated at 1 percent. Japan and West Germany also have benefitted from significantly greater capital investments by their business sector than has occurred in the United States. Furthermore, Tokyo and Bonn have invested in specific areas, often building on initial US research breakthroughs and gaining an economic lead in production.

Perhaps the best example of this phenomenon is the US loss of the microchip market to the Japanese. Bell Labs in the United States developed the concept and produced the first products. The Japanese took the basic research findings and spent their money on refining them and securing a sales base with quality products. They were then able — and willing — to increase their investment in that specific area, thereby leap-frogging US technology and establishing themselves as the world leader.

CONCLUSION

In deterring the Soviet threat to Western security, the United States and its allies have traditionally relied heavily upon qualitative advantages in their defense systems to offset a significant Soviet quantitative edge. If the past is any indication, sophisticated defense systems produced by advanced technology sectors of a nation's industrial base will prove even more important to Western defense in the future. Indeed, through *perestroika*, the Soviet Union has indicated its implicit recognition of this trend.

If the United States is to meet the challenge of increasingly more sophisticated — and formidable — military forces, both in the Soviet Union and in hostile Third World states, it will require a strong research and development effort to sustain a healthy, competitive industrial base, along with an effective technology security program. If the United States proves unable to compete effectively in areas of advanced technologies, it would incur the most severe economic and security consequences: markets would be lost, the US industrial base would erode, and the United States would become increasingly dependent upon offshore technologies for its defense at the same time as its economic health weakens. It is somewhat ironic that, although the Soviet Union constitutes the greatest threat to US security, the greatest challenge to the US technology and industrial base will almost certainly come from the United States' own allies. Thus the United States must succeed in this "friendly competition" with advanced Western industrial states if its economic power, and the West's system of collective security, is to endure. Indeed, an essential part of any US R&D effort will seek to take full advantage of potential technological contributions that can be made by the allies on defense-related programs.

Fortunately, the United States is not faced with the need for radical change of the magnitude that the Soviets are experiencing with *perestroika*. It is, however, evident that the United States cannot persist in its current laissez-faire approach to the competition in advanced technologies without incurring major economic and security problems of its own in the future.

CHAPTER VIII

Prospects for the Future

Moscow's "new thinking" on defense and foreign policy issues has provided the United States with an opportunity to develop constructive military-to-military contacts with the Soviet Union at the highest levels.

THE ORIGINS OF CHANGE

Today the likelihood of conflict between the United States and the Soviet Union is perhaps as low as it has been at any time in the post-war era. There is no longer any question that significant, and in some cases, dramatic changes are occurring in the USSR. For example:

■ Economically, through *perestroika*, the Soviet leadership has embarked on a program to restructure their economy in ways that differ sharply from Marxist-Leninist prescriptions.

■ Politically, through *glasnost*, the Soviets are experimenting with certain aspects of an open society, to include some measure of free speech and, for the first time in some 70 years, elections that offer the Soviet people a limited choice of candidates.

■ Militarily, General Secretary Gorbachev has announced significant unilateral cuts in Soviet conventional forces and has proposed further cuts that merit serious consideration. He also has announced significant reductions in the Soviet defense budget and weapons procurement. Finally, the Soviets claim they are moving away from an offensively oriented military doctrine toward one based on "reasonable sufficiency."

- Socially, the Soviet leadership appears willing to exercise a greater measure of tolerance toward the many non-Russian nationalities and ethnic groups that comprise the Soviet people, and toward religion as well.
- Diplomatically, Gorbachev's call for "new thinking" sees the Soviets moving away from confrontation with the West toward an emphasis on negotiation as a means for resolving disputes. In particular, the withdrawal of Soviet forces from Afghanistan and Moscow's willingness to allow the nations of Eastern Europe some measure of freedom in resolving indigenous problems are positive steps toward the creation of a more stable international environment.

As impressive as these changes are, however, it is only natural that we in the West ask ourselves why they are occurring now, after over 40 years of East-West tension and over 70 years of communist rule in the Soviet Union. We believe that the Soviet leadership is adopting these policies because they are faced with two basic conditions that are leading them in the direction of change.

The first condition concerns the internal breakdown of Soviet communism. This is especially true of the Soviet economy where, a generation after Western Europe and Japan have recovered from the devastation of World War II, the Soviet Union remains unable to compete in a rapidly growing international economic system, unable to maintain the diet of its people without importing large quantities of foodstuffs, and unable to participate fully in a revolution in military warfare because of a deficient technological base. This economic failure, in turn, has led the Soviet people to question their political system's basic underlying assumptions. Under Gorbachev this questioning has manifested itself through the leadership's willingness to view the situation realistically, and in its determination to confront communism's inability to meet the Soviet Union's current and future political, military, and economic goals.

A second major incentive for change in the Soviet Union is the resolve of the Western democracies, demonstrated for over 40 years now, to resist Soviet attempts at intimidation and subversion, and to convince the Soviet leadership that any gains that might accrue through aggression would not be worth the costs incurred. This resolve is rooted in our determination to preserve our common values of democracy, individual liberty, and economic opportunity, and is manifested by a sturdy system of collective security, a strong military deterrent, and the dynamism of a vibrant, innovative economic system. Time has shown the universal power of these values. Today people in communist states are openly expressing their desire to enjoy the benefits of democracy, liberty, and economic opportunity.

In summary, the current Soviet leadership's determination to improve their economic performance, enhance their ability to compete effectively in the rapidly changing international economic environment, and exploit the revolution in military technologies for their own use rests on Soviet self-interest and the Western democracies' determination to protect their own interests from Soviet encroachment.

A RESPONSE FROM THE WEST

Within the context of change, there are opportunities to seek common ground with the Soviets. The United States and its allies should take advantage of the Soviets' current forthcoming attitude toward reducing the threat of war and enhancing international stability. Along these lines we have welcomed General Secretary Gorbachev's "new thinking" in foreign and defense policy. It hopefully represents an approach that the Western Alliance has been looking for since the dawn of the Cold War. President Bush's proposal for a revolutionary conventional-arms-reduction agreement in Europe is one example of our desire to work with the Soviets to reduce tensions, as are our unprecedented agreement with the USSR on avoiding dangerous military activities, and the resumption of the START negotiations.

We can expect implementation of announced Soviet policies to modestly reduce the size of Soviet military forces over the next few years. We can hope that additional reductions will result as the economic benefits of military cutbacks are more clearly perceived, as Soviet "new thinking" about defense needs is taken more seriously, or as the result of arms control agreements negotiated with the West. But for the present we must cope with Soviet military power as it is. We must proceed with caution and prudence in making any changes that would weaken the defense posture that

On 12 June 1989, Admiral William J. Crowe, Chairman of the Joint Chiefs of Staff, exchanged copies of the Prevention of Dangerous Military Activities Agreement with his counterpart, the Chief of the Soviet General Staff, General M.A. Moiseyev.

has underwritten our security throughout the post-war era. It is also clear that we must reaffirm the principles of collective security that have ensured our peace and prosperity. While we laud the Soviets for their professed good intentions, we must deal with the reality of their formidable military might. It is this sobering fact that counsels vigilance and steadiness on our part.

A few facts about recent Soviet policies should serve to remind us that the Soviet military threat is still very much with us:

- Even if the Soviets completely eliminated the forces discussed in Gorbachev's 7 December 1988 United Nations' speech, Warsaw Pact forces would still out-number NATO in tanks, artillery, and divisions by a ratio of over 2 to 1.
- Despite talk of reduced military budgets, Moscow still spends an estimated 15 to 17 percent of its GNP on defense, while the United States spends less than 6 percent.
- Although Gorbachev proposes to reduce the Soviet defense budget by 14.2 percent, since 1985 Soviet defense expenditures have *increased* by an average of

3 percent per year in real terms. In comparison, since 1985 United States defense spending has *declined* in real terms by 11.2 percent. Thus even if Gorbachev makes good on his promise, the Soviet Union will only be following in the wake of our own defense spending reductions.

- While we realize that changes in military production rates typically occur gradually, over time, the fact remains that under Gorbachev Soviet military pro-duction as a whole remains roughly at the level set by his recent predecessors. Of particular concern is the continued modernization of Soviet strategic systems. For example, the Soviets continue to deploy their mobile SS-24 and SS-25 ICBMs, systems for which we have no counterpart.
- The Soviets have been modernizing their short-range nuclear forces for over a decade. For example, they replaced old and inaccurate FROG systems with the advanced SS-21. In fact, under Gorbachev the number of SS-21 launchers has more than doubled. In addition, Moscow is replacing its SS-23 missiles, which it must destroy to comply with the INF Treaty, with Scud missiles. As a consequence of this modern-ization, the Warsaw Pact has a 16 to 1 advantage in

short-range nuclear missiles over NATO.

- The Soviets were recently applauded when Moscow announced its intention to withdraw 500 nuclear weapons from Eastern Europe without replacing them. Less well known is NATO's unilateral reduction of 2,400 nuclear weapons in Europe over the past decade from a significantly smaller stockpile. Thus despite the rhetoric, Soviet cuts are smaller and their residual stockpile considerably larger than NATO's.
- Despite professing a new openness, the USSR has yet to meet Western standards on providing information regarding military spending, weapons procurement, force structure, and the deployment of its forces.

Because of the enormous military forces they continue to deploy, and the uncertain outcome of their reform policies, we must adopt a two-track approach in dealing with the Soviet Union during this period of transition. One track recognizes the importance of continuing to support our successful alliance strategy and collective security efforts, which are based on a strong military deterrent, until we observe a reduction in Soviet military power to significantly lower levels. The second track involves encouraging Moscow in those policies that promote Soviet democratic pluralism and a stable international environment.

It is important to realize that despite their best efforts there is no guarantee that the Soviets will realize the ambitious goals they have set for *glasnost* and *perestroika*. In any case, the process of reform will be arduous and slow. It is possible, therefore, that the West may face a Soviet leadership disillusioned with new ways and willing to return to the old, familiar policies of repression at home and confrontation abroad.

However, the success of the Soviet reform effort — depending on how it develops — may also prove hazardous to Western security. For example, if Gorbachev's economic reforms produce a reinvigorated Soviet technological and industrial base without a corresponding growth of democratic institutions and democratic pluralism, the West could face a far more formidable Soviet threat than it does today. This threat would be even more dangerous if the West, in the interim, allows its defenses to atrophy. Thus Gorbachev's call for change within the Soviet Union cannot be viewed as an unambiguous benefit to the Western democracies. If democratization remains within the narrow confines designed for it by the Soviet leadership, or if the promised shift from an offensive to a defensive military doctrine and force posture does not materialize, successful change in other areas (e.g., economic restructuring, progress in high-technology fields) may well redound to our disadvantage.

Prudence therefore dictates that we maintain our defenses while we wait and see if Soviet capabilities to threaten our security are brought into line with their stated benign intentions. Our experience in this century has shown again and again that, especially with totalitarian states, seemingly friendly relations can change very quickly at the decision of a few powerful individuals. Military capabilities, by comparison, change much more slowly. Until we are able to see clearly what new security environment we are entering, maintaining our military strength and political resolve seem a small price to pay to preserve our security and our freedoms.

SOVIET

MILITARY

POWER

First Edition	September 1981
Second Edition	March 1983
Third Edition	April 1984
Fourth Edition	April 1985
Fifth Edition	March 1986
Sixth Edition	March 1987
Seventh Edition	April 1988
Eighth Edition	September 1989

GLOSSARY

ILLUSTRATIONS

INDEX

GLOSSARY

A

AAA:
Antiaircraft Artillery

AAW:
Antiair Warfare

ABM:
Antiballistic Missile

AFCENT:
Allied Forces Central Europe

AF MD/GOF:
Air Forces of the Military Districts
and Groups of Forces

AFNORTH:
Allied Forces Northern Europe

AFSOUTH:
Allied Forces Southern Europe

ALCM:
Air-Launched Cruise Missile

APC:
Armored Personnel Carrier

ASAT:
Antisatellite

ASCM:
Antiship Cruise Missile

ASEAN:
Association of Southeast Asian Nations

ASM:
Air-to-Surface Missile

ASUW:
Antisurface Warfare

ASW:
Antisubmarine Warfare

ATM:
Antitactical Missile

AWACS:
Airborne Warning and Control System

B

BMD:
Ballistic Missile Defense

BW:
Biological Warfare

C

C^3:
Command, Control and
Communications

CBW:
Chemical Biological Warfare

CEMA:
Council for Mutual Economic
Assistance

CENTAG:
Central Army Group

CENTCOM:
Central Command

CFE:
Conventional Armed Forces in Europe

CGF:
Central Group of Forces

CGN:
Guided-Missile Cruiser, Nuclear-Powered

COB:
Colocated Operating Base

COCOM:
Coordinating Committee for Multilateral Export Controls

CP:
Command Post

CV:
Aircraft Carrier

CVBG:
Carrier Battle Group

CVHG:
VSTOL Aircraft Carrier

CW:
Chemical Weapons/Warfare

D
_____

DDG:
Guided-Missile Destroyer

E
_____

ECM:
Electronic Countermeasures

ECCM:
Electronic Counter Countermeasures

EORSAT:
Electronic Intelligence (ELINT) Ocean Reconnaissance Satellite

ESM:
Electronic Warfare Support Measures

F
_____

FMLN:
Farabundo Marti National Liberation Front

FOFA:
Follow-On Forces Attack

FROG:
Free Rocket Over Ground

FYP:
Five-Year Plan

G
_____

GLONASS:
Global Navigation Satellite System

GNP:
Gross National Product

GOF:
Group of Forces

I
_____

ICBM:
Intercontinental Ballistic Missile

IFV:
Infantry Fighting Vehicle

INF:
Intermediate-Range Nuclear Forces

IRBM:
Intermediate-Range Ballistic Missile

J
_____

JTFME:
Joint Task Force Middle East

L
_____

LOC:
Lines of Communication

LPAR:
Large Phased-Array Radar

LRINF:
Longer-Range/Intermediate-Range Nuclear Forces

M
_____

MAGTF:
Marine Air Ground Task Force

MBT:
Main Battle Tank

MD:
Military District

ME/SWA:
Middle East/Southwest Asia

MiG:
Mikoyan-Gurevich (Soviet-designed aircraft)

MIRV:
Multiple Independently Targetable Reentry Vehicle

MLRS:
Multiple-Launch Rocket System

MM:
Millimeter

MOB:
Main Operating Base

MPLA:
Popular Movement for the
Liberation of Angola

MRBM:
Medium-Range Ballistic Missile

MRL:
Multiple Rocket Launcher

MRV:
Multiple Reentry Vehicles

N

NATO:
North Atlantic Treaty Organization

NCO:
Non-commissioned Officer

NGF:
Northern Group of Forces

NKA:
North Korean Army

NORTHAG:
Northern Army Group

NSNF:
Non-Strategic Nuclear Forces

NSWP:
Non-Soviet Warsaw Pact

NUSN:
Non-US NATO

O

OMG:
Operational Maneuver Group

P

PACOM:
Pacific Command

PLO:
Palestine Liberation Organization

POF:
Pacific Ocean Fleet

POFAF:
Pacific Ocean Fleet Air Force

PRC:
People's Republic of China

R

R&D:
Research and Development

REC:
Radio-Electronic Combat

ROK:
Republic of Korea

RORSAT:
Radar Ocean Reconnaissance Satellite

RV:
Reentry Vehicle

S

S&T:
Science and Technology

SAF:
Soviet Air Force

SALT:
Strategic Arms Limitation Treaty,
Strategic Arms Limitation Talks

SAM:
Surface-to-Air-Missile

SDI:
Strategic Defense Initiative

SGF:
Southern Group of Forces

SLBM:
Submarine-Launched Ballistic Missile

SLCM:
Submarine-Launched Cruise Missile,
Sea-Launched Cruise Missile

SLOC:
Sea Lines of Communication

SNA:
Soviet Naval Aviation

SNF:
Short-Range Nuclear Forces

SNI:
Soviet Naval Infantry

SOVINDRON:
Soviet Indian Ocean Squadron

SOVMEDFLOT:
Soviet Mediterranean Flotilla

SRBM:
Short-Range Ballistic Missile

SRINF:
Shorter-Range Intermediate-Range
Nuclear Forces

SRF:
Strategic Rocket Forces

SS:
Submarine

SSBN:
Ballistic Missile Submarine,
Nuclear-Powered

SSGN:
Cruise Missile Attack Submarine,
Nuclear-Powered

SSM:
Surface-to-Surface Missile

SSN:
Attack Submarine, Nuclear-Powered

START:
Strategic Arms Reduction Talks

STVD:
Southern Theater of Military Operations

Su:
Sukhoy (Soviet-designed aircraft)

T

TEL:
Transporter-Erector-Launcher

TVD:
Theater of Military Operations

U

UAC:
Unified Army Corps

UN:
United Nations

UNITA:
National Union for Total
Independence of Angola

USMC:
United States Marine Corps

V

VGK:
Soviet Supreme High Command

VPK:
Soviet Military-Industrial Commission

VSTOL:
Vertical/Short Take-Off and Landing

VTA:
Military Transport Aviation of
Voyenno Transportnaya Aviatsiya

VTOL:
Vertical Take-Off and Landing

W

WGF:
Western Group of Forces

WP:
Warsaw Pact

ILLUSTRATIONS

V

VII

VIII

INDEX

A

B

C

G

Galosh ABM, 52
Gazelle ABM, 52
General purpose forces
  air forces, 68-73
  challenges facing, 59-60
  chemical and biological warfare and, 67-68
  future of, 81
  ground forces, 64-67
  naval forces, 73-80
  reductions in, 17, 36-37, 58-59, 61, 62, 81, 102-103, 106-107, 113
  theater command structure and logistics of, 63-64
  theater warfighting concepts of, 60-63
General Staff, 13, 17, 22, 43
Geneva Protocol on Chemical Weapons, 91
Glasnost, 11, 140
Global Navigation Satellite System (GLONASS), 54
Gorbachev, Mikhail
  and "common European home," 26
  in Cuba, 24, 125
  defense cutbacks and, 17, 30, 31, 36, 37, 62, 102, 113, 121
  on Krasnoyarsk LPAR, 52
  and military doctrine, 13-17
  military role of, 43
  on NATO force modernization, 49
  and "new thinking" in foreign policy, 9, 17, 141
  and 1968 invasion of Czechoslovakia, 23-24
  and political reform, 11, 12-13
  and revelations on military spending, 32
  on technology, 132
Gorshkov, Fleet Admiral, 75
Greece, 97, 98
Grisha-class corvettes, 35
Ground forces, 59-60, 64-67
  equipment of, 34, 64, 66-67, 109-111
  military balance in Europe and, 109-111, 121
  procurement costs, 32
  reductions in, 17, 58-59, 61, 62, 65, 67, 102-103, 106-107, 113
Guatemala, 127
Guided-missile cruiser, 35

H

Helicopters 66, 69, 71-72, 100, 111
  NATO, 111
  naval, 76, 77, 80

Helix ASW helicopter, 77
Helix A ASW helicopter, 80
Hokum helicopter, 111
Honduras, 127
Hong Kong, 136-138
Hungary
  change in, 23
  military forces in, 58, 59, 62, 98, 107

I

ICBMs. *See* Intercontinental ballistic missiles
Il-76 Candid, 70
India, 28, 29, 121, 123-124
Indian Ocean, 124
Indian Ocean Squadron, 75
INF Treaty, 17, 43, 48-49, 67
Infantry fighting vehicle (IFV), 64, 66, 98, 100, 110-111
Intercontinental ballistic missiles, 35, 49, 85
  deployment of, 42, 43, 142
  modernization of, 43, 44-45
  START talks and, 47, 90
Iran, 28, 122, 123, 138
Iran-Iraq conflict, 123
Iraq, 28, 123, 138
Israel, 27, 28, 121, 122, 123, 124
Italy, 98

J

Japan
  in East Asian conflict, 114, 115, 117
  Soviet Union and, 27, 135
  United States and, 136-138, 139

K

Katyn Forest massacre (1940), 23
Khazikov, V. N., 60
Khrushchev, Nikita, 102

Kiev-class CVHG, 79
Kilo-class SS, 35, 117
Kirov-class CGN, 35, 79
Kohl, Helmut, 26
Korean peninsula, 119. *See also* North Korea; South Korea
Krasnaya Zvezda, 38
Krasnoyarsk radar, 52, 91
Krivak III-class frigate, 36

L

Latin America, 29
Latvia, 11
Lebanon, 121, 122
Libya, 28, 121
Lithuania, 11
Logistics, 64, 73, 80
Long-Range Aviation, 44

M

M1983 MRL, 66
Mainstay AWACS aircraft, 51, 97, 108
Manpower. *See* Military manpower
Maritime balance
  European, 107, 111-112
  overall, 117, 128-131
Mediterranean Sea, 97, 98, 107, 121
Mengistu, President, 25
Merchant fleet, 80
Mi-6 Hook helicopter, 71
Mi-8 Hip E helicopter, 71
Mi-17 Hip H helicopter, 71, 111
Mi-24 Hind helicopter, 71, 111
Mi-26 Halo helicopter, 71
Mi-28 Havoc helicopter, 71-72, 111
Midas air-refueling aircraft, 108
Middle East, 27-28, 120-121, 122-123
MiG-21 Fishbed, 69, 70
MiG-23 Flogger, 69, 70, 108
MiG-25 Foxbat F, 70
MiG-29 Fulcrum, 70, 98, 108, 112, 121
MiG-31 Foxhound, 51, 97, 108, 117

S

T